Light for our Path
2012

International Bible Reading Association

Light for our path 2012

A year of Bible reflections from around the world

Edited by Kate Hughes

IBRA
International Bible Reading Association

Light for our Path aims to build understanding and respect for a range of religious perspectives and approaches to living practised in the world today, and to help readers meet new challenges in their faith. Views expressed by contributors should not, however, be taken to reflect the views or policies of the Editor or the International Bible Reading Association.

The International Bible Reading Association's scheme of readings is listed on the Christian Education website at www.christianeducation.org.uk/about-ibra and the full scheme for 2012 may be downloaded in English, Spanish and French.

Cover photograph: *Trees as Light* by Rosa Wain (see www.veritasse.co uk). We gratefully acknowledge the kind permission of the artist to use this image on our cover.

Editor – Kate Hughes

Published by:
The International Bible Reading Association
1020 Bristol Road
Selly Oak
Birmingham B29 6LB
United Kingdom

Charity number 211542

ISBN 978-1-905893-41-6
ISSN 0140-8267

Designed by Christian Education
Printed and bound in the UK by Mosaic Print Management

Contents

Foreword

Dear Friends

Welcome to this year's *Light for our Path*. The readings are grouped into seventeen themes, which are named in the Contents list on pages v and vi. Some readers value the continuous reading of a biblical book, and several of these are included; others particularly value the insights provided by the wider themes which draw on both the Old and New Testaments. I hope the group that prepares the readings has got the balance between the two types of theme about right this year.

This year we have returned to seven readings for each week. The first page for each week includes a short introduction to the week and notes for the Sunday reading. The questions for group discussion and personal thought can now be found at the end of the week, after the notes for Saturday's reading. Before the first week of notes you will find a page of prayers that you may like to use as you study the Word of God (p. ix).

The year that has been spent on writing and preparing this edition of *Light for our Path* for publication has been marked by a series of natural disasters in different parts of the world. Our writers have not been unaffected. One had her home flooded in India. Another was affected by a tropical storm in the West Indies. Another lost a student in the Haiti earthquake. Reading the Bible is not an escape from reality. Rather, it brings us face to face with the real world, with all its evil and suffering – and helps us to find God there. It is only as we deepen our relationship with God through Jesus Christ that we can resist the evil, share the suffering, and become channels of God's love and peace in his world. Reading God's Word helps us to do this, and I hope that your faith will grow this year as you read these notes in the company of our writers from around the world.

Kate

Kate Hughes – Editor

Reading *Light for our Path*

Before reading, be quiet and remember that God is with you. Ask for his Holy Spirit to guide your reading.

- If you do not have a Bible with you, you can work solely from *Light for our Path* by referring to the short Bible passage printed in bold type. (Only the editions printed in English have this.)

- You can begin by reading just the short extract from the daily Bible passage which appears in the notes. Or you may prefer to read the full text of the daily passage from your Bible. The weekly notes use a variety of Bible translations, which are named at the beginning of each week. You may like to see how the extract in bold type compares with the same passage in your own Bible. And if your Bible mentions parallel passages in other places, comparing these passages can widen your thinking.

- The week of notes begins on Sunday, with a short introduction and notes on the day's reading.

- When you finish each day's reading, spend a little time reflecting on it. What does it say to you about God? About yourself? About others? About the world in which we live? Has it changed your thinking? Does it suggest something that you should do? Then use the final prayer (marked with a cross), or any prayer of your own you need to make.

- At the end of each week there are questions and suggestions for group discussion or personal thought. These are only suggestions – your own reading and prayer may have drawn your attention to other aspects which you would like to explore further. The important thing is that you should let God speak to you through his Word, so that as you read steadily through the year you will be able to look back and see that you have got to know him better and have grown spiritually.

Prayers

O Lord,
As I open my Bible today
Open my eyes to read your word
Open my mind to understand your word
Open my heart to love your word
Open my life to the working of your Holy Spirit
That through your word in the Bible
I may come to a greater love of your Word Jesus.

The discussion group

God our Father, Creator and Redeemer,
reading the Bible is like taking part in a divine discussion group,
as your people over the centuries share their experience of you:
'This is the God we see in his creation'
'This is the God who rescued us from Egypt'
'This is the God we met as we wandered in the desert for forty years'
'This is the God who went with us into exile'
'This is the God who revealed himself to Isaiah, Jeremiah, Hosea and the
other prophets'
'This is the God who made himself known in Jesus'
'This is the God we saw crucified'.
As I meditate on your word, may I add my experience to theirs:
'This is the God I have known in my own life.'

Abbreviations and acknowledgements

We are grateful for permission to quote from the following Bible versions:

CEV   Scripture quotations are from the *Contemporary English Version* Copyright © 1991, 1992, 1995 by American Bible Society, Used by Permission.

GNB/TEV Scriptures quoted are from the *Good News Bible: Today's English Version* © 1994 published by the Bible Societies/HarperCollins Publishers Ltd., *UK Good News Bible* © American Bible Society 1966, 1971, 1976, 1992. Used with permission.

NIV   Scripture taken from the *Holy Bible, New International Version®*. Copyright © 1973, 1978, 1984 International Bible Society. Used by permission of Zondervan. All rights reserved.

NLT   Scripture quotations are taken from the *Holy Bible, New Living Translation*, copyright 1996, 2004, 2007. Used by permission of Tyndale House Publishers, Inc., Wheaton, Illinois 60189. All rights reserved.

NJB   *The New Jerusalem Bible*, published by Darton, Longman & Todd, © Darton, Longman & Todd Ltd and Doubleday & Company, Inc., 1985.

NRSV   Bible selections are from the *New Revised Standard Version of the Bible*, copyright 1989 by the Division of Christian Education of the National Council of the Churches of Christ in the USA. Used by permission. All rights reserved.

TNIV   Scripture taken from the *Holy Bible, Today's New International Version®*. Copyright © 2001, 2005 by Biblica®. Used by permission of Biblica®. All rights reserved worldwide.

The Message Eugene H. Peterson, *The Message*. © 1993, 1994, 1995, 1996, 2000, 2001, 2002. Used by permission of NavPress Publishing Group.

Faces of the Divine

1 Creating God

Notes based on the *New International Version* by

Marian Strachan

Marian Strachan has taught in Papua New Guinea, Samoa and England. She is married to a Baptist minister who has also served in the United Reformed Church and as a university chaplain. Recently retired, they now look to serve God wherever, and however, they are able.

Introduction

God wants us to know him. He is not remote, far away, and unconcerned about us. Each one of us is valued and loved by him. Scripture is full of God's revelations of himself. In the Bible, he makes himself known through individuals, stories and events, as he works for the growth and well-being of his people. We are in the world to see, discern, and respond to the divine. Today we start with the familiar image of God the creator. This leads us on to discover other aspects of the nature of God.

Sunday 1 January: *Genesis 1:1-19*

Creating God, yesterday, today and forever

For many people the start of a new year is an opportunity to make resolutions and decisions, to try new activities, to be more creative. People often see the hand of God in new beginnings. We can welcome the New Year as an opportunity to dedicate ourselves to be more open to God, to learn more of him, and to trust him to be with us through the difficult times.

Scripture shows God creatively at work in many exciting new beginnings. The great opening statements of faith in Genesis: 'In the beginning God' and 'God created' set the scene for God's activity and self-revelation.

> *In the beginning God created the heavens and the earth . . . And God saw that it was good.*
>
> (verse 1 and part of verse 10)

Throughout history and today, God tells people about himself – who he is, what he has done and is doing, and what he will do. God's involvement and delight in his creation is ongoing, and we are invited to share in it.

† Creating God, we trust in you for all that this year will bring, and thank you because you are active in your world and in our lives.

Monday 2 January

Numbers 6:22-27

A blessing God

'The LORD bless you
and keep you;
the LORD make his face shine upon you
and be gracious to you;
the LORD turn his face towards you and give you peace.'

(verses 24-26)

What a wonderful, powerful blessing this is! When the people of Israel called on the name of the Lord with faith and reverence, God's power and presence became a reality for them, as it does for us today. The first part of each line of the blessing calls for God's personal act upon his people. He is asked to bless and protect them, to be gracious by showing love and mercy in dealing with their failings and weakness, and to bring them peace, which involved their total welfare and salvation as the people of God. The blessing reveals a God who turns his face towards his people in love as he looks on them for good.

This priestly blessing from the Old Testament is many centuries old and is probably the best-known benediction that comes to us from the Bible. Traditionally, the priests blessed the people every morning after the sacrifice at the Temple. Today many synagogues end their service with this blessing or benediction, and in Jewish homes it is used on the Sabbath to bless the household.

It is familiar to many of us because we are regularly blessed with these words in our churches at the close of worship. We also hear it during wedding services, and in infant baptisms or dedications. At our city church in Exeter, we often sing the blessing as we welcome children into the church family.

God's blessing is for people of every generation. It is given to us so that through us God can bless his whole creation. God's blessing, care and involvement with his people continue his creative work. He seeks to share and bless our lives, and to bless others through us.

† Pray for a family member, a friend or someone in need, using this blessing for them.

Marian Strachan   Creating God

2

Tuesday 3 January

Isaiah 65:17-25

A God who creates anew

'Behold, I will create new heavens and a new earth.
The former things will not be remembered,
nor will they come to mind.
But be glad and rejoice for ever
in what I will create.'

(verse 17 and part of verse 18)

In a popular UK television programme, damaged pictures, clocks, pottery and furniture are carefully and lovingly restored by craftsmen and experts until they look new. On many occasions in the history of God's people, God patiently and lovingly restores damaged relationships and situations. But Isaiah's vision seems to move beyond restoration. The recurring unfaithfulness and disobedience of the nation required a radical new beginning. There would be a new creation for God's people.

The new earth and new heavens that Isaiah sees leave the past behind and the people are made new. Peace, security, justice and a new intimacy of communication with God are present. There will be gladness and rejoicing because of the new creation and God himself will be full of joy. The renewed people of God, with all the blessings they have received, will bring blessings for their descendants and for the whole creation.

This vision is echoed in John's Revelation, chapter 21, where he describes the new heaven and the new earth. Both Isaiah and John lived in difficult and tragic times but through their visions they saw and believed that God was able to bring change and make all things new.

There is a song enjoyed especially by the young people in our churches in the UK that speaks of becoming a new creation, a new person through Christ, which is the gift of God for all who will receive it. We know that God can change people and situations and make them new. Very often God uses other people to bring new possibilities and opportunities to us. Sometimes, he seeks to use us, and what we can give, to bring change and new beginnings for others.

† God of new creations and possibilities, grant us wisdom and your help for all the new challenges, new opportunities, and new insights of the coming year.

Creating God   Marian Strachan

Wednesday 4 January

Psalm 104:24-35

A supporting, sustaining God

Good News Bible introduces Psalm 104 with the title, 'In Praise of the Creator'. The psalm celebrates the order, symmetry and majesty of creation. It recognises God's ongoing support as he provides and cares for his world.

> *How many are your works, O Lord!*
> *In wisdom you made them all; the earth is full of your creatures . . .*
> *These all look to you to give them their food at the proper time.*
> *When you give it to them, they gather it up;*
> *When you open your hand, they are satisfied with good things.*
>
> (verses 24, and 27-28)

God's sustenance is a daily gift to the world. Do we believe this? The psalmist certainly did. The God of Psalm 104 continues his activity in the world, giving new life. But what does this mean for us? How does our creating God sustain us today? Are the wonderful advances in agriculture, science, medicine and knowledge God's gifts? Is our creativity, inspiration and work our sharing in God's work?

Sustaining means 'giving strength to', 'encouraging', 'supporting', 'giving nourishment to', 'maintaining', 'keeping', 'bearing the weight of – particularly for a long period'. God did not create and then abandon his creation. Certainly, he risked allowing free will and rejection. But through the centuries Christians believe that God has sustained and supported his creation and this continues for us.

In our modern world there is a lot of discussion about sustainability. This is concerned with our sustaining and renewing of the world's resources. It is a challenge for everyone. We are called to be partners with God, helping to sustain his creation by conserving and sharing its resources, which can lead to a fairer and just world for all its peoples.

† Sustaining God, you give us the tools to maintain our lives and you stimulate in us gifts of creative vision and inventive skills. Grant that we may use these for the sake of all your people and the world around us.

Marian Strachan   Creating God

Thursday 5 January

Genesis 9:1-15

A remembering God

And God said, 'This is the sign of the covenant I am making between me and you and every living creature with you, a covenant for all generations to come. I have set my rainbow in the clouds, and it will be a sign of the covenant between me and the earth . . . I will remember my covenant between me and you and all living creatures of every kind.'

(verses 12-13 and part of verse 15)

Remembering can be a very positive thing. We remember people not because we have forgotten them but because we are thinking about them. We remember to do things because we want or intend to do them. Having learned a skill, we remember and can repeat it. The dictionary definition includes 'keeping in the memory', 'mentioning in prayer'. Remembering is not always the opposite of forgetting.

In the story of Noah and the Flood, God's remembering of his covenant is about his renewing of life on earth, following judgement on wickedness, corruption and violence.

God's making and remembering of his covenant is another instance of his creative activity for his people of all generations. The covenant is the gift of God to his people that guarantees his faithfulness and calls for them to be his people. In the New Testament Jesus is revealed as God's gift for our salvation, God's new covenant.

If we forget God and forget to allow him the creative space he longs for in our lives, we can be sure that he does not forget us. His remembers us, he is faithful, loving and forgiving, always reaching out to us, seeking to challenge us to receive from him and to grow in him.

† Remembering God, thank you for the assurance that we are lovingly held in your memory. May we remember those who, for whatever reason, need our support, love and prayer.

Creating God   Marian Strachan

Friday 6 January (Epiphany)

Isaiah 40:1-5

God manifests his glory

*And the glory of the L*ORD *will be revealed,*
and all mankind together will see it.

(verse 5a)

In this passage, Isaiah speaks of the return of God's people from exile. The Exile had been a time of darkness for the nation, both socially and spiritually. Now the prophet suggests that this dark time is coming to an end. There is light at the end of the tunnel. The people will return to their own land. God has not abandoned them.

In everybody's life there will be periods of darkness, and it is easy to feel abandoned. Sometimes there is no one to blame for this – we may be going through a time of illness or depression, or the darkness may have been brought on by unemployment or family worries. At other times we may have brought the darkness on ourselves through our own actions and attitudes, as God's people had done. In any case, God had not abandoned them, and he promises never to abandon us.

Isaiah says that when the people are rescued from exile and return home, 'the glory of the Lord will be revealed', not only to Israel but to all humankind. This is an 'epiphany', a shining light. Centuries later, the gospel writers saw the birth of Jesus as an epiphany in which God revealed himself not only to Israel but to the whole world. That is what we remember when we hear the story of the visit of the Magi on the feast of the Epiphany.

When God brings us out of darkness and into light, it is so that people will see him and be drawn to his light.

† When I am going through tough times, Lord, help me to know that you are there with me. Through these experiences, may I learn new things about you and about myself, and so grow in my faith and understanding. Then, when the light comes again into my life, may I not forget you, but remain humble and thankful. Through Christ, who suffered for me, Amen.

Marian Strachan

Creating God

Saturday 7 January

Genesis 2:1-3

A resting God

God had finished the work he had been doing; so on the seventh day he rested from all his work. And God blessed the seventh day and made it holy.

(part of verses 2 and 3)

I have a very amusing and useful book in which prominent church leaders, well-known musicians and others write about how they relax. It gives me hope to read it because these people provide creative, honest insights into the many and varied ways in which people can relax, rest and be re-energised. Do we see rest as one of God's special gift to us?

God's people down the centuries have observed time for rest and worship, a holy day. Sometimes strict rules and censorship on how this time should be used were negative and unhelpful. Today, we can be more positive and imaginative, and we need to be if we believe that rest and time with God are essential for health and faith. Working shifts, schedules, targets, church commitments and that essential time for family and friends have to be taken into account, but we all have to consider what is essential for us to have a balanced, healthy, God-centred life.

† Loving Lord, creator of all good things, forgive us when we neglect to rest, relax and take time out to be with you. Draw us closer to yourself and help us in the decisions we make, for our sakes and that of others.

For group discussion and personal thought

• Which image of God in our week's readings do you find the most interesting or helpful?

• In what ways has God sustained your life and faith during the past year?

• How do you relax and rest, and how can you help others to relax and rest?

Creating God   Marian Strachan

Faces of the Divine

2   Divine lover

Notes based on the *New International Version* by

Peter Ibison

Married, with two children, Peter is a member of the Anglican Church in Buckinghamshire where he lives with Margaret his wife. He works in the telecommunications industry and leads worship at his local church.

Introduction

Our Lord is a God who watches over us for our good. This week we will read of different 'faces of the divine': our God as healer, leader, one who hears our cries, seeks our devotion, and embraces all. As we reflect on passages of Scripture this week, let us pray that the Holy Spirit will reveal to us more of the character of our loving heavenly Father.

Sunday 8 January: *Exodus 3:13-17*
God who hears us

When God commissioned Moses from within a burning bush to speak to the Israelites, Moses had some concerns. Did God understand the people's predicament? Would he save them from their oppression? So Moses asked God not only his name but also its significance for him. God's answer was 'I am who I am' (verse 14), the God who had been with them, was with them now and would be with them in the future. When we face trials and difficulties we seek specific answers about our deliverance. God's assurance will be the same to us as to Moses: 'I will be with you' (Exodus 3:12):

> *I have watched over you and have seen what has been done to you in Egypt. And I have promised to bring you up out of your misery.*

(part of verses 16 and 17)

Moses needed to be confident that the people would listen and respect his authority. Years of tending sheep had drained his confidence. God did not respond by showing Moses what he was capable of doing, but by lifting his eyes to see himself in relation to God. The clearer our understanding of our relationship to God, the better resourced we will be to do his work.

† Help us, Lord, to remember that what you did for the Israelites you can do for us, because you are always with us.

Monday 9 January

Exodus 20:1-6

A jealous God

God gave the Ten Commandments to Moses for three purposes: to show our moral distance from God, to show our need for a mediator in approaching God, and to show us how to live a more abundant life. In today's passage God commanded:

'You shall have no other gods before me. You shall not make for yourself an idol.'

(verse 3 and part of verse 4)

How can we understand these commands today – addressed to a people who had been redeemed, who had been in bondage and were now free?

Firstly, when an evil is forbidden in one of the commandments, its opposite good is being encouraged. To have no other gods means to have only one God and only one focus for our devotion and worship. In practice this can mean not allowing ourselves to be drawn away by the anxieties of life, our wants and worldly ambitions, but instead to be wholehearted in our affection and devotion to God.

Secondly, idols are forbidden; this command is not meant to stifle artistic talent but only to avoid improper substitutes that, like the idols of Canaan, would steal hearts away from the true worship of God. God's jealousy can be seen in this context – it is an expression of love. He wants us to be devoted to him alone, knowing that we cannot share that devotion with other sources of affection. He must be loved first to be truly worshipped.

† 'Who is he who will devote himself to be close to me?' This was the call of the prophets. Lord, may I love you first, above all other loves. May you have first place in my heart. May I never lose the first love which I had at the beginning. Amen

Divine lover   Peter Ibison

Tuesday 10 January

Luke 17:11-19

The God who heals

Today's passage teaches us not only that God, in Jesus, is our healer. It also shows us the role the church has today in bringing healing to those outside the family of faith. Jesus steered a course through two countries at enmity with one another and saw ten lepers standing at a distance: outcasts, and a mixture of Jews and Samaritans. These ten men called in unison for healing from Jesus. Their theology might have been wanting but their cry was heartfelt:

'Jesus, Master, have pity on us.'

(verse 13)

Jesus did not immediately heal the ten but instead instructed them to go to the priests as a witness of their healing. This required faith on their part and as they went, they were cleansed. Today, Jesus calls his church to respond to the outcast and the marginalised, and to listen well. Many will experience God's grace through the church. Some will 'return', as did the Samaritan leper, and encounter a fuller healing. As he turned to the author of his healing, his cleansing and restoration were complete. Let us not be discouraged if only one out of every ten who hears of the restorative love of Jesus returns to know more. God is kind to the ungrateful; so let us not hold back from loving the outcast – even to those who show no gratitude, for as we do this we model the love of Jesus.

† Lord, you call your church to bring healing in your name to a lost world. Thank you for your grace which overflows to many. Help your church to show to others that same love, bringing your healing in relationship, in body and in soul.

Peter Ibison

Divine lover

Wednesday 11 January

Psalm 121

Watching over

Mountains surrounded the psalmist as he travelled, his life in danger from attackers and robbers. No obvious signs of help were visible. He chose, however, not to focus his attention on the threat, but rather on the God who made heaven and earth. When we face trials and difficulties our best starting place is to focus not on the magnitude of our problems but on the greatness of our God:

My help comes from the LORD,
the Maker of heaven and earth.

(verse 2)

How often we need to remind ourselves of the greatness of God when faced with life's challenges. The psalmist also reminds himself that God's love did not stop with a single creative act. He 'who watches over Israel' (verse 4) cares about nations, but is also the Lord who 'watches over you' (verse 5) as an individual. Note the direction of travel, from the general to the more specific, and the implications for our own prayers. If we start with our problems, we will not reach heaven's perspective. If, however, we start with heaven, then our problems are seen in true perspective.

Earlier in the week we read how Moses sought to understand the significance of God's name for his situation. Here the psalmist reminds himself of another aspect of God: he meets the need of the traveller, he is our shade at our side (verse 5).

† Lord, thank you that you are a God who watches over us. You never sleep or slumber. You hear our prayers, in whatever situation we find ourselves. Help me today to be mindful of your presence in all I do. Amen

Divine lover   Peter Ibison

Thursday 12 January
Psalm 77:11-20

Leading through

The psalmist speaks of his cry to God for help, at a time when God appeared to be silent. He tried with all the ingenuity he could muster to recapture his sense of God's presence, but neither his heartfelt prayers nor his acts of worship seemed to work. But when the psalmist reflected on the past and God's miracles and acts of mercy (in particular the crossing of the Red Sea) his hope for the present situation was restored.

I will meditate on all your works
And consider all your mighty deeds.

(verse 12)

Why was the psalmist encouraged by the account of the crossing? Was it the evidence of God's power over wind, storm and waves? Or was it the story of how God had raised up individuals (Moses and Aaron) to lead the people out of Egypt? When the children of Israel crossed the Red Sea, they thought that God had abandoned them and it was only later that they understood that God had been with them throughout their trials. Before the people crossed the Red Sea, Moses confidently asserted, 'God will surely come to your aid' (Exodus 13:19); but in their anxiety the people of Israel responded, 'What have you done to us by bringing us out of Egypt?' (Exodus 14:11). Their minds were confused and their anxiety levels high. In the same way, when we are in the midst of a crisis all we can see are the crashing waves, the wind and the storm; we cannot see the God whose 'footprints' are invisible. The true closeness of God was only seen later. The psalmist reminded himself of this, and so can we.

† Lord, whenever I see friends and family buffeted by the storms of life, help me to show your compassion and love. When others express confusion and doubt in the trials they face, help me to be patient and hold onto the hope that you will redeem your people, whether in this life or the next. Amen

Peter Ibison

Divine lover

Friday 13 January

Psalm 27:7-14

Abounding goodness

This psalm finishes with an expressed confidence in the goodness of God:

I am still confident of this:
I will see the goodness of the Lᴏʀᴅ in the land of the living.

(verse 13)

Such expressions of confidence do not occur in a vacuum; there are stepping stones to get there. Firstly, the psalmist understood his part in seeking God's presence. While he yearned to see more of the Lord in his life, he knew that such yearning was not sufficient in itself. The desire needed to be matched with activity on his part. David not only listened to his heart, but he acted on that inner prompting: 'My heart says of you, "Seek his face! Your face, Lᴏʀᴅ, I will seek." ' (verse 8). Many of us find ourselves unable to appreciate the goodness of God because we are waiting for God to do something which we must actually do for ourselves. We need to seek his face – and as we do, we will see his goodness.

Secondly, the psalmist did not allow himself to become embittered by life's interpersonal disappointments; for David, this involved the experience of rejection by his family. The effect of such experiences can run deep in our lives. But they can also serve to point us to a more permanent and secure source of love: 'Though my father and mother forsake me, the Lᴏʀᴅ will receive me' (verse 10). If we allow them, human disappointments can draw us to a deeper appreciation of the goodness of God.

† Lord, I praise you for your goodness, your love, your compassion and grace. My heart seeks after you: may my choices reflect that desire. Wherever I have faced rejection, may I instead be reminded of your loving acceptance. Amen

Divine lover   Peter Ibison

Saturday 14 January

Acts 10:23-35

Embracing all

Our final passage this week is the story of Peter's vision from heaven, which he later recounted to Cornelius, a Gentile. Its message was that God shows no favouritism in his multicultural dealings with men and women. God sets the scene. He reveals himself in a dream to Peter, and in a vision and prophetic word to Cornelius. Peter's dream concerned the eating of animals he believed to be unclean. Peter pondered the meaning of the vision and Cornelius provided the key to it. We can observe how the 'dividing wall of hostility' between Jew and Gentile began to be dismantled as both Peter and Cornelius realised the inclusiveness of God's embrace:

'God does not show favouritism but accepts men from every nation who fear him and do what is right.'

(verse 35)

This acceptance by God extends beyond human barriers of race, colour and gender. The key to overcoming our own prejudices is not to begin with ourselves, but with God, asking ourselves how he sees others who are different from us. As we ask him that question, then the barriers will begin to come down.

† Father, thank you for your loving embrace of all humankind. Help me today to see others as you see them and to show them your love. For Jesus' name sake. Amen

For group discussion and personal thought

Many of this week's readings have described the promise of God's constant presence in all aspects of our lives, especially in storms and strivings.

• What have you personally found most helpful in restoring your faith when you have gone through difficulties?

• In what circumstances have you felt closest to God?

• Do you know someone who would be encouraged by being reminded of the loving God who watches over them?

Peter Ibison

Divine lover

Faces of the Divine

3   Incarnating saviour

Notes based on the *Revised Standard Version* Catholic Edition by

Paula Fairlie OSB

Paula is a Benedictine nun and lives in Chester, England. She is now seventy, enjoying the spiritual freedom of older age.

Introduction

When we first meet people we notice their appearance. When we smile at them we notice their facial response. When we speak to one another, we hear the voice, see the gestures. When we leave them, what do we remember? It may be their appearance or a hidden quality we have perceived. When God became man he could only communicate with us on the level of our humanity and our ability to understand. When we receive the Spirit of Christ, we too may be able to incarnate some qualities of the saviour in our relationship with others.

Sunday 15 January: *John 3:16-21*
Sacrificing

> *For God so loved the world that he gave his only Son, that whoever believes in him should not perish but have eternal life.*
>
> (verse 16)

Every day we are silently asked: Do you believe in the Son of God? Our answer affects our heart, mind, conduct, and judgement. We are given a choice, even when our faith is weak, to want to believe, to desire eternal life, to be enlightened, to avoid sin and inner darkness. If God could send his Son into our darkness, surely we can respond with a glimmer of hope amid our confused state, often touched by sin and despair? As light shines on clear water, may the glory of God shine out of our loving eyes.

† Dear Lord, we find it difficult to live in the light, and we shield our eyes. Grant that we may respond to your sacrifice in the dim, dazzling light of faith. Amen

Monday 16 January

Philippians 2:5-11

Incarnating: finding a human face

Have this mind among yourselves, which was in Christ Jesus.

(verse 5)

Although we cannot 'incarnate' Jesus in our own flesh, we are called to receive him in our mind and heart. If we allow him to live within us, our attitude and behaviour may then reveal him wordlessly to others. We are reminded here that he came down to earth, renouncing his divine attributes, discovering the joy of being formed from the earth, of living among us like a servant. He also lived through the consequences of being human: he was hungry and tired, misunderstood and rebuffed. These are often our experiences, which we have not chosen to suffer. There are many people who suffer death on account of their belief or race – something which most of us hope to avoid. Jesus plunged into the mystery of pain and suffering, actually and truly suffering, while we hope that our lives will be long, spent in service, and with a peaceful end. At the conclusion of today's reading we are told that God 'exalted' Jesus, giving him the highest honour possible, so that 'every tongue will confess that Jesus is the Lord, to the glory of God the Father' (verse 11). Did Paul see this in a moment of ecstatic exaltation? Was it a moment of intense revelation in faith? Then the question comes: 'Is this really what "heaven" is like?' For those of us who don't share Paul's vision, this contrast between loving humility and regal exaltation is too great. Is Jesus really like that? Is he not still among us, lowly, suffering, loving and faithful in our afflicted humanity – in us?

† Dear Lord Jesus, human power and authority can be terrifying. Please remain among us as a lowly and humble Son of Man. Amen

Tuesday 17 January

John 10:1-10

Offering full life

I came that they may have life, and have it abundantly.

(part of verse 10)

It is rather strange to be likened to sheep! Like fish, they are for most of us ultimately food. We can only hope that we are destined to share the bounty of God with the rest of creation, neither eating nor drinking in the place where there is no giving in marriage! Sheep are looked after because they are useful, yet they form a trusting relationship with those who care for them. Is it really in God's interest that we should relate to him as sheep in this way? I would like to think not – especially as the theme of this section of the gospel is about having 'abundant life'. So we are kept safe in a sheepfold, with high walls and a gate, which robbers cannot easily enter. Does this mean that we are protected from evil? Not fully, for we retain our own free will. Elsewhere in John's Gospel Jesus is described as the Lamb of God, the sacrificial lamb. So life and death are intimately connected in Jesus – and in us. Some aspects of our life have to pass through 'death' in order to become fully alive. The ancients used to regard the body as a 'prison'. Later, this was not considered correct: we are only fully human within our human limitations. However, scientific discoveries have revealed that everything created is pulsating with energy. The whole universe is pulsating with invisible – and abundant – life. As matter decays, that energy flows free and God directs it as he wills.

† Dear Lord, we are people with little understanding, incapable of fully knowing how to live in your presence. Please guide and protect us until we are fully united with you. Amen

Incarnating saviour   Paula Fairlie

Wednesday 18 January

Matthew 17:1-8

Transfiguring

[A]fter six days Jesus . . . led them up a high mountain . . . and he was transfigured before them, and his face shone like the sun, and his garments became white as light.

(part of verse 1, and verse 2)

This wonderful text first of all brings to mind the account of creation in Genesis 2, when after six days the Lord God rested. It is also a wonderfully poetic allusion to what happened to Moses on a high mountain, though without the thunder, flashes of lightning and primeval terror, although terror was there in the three disciples who accompanied Jesus. Jesus is represented as the new Moses, as he speaks to Moses and Elijah, who both received new revelations about the law and prophecy. Jesus was overshadowed by a bright cloud, as Mary had been overshadowed by the power of the Most High when he was conceived. Yet when the vision ended, instead of trailing 'clouds of glory', Jesus was outwardly just the same.

We may not have seen, heard or experienced the same as Peter, James and John, but there are times when the Word of God both touches and transfigures us. This is when a certain energy of new life possesses us: we are in love, and we are radiant; we have made a new discovery, and bubble with excitement; we may have learned to see God in the ordinary events of life, and our peaceful face and calm smile radiate serenity. It is through this quiet experience that lives are touched, that men and women become sons and daughters of the God whose words heal and bring both purpose and hope.

† Dear Lord, thank you for the small revelations you give us in daily life, for the love which transfigures us and those whom we meet – without a word being spoken. Amen

Paula Fairlie

Incarnating saviour

Thursday 19 January

Ephesians 2:11-22

Reconciling

But now in Christ Jesus you who were once far off have been brought near in the blood of Christ. For he is our peace, who made us both one, and has broken down the dividing wall of hostility.

(verses 13-14)

This whole passage makes me feel sad. It describes what Paul believed had happened through the redemptive death of Christ. His imagery comes from the Temple in Jerusalem, before it was destroyed. It had different areas for different people. The Jews could come closer to the Holy of Holies than the Gentiles who did not share the Jewish faith. This segregation of peoples in religious matters was important to ensure purity of practice in the faith. It did not include separation for converts to Judaism from other races: the unifying factor was a common belief, as it should also be in Christianity and Islam. However, all three monotheistic religions are now riddled by divisions, controversies and even violence and persecution.

Paul knew that potentially this alienation was over: Christ had created a new human race in himself – one body, as man and woman had been created to be one body. However, these intentions have not been visibly fulfilled. Despite Christ's atoning death, hostility has not been brought to an end, as we are reminded in this Week of Prayer for Christian Unity. We may have access to the Father in one Spirit but our holy temple has become a torn garment which does not cover the nakedness of difference.

† Dear Lord, forgive us for not obeying your intention for our unity in Christ. We are a fragmented people, scattering ourselves over the earth, as you once scattered the people who tried to usurp your place at Babel. Please call us back, so that we may be truly one in Christ through the power of the Holy Spirit. Amen

Incarnating saviour   Paula Fairlie

Friday 20 January

1 John 4:7-12

Atoning

No man has ever seen God; if we love one another, God abides in us and his love is perfected in us.

(verse 12)

This is a most wonderful affirmation of love, and extremely reassuring to those who feel bewildered about their relationship with God: 'If we love one another, God abides in us and his love is perfected in us.' Isn't it wonderful that people who do not know God are blessed by him through their loving concern for others? 'Truly I say to you, as you did it to one of the least of my brethren, you did it to me' (Matthew 25:40). Like me, you have probably experienced in your own life being blessed by inexplicable acts of kindness and concern by virtual strangers, who simply sensed our need and quietly responded. There was no intrusion, no sense that we were indebted, simply a generous act on their part and thankfulness on ours. To me, that is how God acts in our lives, and – to my shame – I realise that I almost take it for granted. I still pray for these kind strangers, knowing that my prayer can reach back to times when they too were in need, times when they too were inexplicably touched by God through the prayers of others.

However, this gift of love – which is a free gift to us – required a definitive act from God. His Son became incarnate 'for the expiation of our sins'. Why should God suffer on our behalf? Why do parents sacrifice their lives for their children? It can only be because they are motivated by love, and believe in the value of life. This remains a mystery, found even in other creatures. Is it a God-given instinct, blessed by love?

† Thank you, Lord, for the wonder of your love. Amen

Paula Fairlie

Incarnating saviour

Saturday 21 January

Mark12:28-34

Practising love

'[T]o love [God] with all the heart, and with all the understanding, and with all the strength, and to love one's neighbour as oneself, is much more than all whole burnt offerings and sacrifices.'

(verse 33)

Does the building of large churches, beautifully decorated and maintained at great cost, demonstrate true love of God, if the people around them live in abject poverty? Not according to this reading, in which unblemished animals had been reared not to provide food but to be consumed by fire as 'whole burnt offerings and sacrifices'. God doesn't want that sort of sacrifice. Don't we get things wrong if we put elaborate and costly ceremonies before worship in spirit and truth, and leave people to starve around us? Shouldn't we be feeding the hungry, clothing the naked, nursing the sick? Worship from the heart in a simple meeting place can unite rich and poor alike in the giving and receiving of spiritual gifts. We need to listen to this text with our hearts. God wants us to care for each other, and also to care for ourselves: this is how we show him love.

† Dear Lord, may we love you with understanding hearts and concern for all your creation. Amen

For group discussion and personal thought

• Have you caught a glimpse of God today and seen him at work in the people around you?

• Take a moment to look quietly around you, listen to the sounds, and feel the air – the air we all need and share. What have you done to make this world, this home, this workplace a better place to live in?

• How has God touched you today, and shown you how to act with love?

Incarnating saviour   Paula Fairlie

Faces of the Divine

4 Faithful companion

Notes based on the *New International Version* by

Meeli Tankler

Meeli Tankler lives in Estonia. She is a President of the Baltic Methodist Theological Seminary in Tallinn, Estonia. Married to a Methodist pastor, she is mother of three grown-up children, and a grandmother.

Introduction

While exploring the richness of scriptural images of the divine presence among us, we can experience the comforting assurance that this presence is faithful and stable. In the various stages of our life, and in good or bad situations, we encounter God as our companion on the road – sometimes encouraging us, sometimes reminding us about something important, sometimes stepping right into our troubled and scattered life – and sometimes just being silently present so that we need not feel alone.

Sunday 22 January: *Jeremiah 31:10-17*
Hope revealed

> *'So there is hope for your future,'* declares the LORD.

(part of verse 17)

We are suspicious of declarations because we have so often been disappointed, watching beautiful words turn into nothing and those who made the declarations failing to carry them through. With God it is different. His words are never empty words – he declares that 'my word that goes out from my mouth . . . will not return to me empty, but will accomplish what I desire' (Isaiah 55:11). What will it accomplish then, as a word of hope?

In today's reading, the reality of divine hope begins to unfold. The beauty of life with God – and the abundance of his grace – becomes very vivid. There are pictures of people all ages dancing and shouting for joy, abundant harvests of grain, wine and oil, and the satisfaction of being rewarded for heavy labour. All this is brought before our eyes as a testimony about the mighty God whose presence can and will change everything.

† Lord, thank you for this wonderful assurance that we do have a living hope even in the midst of our tears. You alone have the power to turn our mourning into gladness. Help us to stay close to you. Amen

Monday 23 January

Romans 8:18-27

Groaning for creation

Ajith Fernando, a theologian from Sri Lanka, speaks about 'the theology of groaning' as something we have almost forgotten in our success-driven ministry. He points out that the biblical view of praise does not exclude the real need to complain now and then as we experience the depths of human misery. However, as Fernando says, these complaints are 'the cries of those who believe that God is good and cannot now see this goodness in what they are experiencing. They cry out to God, but their cries are tinged with hope' (*Jesus Driven Ministry*, Crosswaybooks 2007, p.142). We become more and more aware of this 'ecological misery' these days as we see and hear nature around us groaning as it

> *waits in eager expectation for the sons of God to be revealed . . .*
> *in hope that the creation itself will be . . . brought into the glorious*
> *freedom of the children of God.*
>
> (part of verses 19-21)

This groaning should remind us that as human beings we have been called to take care of the earth from the very beginning of time, and God has not yet changed this calling. How worried are we about God's creation? Do we see the world as God's, created to be good but suffering the consequences of human sinfulness? Are ecological problems sometimes shaking our faith in almighty God?

We can still keep in mind the image of the good God as our daily companion who has sent his Spirit to intercede for us and the world around us, even when we 'do not know what we ought to pray for' (verse 26) and are just groaning together with the whole creation.

† Our Creator God, thank you for this world you have created so we can live in it. Help us to see it with the eyes of a good steward, and act in it in a responsible way. Thank you for your Spirit who guides our prayers for this world. Amen

Faithful companion   Meeli Tankler

Tuesday 24 January

Luke 2:1-7

Becoming vulnerable

[S]he gave birth to her firstborn, a son. She wrapped him in cloths and placed him in a manger, because there was no room for them in the inn.

(verse 7)

We almost certainly heard this text just a month ago, at Christmas, but then it was in a special setting of great joy and celebration, and perhaps we did not listen very carefully. But as you read it again in the midst of your daily life, have you ever pondered why God actually did such a risky thing as sending his Son to this world in exactly the same way that every human being begins their earthly journey?

The Son of God could certainly have stepped down from heaven as a full-grown man, ready and fit for his earthly ministry. However, God chose another way to reveal his real closeness to us as human beings, created in his image. As Jesus was born into this world, and grew up as a Jewish boy in a little village, he experienced everything that was human, from birth to death, and reflected his Father's glory in the midst of it.

Wherever we are in our life journey – in childhood, youth, adulthood, old age, experiencing joy, sorrow or suffering – we can be sure that the incarnated Christ has also been there. He knows the human life fully. And in this blessed assurance we can rely on God's faithful presence in our life, as an experienced companion who has made himself vulnerable by feeling human pain and sorrow just like any of us.

† Father in heaven, your love for the world is incredible: you did not hesitate to give your son into human hands as a helpless newborn baby for our sake. He became one of us, and led an ordinary life among ordinary people. We stand in awe before your love, revealed to us in such a special way. Amen

Meeli Tankler   Faithful companion

Wednesday 25 January

Amos 5:11-15

Hating evil

Today Amos brings us a word from God that is addressed to everyone living when 'times are evil' (verse 13): we should be very clear about our attitudes, we should hate evil and love good if we want to live the life that God intends for us. But even this is not the ultimate guarantee of God's mercy, because we can never manipulate God with our deeds or words. So after his admonishing words, Amos gives us this very carefully worded almost promise:

> *Perhaps the LORD God Almighty will have mercy*
> *on the remnant of Joseph.*

(part of verse 15)

When we walk with God as our faithful companion in our daily life, and try to learn and do his will, we hopefully become more and more influenced by his holy character. In this process we gradually learn to see our life through different lenses. And though we may not like the idea of hating something, as we begin to reflect God's character in our lives, we realise that hating evil is the only way of truly loving good, because these two poles cannot coexist. So we need to make constant choices – we need to 'seek good', as Amos puts it, and here God's Spirit will gracefully guide us.

Perhaps the Lord will have mercy? I sincerely believe he will, as we continue our journey in 'seeking good' together with him, so that we can live. But even as we become better in our search for good by practising hard, we can never earn God's mercy just by hating evil and loving good. His mercy always remains a divine gift from above.

† Thank you, Lord, for your companionship that guides us in our daily living. Help us to learn from you and to reflect your holy character in our lives. Amen

Faithful companion

Meeli Tankler

Thursday 26 January
Habakkuk 1:1-6

Trusting God's answers

In a true relationship, communication is a key issue. We expect our loved ones to listen to us and respond to our pleas, just as we try to do the same for them. In our relationship with God we tend to be more eager to speak than to listen, and we do not hear the responses as clearly as we would like. But sometimes we get a feeling that God's answers do not quite match our prayers. He seems to hear something other than what we are telling him, and his answers may even confuse us.

Perhaps we are then tempted to say that he has not answered at all. As our expectations are not met, and the encouragement and support we were waiting for is not there, we try harder, making our requests again and asking for 'another' or better answer.

But perhaps the first answer we got was the best available answer. God's ways are not our ways, and as he faithfully stays with us no matter what happens, his presence is always the best answer.

In today's passage we can see how the human eye and God's eye are looking in the same direction but seeing different things. While the human eye can see only destruction, violence, strife and conflict, God is pointing to the future where he can already see clearly everything that he is going to do:

> 'For I am going to do something in your days
> That you would not believe,
> Even if you were told.

(part of verse 5)

What a wonderful companion to have on our daily journey!

† Almighty God, as we pray in desperate situations we hope to receive consolation and help from you. Teach us to trust your vision of the future as you guide us towards your greater goals for our life, and not to grasp only at the moment. Teach us to lean on your everlasting love. Amen

Meeli Tankler   Faithful companion

Friday 27 January
Psalm 11

A companion who loves justice

We generally appreciate friends who are sincere with us, whom we can trust to treat us fairly and tell us the truth. This is not always pleasant, of course, because those friends may point out things in our lives that need attention. But they do it in order to help us to recognise our failures – sometimes just little slipping moments when we have not been fair to others around us. But insofar as we trust their love for us, we can appreciate their candidness.

In today's passage, the psalmist reminds us that the Lord carefully observes and examines all people on the earth – but this is always a fair and just examination. Human beings are capable of righteousness and justice; God is continually looking for it, and is pleased whenever he finds it.

> For the LORD is righteous,
> he loves justice;
> upright men will see his face.

(verse 7)

We are walking daily with a divine companion who loves justice and is sincerely committed to it. It is part of his innermost being. So there may be times when we hear a loving reproach or reminder from him, just to keep us on the path of righteousness. But we can always be sure that it comes from a loving friend who treats us fairly, and as we try to seek justice on our walk, God will be our support and guide.

† Lord, thank you for leading us towards righteousness. Let us learn to love justice just as you yourself love it. And keep us close to you so that we can find our refuge in you in the midst of the injustice of this world. Amen

Faithful companion   Meeli Tankler

Saturday 28 January
Acts 2:14-24

Dying and rising

Peter's sermon at Pentecost points out the magnificence of God's presence in the whole of human history. The divine presence is not easy to describe, because it can be experienced in countless ways, and during human history multitudes of people have given their testimonies about unique encounters with God. And yet, 'in these last days he has spoken to us by his son' (Hebrews 1:2) and Peter is standing here, explaining to us the significance of this great event. For Peter, Jesus Christ is not just a historical person – he is a living companion, and lo and behold, even as he has died, he is still a living companion because God has raised him,

> *freeing him from the agony of death, because it was impossible for death to keep its hold on him.*

(part of verse 24)

This very personal experience of Jesus, and of the Holy Spirit, gives strength and power to Peter's sermon. He does not preach a nice theory about living in the presence of God; he tells a true personal story, Peter's own story that continues to be the focus and treasure of his life.

† Thank you, gracious God, for offering us your presence in the person of your Son Jesus. Thank you for raising him from the dead to be our faithful companion for ever through his Holy Spirit. And thank you for the opportunity to have this personal encounter with Jesus today. Amen

For group discussion and personal thought
- How has the rich and diverse imagery of God's presence helped to shape your knowledge of God's character?
- How have you experienced God's presence in your life – has it been surprising, comforting, challenging?
- Have you experienced God's confusing answers to your prayers, or situations in which God has challenged you on issues of justice?

Meeli Tankler   Faithful companion

Faces of the Divine

5 Inviting host

Notes based on the *New Revised Standard Version* by

David Huggett

David Huggett is a Baptist minister. He has had pastoral experience and worked with the Bible Society, the Leprosy Mission, as an editor, and in adult Christian education. Now in active retirement, he lives with his wife in Somerset.

Introduction

In his hymn 'There's a wideness in God's mercy', F.W. Faber wrote that 'the love of God is broader than the measures of our mind'. Such love makes God vulnerable. This week we explore some of the ways in which the biblical writers express their understanding of this as God invites us to enjoy his blessings.

Sunday 29 January: *John 1:35-39*

A wide welcome

Jesus, the wandering peasant preacher from Galilee, knew what it was to be excluded (verses 10 and 11), as he gained a reputation for consorting with others who were excluded by society. The very people who should have been offering hospitality to this homeless preacher criticised him for mixing with undesirable characters like tax gatherers and prostitutes (Luke 5:30). It is therefore significant that at the outset of his ministry Jesus gave a generous welcome when two of John the Baptist's followers asked where he is living. He simply says,

'Come and see.'

(part of verse 39)

No conditions were laid down. No statement of faith was required; no commitment; no character reference. The standard is set for the rest of his ministry. Later he will talk openly to a Samaritan woman by a well, refuse to condemn a flagrant adulteress, offer bread and wine to a traitor, and promise a place by his side in Paradise to a convicted terrorist. Polite society excludes them; Christ does not. Without any stipulations, he welcomes them.

† Lord God, thank you for loving all, including me, without any preconditions. Help me to remove my prejudices against people who are different from me, and who don't always see things as I do. May my love grow daily wider and more undemanding.

Monday 30 January

Job 28:12-28

Wisdom for all

The Industrial Revolution of the early nineteenth century changed our world. The Technological Revolution of the twentieth and twenty-first centuries is changing it again. Such human achievements are considerable and we celebrate them. Job too celebrated the achievements of his day. In the first eleven verses of this chapter he describes some of the technological achievements seen in his day, largely in terms of mining. In verses 14-19 he celebrates economic achievement. But Job also knew that however great the skill, expertise and knowledge accumulated by human beings, much more important is what he called wisdom. Technology has often been misused. Economic success can be indulged selfishly. Mind-blowing discoveries can be used in evil ways. What we human beings need is wisdom. The source and giver of that wisdom is God:

> And he said to humankind,
> 'Truly, the fear of the LORD, that is wisdom;
> and to depart from evil is understanding.'

(verse 28)

Fear, of course, is not to be understood as dread, but rather as respect and reverence. And the breadth of God's love is once again made clear as the offer of wisdom is made to humankind, not to a favoured few. The psalmist agrees that this kind of fear is the first step to real wisdom (Psalm 111:10). Knowledge is precious but wisdom is more important. And the closer we come to God, the more we enter into the experience of true wisdom.

† 'If any of you is lacking in wisdom, ask God, who gives to all generously and ungrudgingly, and it will be given you' (James 1:5). Thank you, Lord.

David Huggett   Inviting host

Tuesday 31 January
Exodus 16:1-16

Satisfying hunger

Just six weeks into their adventure the Israelites faced another crisis. As far as they were concerned, on both previous occasions – the escape from Egypt and the parting of the Red Sea – the solution had been miraculous. Perhaps it was time for another miracle. Sometimes as Christians we seem to live looking for the next miracle. We expect God to step in, intervening in life in supernatural ways. Rather like base jumpers launching themselves off skyscrapers with only a parachute in order to enjoy ten seconds of extreme excitement, we look for our next spiritual adrenaline rush. God's immense patience is emphasised four times in these verses, as Moses assures them:

'Draw near to the Lord, for he has heard your complaining.'

(part of verse 9)

But maybe the answer, when it came, was not quite the miracle they may have expected. The manna was no magical, supernatural creation, but something that still occurs naturally in the region. Insects cause the tamarisk tree to excrete a sticky substance which the Bedouin still call manna. The quails are birds that fly in great flocks and sometimes get blown off course. Landing exhausted, they can easily be collected and slaughtered. The miracle consisted rather in the guidance the people were given, first of all to realise that these naturally occurring things are edible, and then to know how to handle and prepare them for their use. Perhaps we too need to be reminded that God is present and active in the ordinary and the natural. If we spend our time looking always for the extraordinary, we may easily miss him.

† Lord, open my eyes to see you working in ordinary ways in my life, and when the going gets tough help me to replace my complaining with trust in your great generosity.

Inviting host   David Huggett

Wednesday 1 February

Psalm 23

A royal feast

In the ancient world kings and other rulers were often described as the shepherds of their people. So it is not surprising that from the early days of Israel's monarchy David, with his background as a shepherd boy, should be described in this way. Later the idea of the 'shepherd-king' was applied to the promised Messiah (Micah 5:7). In John 10 Jesus applies the title of shepherd to himself. The theme of the shepherd-king is clearly applied to God himself in this most beautiful psalm. The first four verses are full of rural pictures – the rich pastures, running streams and rocky valleys are the backdrop of a shepherd's life. They are also a reminder of a God who protects his people, risking and even laying down his life for them. But then in verses 5 and 6 we are transported to the king's palace. There he bestows his hospitality upon his servants. He provides not just the bare essentials but includes them in his banquet. The feasting, the eastern welcome signified by the rich perfumes on offer, and the flowing wine (verse 5) are all eclipsed by the permanent home in the palace that the king provides for his followers (verse 6). The symbols of this twofold nature of a true shepherd-king are the 'rod' or sceptre, and the 'staff' or shepherd's crook. As we recognise the psalmist's picture of God, fulfilled supremely for us in Jesus, we can agree, whatever our current situation, that

I fear no evil;
for you are with me;
your rod and staff –
they comfort me.

(part of verse 4)

† I thank you, Lord, for my personal experience of your protection and rich provision; thank you too that I am part of the flock.

David Huggett

Inviting host

Thursday 2 February
Matthew 14:13-21

More than enough

To understand the full impact of this familiar story we need to notice that Matthew places it immediately after the account of John the Baptist's death. We have here the record of two very different meals. First there is Herod's birthday party (verses 6-11). As ruler of Galilee he could afford a lavish affair with an impressive guest list. Course after course of rich food was brought in; the wine flowed; the dancing became ever more erotic; and the ruler displays his power in the grisly trophy brought in on a plate. What a contrast with the meal Jesus hosted. Quite naturally, the news of John's murder upset him and he wanted to be alone. But, as always with Jesus, the needs of people were paramount. Faced with a very large crowd who had followed him to an isolated spot Jesus revealed his power. But it wasn't a power like Herod's: it was the power of compassion expressed in healing (verse 14), and in providing food for the hungry.

And all ate and were filled; and they took up what was left over of the broken pieces, twelve baskets full.

(verse 20)

It was very basic. Nothing like Herod's banquet. No flowing wine. And I've often wondered what happened to those leftovers. We are not told, but it was a comparatively small amount considering the largeness of the crowd. This reminds us that while God gives enough and some to spare he is not wasteful – a lesson that is sadly ignored in our wasteful western society.

† Lord, we remember those who today are living in their own personal wilderness – hungry for food, thirsty for clean water, longing for freedom. Help us to rise to your challenge to 'give them something to eat'.

Inviting host   David Huggett

Friday 3 February

Philippians 4:1-7

Peace to share

Paul lived during that period which historians have dubbed the 'Pax Romana' – the Roman peace. Yet the Roman empire had been built on war, conquest and brutal suppression. Although now they were experiencing a time of relative peace, Paul understands the irony of it as he languishes in prison. The Philippian Christians are also facing opposition (Philippians 1:28, 30), and conflict has even found its way into the church (verse 2). Yet Paul is also clear that God's gracious invitation includes the experience of a deep inner peace that does not rely on outward circumstances, and cannot be engineered by human ingenuity.

The peace of God, which surpasses all understanding, will guard your hearts and your minds in Christ Jesus.

(verse 7)

Conflict, in whatever form it may affect us, is never pleasant; so to have the opportunity of a deep inner sense of peace is a prize that is highly valued. The tone of this letter shows that Paul had discovered this experience for himself, so it is worth asking how he achieved it. The simple answer, which we forget all too quickly, is to develop the habit of conversing with God (verse 6). This has the effect of opening up our innermost being to a deep and mysterious sense of wholeness and calm. C.S. Lewis once said, 'God cannot give happiness and peace apart from himself', so however difficult we may find it, however time-consuming, it is clearly worth cultivating that relationship with God.

† Lord, in a world that, in spite of our pious hopes and our best efforts, is often afflicted with cruel conflict, may your peace rule in our hearts, and may our lives be so governed by your Spirit that we may be true peacemakers in our world today.

David Huggett   Inviting host

Saturday 4 February

2 Corinthians 3:1-6

The letter and the Spirit

Some people regard the Russian Anton Chekov as the greatest ever writer of short stories, although perhaps he is best known for his play *The Cherry Orchard*. He died at the early age of 44 but we learn much about his complex character from the intriguing record he left us, entitled *A Life in Letters*. With our modern electronic communication, the great age of handwritten letter writing may have passed, but still we reveal something about ourselves in the letters we write. Paul takes up this image and applies it to the Christian. He suggests that our lives are themselves letters, sent out for all to read. When we are followers of Jesus Christ, people will 'read' us, not only to discover the kind of people we have become, but also to reflect on the one we claim to follow. True, some people may be sufficiently curious to pick up a Christian book or a Bible, but everyone will read the letter of our lives. The challenging thing is to ask ourselves honestly, 'What will they read?' If the only picture they ever gain of Jesus Christ is from looking at us, will they be attracted or repelled? This may seem too great a responsibility. But we are not to be discouraged, for,

> *you are a letter of Christ . . . written not with ink but with the Spirit of the living God.*

> (part of verse 3)

† Thank you, Lord, that your Spirit gives life.

For group discussion and personal thought

- In what ways could you help your church to become a more welcoming community?
- 'Half the world is starving; the other half is on a diet' (Madeleine L'Engle). How do you respond to that?

Inviting host   David Huggett

Readings in Mark

1 Jesus: teacher and healer (1)

Notes based on the *New International Version* by

Susan Hibbins

Susan Hibbins is a freelance writer and editor who endeavours to apply the Christian faith to everyday living in the twenty-first century. She is especially interested in history and choral music, and is secretary of a local community choir.

Introduction

In these passages from Mark's Gospel, we see Jesus meet with many different people. Each encounter is vividly described: we can feel the heat of the sun and the pushing and jostling of the crowd desperate to reach Jesus. We can smell fear and anguish, and hear the groans of the sick. We feel afraid among the rocky tombs where Legion dwells, helpless and alone. And in the midst of all this is Jesus, listening and healing, and reaping a rich harvest for his Father's kingdom.

Sunday 5 February: *Mark 1:29-39*
Many people, many needs

> *Very early in the morning, while it was still dark, Jesus got up, left the house and went off to a solitary place, where he prayed.*

(verse 35)

Early in Jesus' ministry, people turn to him for help. Simon's mother-in-law is ill and Jesus heals her; after sunset, crowds turn up, seeking him. And even though he must have been tired himself, he deals patiently with them all. Jesus never puts his own need for rest and comfort before that of others. How did he keep going?

The clue lies in verse 35: prayer and quiet waiting upon God's will were essential to Jesus. We can imagine him slipping out before dawn while others slept, to pray and draw on that refreshment and peace that he found in communion with his Father – before the world once again sought him out.

---

† Dear Lord, when life is busy and we have much to accomplish each day, remind us first to enter your presence in prayer. In this time of refreshment and renewal help us to know your will, and then to do those tasks you ask of us, one at a time, knowing that you will give us the strength we need.

Monday 6 February
Mark 4:1-20

Sowing the seed of God's word

A farmer went out to sow his seed.

(part of verse 3)

The subjects of Jesus' parables are just as relevant now as they were when he first spoke them aloud to people. Most people today have seen at least pictures of crops growing and farmers sowing and reaping, even though a great deal of our food is imported. I wonder if Jesus, during the years that he worked in the carpenter's shop in Nazareth, stored up images in his mind that later helped him in his teaching? And whether he watched the sower in the fields around his home, flinging the seed wide so that it fell on all kinds of ground? Jesus knew that such images would have been seen and remembered by his audience, and he spoke so vividly that his words would stay with them long after he had finished speaking.

His disciples needed to hear Jesus' teaching explained in more detail. It was they who would go out to sow the seed of God's word, and they needed to know that although many would hear them with enthusiasm, the results in their lives might be brief or non-existent. Much seed would be sown for apparently little harvest. Yet from that harvest, more good seed would grow, the yield increasing as the harvest became greater.

And what about us? Is our harvest increasing as the years go by? Are we tending the seed in our own lives so that it becomes a source of food for others? Each time we see the shoots of new growth, or the harvest gathered in, we are reminded of this parable, just as Jesus intended.

† Help us, Lord, to sow your word in the hearts of those with whom we live and work and meet day by day. May your word fall on fertile ground, and reap a rich harvest for your kingdom.

Jesus: teacher and healer 1   Susan Hibbins

Tuesday 7 February

Mark 4:21-25

A shining truth

'Do you bring in a lamp to put it under a bowl or a bed?'

(part of verse 21)

Once again Jesus uses an everyday image to explain an important truth. No one would put a lamp under cover, where its light would not be seen. Even more, the light that Jesus brought into the world can do no good if it is hidden. 'For whatever is hidden is meant to be disclosed' (verse 22). Is our Christianity kept hidden from view? Is it a Sunday faith, brought out once a week and then kept out of sight for the other six days? I asked myself this question recently: how many people I know see Jesus in me? Does my behaviour always reflect my Christian belief? The answer was not a comfortable one. Christianity in theory and not in practice is not what Jesus asked of his followers, or of us. But the more we put into our faith, the more we will receive from it. Once the light of our faith is put to work in the world, its rays reflect back to us as well as others. Paradoxically, the more we give the more we get back.

The final two verses of today's reading may seem a harsh saying of Jesus; they are not, but they do contain a warning. Anyone who has a gift knows they have to keep working at it, or they will not improve or, at worst, will lose what skill they have. It is the same with our faith. Forgetting our prayers, discontinuing our Bible study, drifting away from our discipleship, will have one end result: we will lose what little faith we had in the first place. We need to be careful that our light does not go out.

† May our lives reflect the light of your truth, O Lord. Challenge us to bring your light into the darkest corners of our world, to be unafraid in proclaiming your word in our own situations, so that all may see your glory through us.

Susan Hibbins

Jesus: teacher and healer 1

Wednesday 8 February

Mark 4:26-32

From small beginnings

'What shall we say the kingdom of God is like . . .? It is like a mustard seed, which is the smallest seed . . . Yet when planted, it grows and becomes the largest of all garden plants, with such big branches that the birds of the air can perch in its shade.'

(part of verses 30-31, and verse 32)

One autumn my husband pushed a little acorn into the border of our garden. 'Who knows,' he said jokingly, 'one day we might have an oak tree big enough to build a ship.' Nothing happened for many months, and then one day we noticed two small, crumpled leaves on a slender stem, just about holding their own against all the weather threw at them. The following year several other leaves and even thinner stems survived. Three years later our little oak sapling is still clinging on, a little bigger but still very fragile. It seems impossible to believe that mighty oak trees, once used to build ships for the British Navy, started their lives like this.

We may feel that our faith is similar, that our contribution to the work of the kingdom is very small and easily threatened. We may feel frail at times, that we are not growing in our faith. But we have no way of knowing how our actions, and the things we try to do for the Lord, are received and acted upon. A word of ours to comfort or cheer another may grow as it is passed on to someone else. A letter we write to someone who is bereaved may have far-reaching consequences for that person, who in turn may comfort others. So the kingdom of God grows, in secret and slowly, but each action, each kindness adds to its branches and strengthens its roots.

† Lord, we sometimes feel that our work for your kingdom is inadequate. Help us not to worry about results, but only to continue in loving service, leaving the rest to your care.

Jesus: teacher and healer 1   Susan Hibbins

Thursday 9 February

Mark 5:1-20

Change and challenge

Then the people began to plead with Jesus to leave their region.

(verse 17)

If we look back at the end of Mark 4, we can see that this encounter took place late in the evening. The shadowy darkness and the cries of the man who shouted at Jesus and his disciples would have increased the atmosphere of fear in what was already a disturbing situation. We feel only pity for the man whose violent insanity had driven him beyond normal society, to live among rocky tombs, alone with his misery – and his demons. Even for Jesus this was a tough case to deal with. The man was so ill that perhaps the only way Jesus could convince him of healing was to destroy the pigs: a solution that we may feel uneasy with today. Yet soon the man was calm, clean and healed, his mental battle at an end.

The people who lived nearby were understandably disturbed about the loss of the pigs. They were alarmed at what Jesus had done, and panic set in. There is no mention that they were pleased to see their one-time neighbour restored to health. There was something here they did not understand, that threatened their way of life, and they wanted none of it. Turning away their chance of meeting and talking with the Son of God, they asked him to leave.

The presence of Jesus is not always comfortable. It threatens to overturn our settled way of life, bringing new ideas, new challenges for which we may think we are ill-equipped. We may think that our life is all mapped out, safe, well ordered, predictable. And then along comes Jesus, with different priorities which he asks us to share with him. What will our response be?

---

† Lord Jesus, sometimes I am afraid to let you into my plans, for fear of the result. Help me to trust you, for life now, and for life in the future.

Susan Hibbins

Jesus: teacher and healer 1

Friday 10 February

Mark 5:21-34

Jesus' full attention

[Jesus asked] 'Who touched my clothes?'

(part of verse 30)

Have you ever been talking to someone, perhaps at a wedding or a conference, when you had the uncomfortable feeling that they were only half listening to what you were saying? One eye seemed to be on you and the other looking at someone else over your shoulder, and you felt that they could not wait to escape from you in order to go and talk to the other person.

Jesus never made anyone he met feel like that, and here we have a perfect example of his full attention focused on one person at a time. Jairus was important to Jesus, but so was the desperate woman in the crowd, who felt that if she could just touch Jesus' clothes, she would be healed of a long and debilitating illness.

We can almost feel Jairus' unspoken but seething impatience as, quite unhurried, Jesus stopped when he knew that someone seeking healing had touched him. The disciples were incredulous, given the number of people pushing and shoving in the crowd. But Jesus was insistent: he was going nowhere until he had seen and spoken to the trembling woman, who found herself thrust forward to give an account of herself. Jesus, undoubtedly aware of Jairus waiting desperately by his side, blessed the woman in front of him for her faith. He did not, as we might have done, speak hurriedly to her and dash away to where Jairus' daughter lay seriously ill. Jesus never did anything in a hurry. One person at a time received his full attention, for as long as it took. And today, when we seek communion with him in our prayers, we find the same loving response. Every time we seek him out, he is there waiting to receive us.

† Thank you, Lord Jesus, that you are always by my side, that I never have to wait to talk to you, and that you understand me as no one else can. Help me always to have faith in you, and to entrust my body and soul to your care.

Jesus: teacher and healer 1   Susan Hibbins

Saturday 11 February

Mark 5:35-42

From death to life

'Don't be afraid; just believe.'

(part of verse 36)

Poor Jairus. He knew that all hope had gone when he saw his servants. His daughter was dead. No need for Jesus now. But Jesus, in complete contrast to the anguish and despair around him, went to Jairus' home with him, kindly removed the distressed family, and restored the little girl to her parents.

'Don't be afraid; just believe.' Jesus' words were scorned by this grieving family. Many families would feel the same. Others' loved ones are not restored to life; many people die in spite of earnest prayer for their healing. Anyone who has lost someone close understands Jairus. Grief can be all-consuming, a constant heartache that we sometimes feel will never be healed. And yet, as Christians, we can hold fast to these words of Jesus in our dark days. Jairus' story tells us that there is nothing that we cannot face, even death, if we put all our trust in our Lord, giving him our fears and grief. Though our hope in the future may be slender, in Jesus' hands it will strengthen and grow.

† When I face grief and loss, Lord, help me to remember your words of hope and put my trust in your promises.

For group discussion and personal thought

- How much time each day do you spend in prayer and meditation? How do you spend that time? Do you make a point of listening to what God has to say to you?

- How do people know you are a Christian? Is your faith limited to going to church on Sunday? Do you meet only with other Christians to talk about your faith?

- Do you give your close attention to the people you meet each day? Do you treat every individual as a precious child of God?

Susan Hibbins   Jesus: teacher and healer 1

Readings in Mark

2 Jesus: teacher and healer (2)

Notes based on the *New Revised Standard Version* by

Robert Draycott

Robert Draycott has had a varied ministry, working in the local church in Britain and in Brazil, in theological education, and more recently as a school chaplain.

Introduction

Although Mark is my favourite gospel, these notes have been a challenge to write, partly because of the hidden depths in what appears to be a simple action-packed narrative. At first we see the 'physical events', especially through the healings. But as we continue through to the day before Lent begins, we see the 'spiritual' aspects of the ongoing ministry of Jesus as references are made to his sacrificial death.

Sunday 12 February: *Mark 1:40-45*

Touching the untouchable

This description of how Jesus healed a leper is memorable, powerful, and vivid. Memorable, because the leper does the unacceptable in approaching Jesus, who responds by doing the unthinkable and touching him.

> *Moved with pity, Jesus stretched out his hand and touched him, and said to him, 'I do choose. Be made clean!' Immediately the leprosy left him, and he was made clean.*

(verses 41-42)

Powerful, because Jesus' touch heals the leper. Vivid, because we can clearly imagine the scene: the approach, the response of Jesus, and the result. The key issue is that Jesus touches the untouchable. This challenges us today, firstly to recognise those people who are considered 'unclean' in our own community, our nation. The second challenge is for us to find ways of 'touching the untouchable'. Christian churches all over the world today have a wide variety of ministries that reach out to those on the margins of society. On a more personal level, how can we play our part in continuing the healing ministry of Jesus at the point that our lives touch those of others?

† Lord, give us eyes that see the needs of those around us, and hands that reach out in your name. Amen

Monday 13 February
Mark 7:1-8

Rituals, their place and their purpose

Washing our hands before preparing or eating food is a ritual with a point and a purpose: it gets rid of germs.

> [T]he Pharisees and some of the scribes ... noticed that some of his disciples were eating with defiled hands, that is, without washing them ... So the Pharisees and the scribes asked him, 'Why do your disciples not live according to the tradition of the elders, but eat with defiled hands?' He said to them, ... 'You abandon the commandment of God and hold to human tradition.'
>
> (part of verses 1 and 2, verse 5, and parts of verses 6 and 8)

For the Pharisees and scribes, ritual handwashing also had a point and a purpose, but its purpose was religious rather than hygienic. Christians today tend to see themselves as either having or not having rituals. For example, some worshippers will bow to the altar and cross themselves and others do not feel the need to do this. The important thing, whether one follows rituals or not, is to see beyond the actions to what they mean. However, although some of us think that we don't have rituals and that our worship and devotion are a 'ritual-free area', as Christians we do all have rituals of one kind or another, even if we do no more than close our eyes or fold our hands when we pray. It is simply that some have fewer and generally simpler rituals than others.

Today's reading can remind us that we belong to a world-wide family that encompasses a tremendous range of worship styles, some of which are full of elaborate rituals while others are much simpler. These differences are real; the secret is to recognise the underlying unity that binds us together as followers of Jesus.

✝ Lord, thank you for all the ways in which ordinary everyday rituals enrich our daily lives. Amen

Robert Draycott   Jesus: teacher and healer 2

What is the commandment of God?

Yesterday we thought about the point and purpose of rituals, and that every Christian follows some sort of ritual, even if rarely and simply. Rituals need to point beyond themselves to the commandment of God. When they cease to do this they have become human tradition.

> *Then he said to them, 'You have a fine way of rejecting the commandment of God in order to keep your tradition!*

(verse 9)

This verse challenges us to grasp what the commandment of God actually is. Jesus does not spell it out here, but later on in the gospel, when he is specifically asked 'Which commandment is the first?' (Mark 12:31), we can summarise his answer as the threefold 'Love God and your neighbour as yourself': love for God expressed through worship, love for our neighbour expressed through service, and a proper measure of self-love. Christians often overlook this third element, loving ourselves. There is a temptation to be driven and to feel that we are not 'wholehearted' in our devotion to God if, for example, we spend time on hobbies and interests. This is to misunderstand God's gifts in creation, such as music, art, sport and other interests. These are literally recreations that re-create and renew us.

Perhaps we need reminding that God is generous and wants us to love both our neighbour and ourselves. Love is for sharing, as Jesus points out in today's passage, when he teaches that devotion to God involves honouring parents and caring for them (verses 10-13).

† Lord, thank you for our recreational activities, for everything and everyone that contributes to your ongoing work of re-creation. Amen

Jesus: teacher and healer 2   Robert Draycott

Wednesday 15 February

Mark 7:14-23

Eyes, ears and imagination

Have you ever had the experience of talking to someone who outwardly appears to agree with every word you say, yet feeling that inwardly it is a very different story? A similar type of experience comes when we discover a darker side to someone we thought we knew well, someone we thought we could trust. Furthermore, many people are aware of things about themselves that they would prefer not to be there.

> '[T]here is nothing outside a person that by going in can defile, but the things that come out are what defile.'

(verse 15)

When the disciples ask Jesus to explain this saying, he makes his point even clearer:

> 'It is what comes out of a person that defiles. For it is from within, from the human heart, that evil intentions come.'

(part of verse 20)

Even if Christians are not required to obey food laws, we still need to be concerned about what we receive via what we might call the 'eye gate' and the 'ear gate' of the body. There are some things it is better not to gaze upon or listen to. Jesus also challenges us to use our imagination positively and healthily, not even to contemplate some actions, the evil intentions that he lists in verses 21-22. To some extent we all have these tendencies or attitudes within us. The challenge is to recognise their potential within us and aim for moral cleanliness. As children show, the ability to imagine is a great gift to human beings; as adults we need to use this gift wisely, imagining what is good and refusing to contemplate wickedness.

† Lord, we thank you for the gift of imagination. Help us to use it creatively and constructively. Amen

Robert Draycott   Jesus: teacher and healer 2

Thursday 16 February
Mark 7: 24-30

Proper pride

The story of the Syrophoenician woman is well known because of the dialogue she had with Jesus, which began rather badly with Jesus pointing out that his first responsibility was to the Jews (verse 27). This is a fascinating story which raises all sorts of questions that do not have clear answers. Jesus appears to speak harshly to someone who was doubly an outsider, being both a Gentile and a woman. One reaction might have been for her to feel offended and insulted. Instead she reacted with a proper pride in both who she was and in the reasonableness of her request. It was reasonable because she was motivated by love for her daughter, and by her faith in Jesus. Love meant that she did not take offence; instead she came back with her memorable line:

'Sir, even the dogs under the table eat the children's crumbs.' Then he said to her, 'For saying that, you may go – the demon has left your daughter.' So she went home, found the child lying on the bed, and the demon gone.

(part of verse 28, and verses 29-30)

Traditionally, pride has been considered the first of the deadly sins, and in many ways it has potential to be a negative aspect of our characters. Yet the Syrophoenician woman reminds us that there is also a 'proper pride' which Jesus recognised and responded to. Once more we are reminded that as daughters and sons of God we have a basic dignity. We are much more than 'mere worms', we are people who are called to be motivated by love and to act in faith.

† Lord, give us a proper pride in ourselves as your daughters and sons, and in the gifts you have entrusted to us.

Jesus: teacher and healer 2   Robert Draycott

Friday 17 February

Mark 8:22-26

A second touch

Although they seem to have used much of Mark's material as the basis of their own gospels, both Matthew and Luke omit this healing miracle, perhaps because they felt it showed Jesus in a poor light: he didn't complete the cure the first time he touched the blind man. He had to try again.

> [W]hen he had put saliva on his eyes and laid his hands on him, he asked him, 'Can you see anything?' And the man looked up and said, 'I can see people, but they look like trees, walking.' Then Jesus laid his hands on his eyes again; and he looked intently and his sight was restored, and he saw everything clearly.
>
> part of verse 23, and verses 24-25)

Today's account is of the healing of a unnamed blind man; tomorrow's reading is about a man with a name. Both stories are delightful in themselves and we can find them encouraging and inspiring simply because two blind men have their sight restored. We can imagine both the misery of becoming blind and then the joy of being cured.

But why did Mark include this two-stage cure? One explanation is that this was an 'acted parable' which illustrated something important about faith. Faith demands patience. It often requires us to wait for God to act, believing and trusting that he will do so when the time is right. This man could have been upset when, after Jesus had laid hands on him, he still couldn't see properly. He could have despaired and told his friends to lead him away. Instead, he waited quietly, and was rewarded for his faith. Mark has at least one other story in his gospel in which the suffering person, like this blind man, doesn't actually ask Jesus for healing (see 3:1-5). But the process of being healed taught this man faith.

---

† Lord, help us to have the faith to trust you and wait for you to act, even when we cannot understand what you are doing. Amen

Robert Draycott   Jesus: teacher and healer 2

Saturday 18 February

Mark 10:46-52

Purposeful healings

Today's healing is full of deeper meaning. Despite his blindness Bartimaeus recognises Jesus as 'Son of David', as the one sent by God. He is not discouraged by those who tell him to be quiet, he knows his need and voices it.

Jesus stood still and said, 'Call him here.' And they called the blind man, saying to him, 'Take heart; get up, he is calling you.' So throwing off his cloak, he sprang up and came to Jesus.

(verses 49-50)

Unlike yesterday's blind man, Bartimaeus already had an active faith in Jesus. His faith leads to action: keeping on calling out, springing up and walking towards Jesus, asking to have his sight restored, following Jesus on the way. Bartimaeus already thought positively; now, with the words 'Take heart', other people encouraged him. Faith in God is rooted in our inner belief, yet often even as Christians we find that inner trust difficult. Take heart, God does love us.

† Lord, we give thanks for all those who encourage us, may we in our turn seek to encourage others.

(The questions 'For group discussion and personal thought' can be found at the end of this theme, on p.52.)

Jesus: teacher and healer 2   Robert Draycott

Sunday 19 February

Mark 9:2-9

A glimpse of glory

Sometimes we have the strange experience of seeing friends that we know well in an unexpected light. We see something previously hidden from us. This is what happened to three of the disciples.

Six days later, Jesus took with him Peter and James and John, and led them up a high mountain apart, by themselves. And he was transfigured before them, and his clothes became dazzling white, such as no one on earth could bleach them.

(verses 2-3)

Peter, James and John had a glimpse of glory; they saw something, but were unable to grasp what it meant. But then they heard something.

Then a cloud overshadowed them, and from the cloud there came a voice, 'This is my Son, the Beloved; listen to him!'

(verse 7)

There is a saying in English about not being able to believe one's eyes. Fortunately for the three dazzled disciples, the explanation followed: an explanation of who Jesus is – Son of God; followed by a call to action – the need to listen to Jesus. These are two sides of the coin of faith. Jesus can be trusted because he is the Son of God, and the Christian life involves seeking to know the mind of Christ. This is a life-long process both for the Christian community, through its worship and the daily lives of its members in the wider world, and also for the individual journey of every Christian, inspired by the insights of scripture.

† Lord, remind us of all those times when we have been lost in wonder, love and praise. Amen

Robert Draycott

Jesus: teacher and healer 2

Monday 20 February

Mark 9:30-37

True greatness: putting others first

We live in a world that values greatness. We revere great leaders, we honour great achievements, we admire great sportspeople, we consider some people to be great artists or musicians. In history we learn about great military leaders, about kings and emperors who are now called 'the Great'. It is easy to understand greatness in terms of power, status, wealth, dignity, titles, and honour.

Long ago Pope Gregory I was called 'the Great'. One reason was because he understood his position as the Bishop of Rome as being that of 'the servant of the servants of Christ'. This phrase encapsulates something fundamental about true greatness: the need to put others first.

> *He sat down, called the twelve, and said to them, 'Whoever wants to be first must be last of all and servant of all.'*

(verse 35)

Jesus used a child to illustrate his point, perhaps because a child has not 'achieved' greatness through what he or she has done in life. Children accept their lowly place in the scheme of things. Seeking to get to the top is a 'learned' activity that Jesus challenges. We can also say that children have an innate greatness simply by being who they are, and by being essentially powerless. True adult greatness may involve power, but it does not abuse it. Are the people you particularly admire the sort of people who 'would do anything for you', who are happy to serve? Do other people see us like that?

† We give thanks for all who have been great enough to serve us; may we in our turn serve others in your name. Amen

Jesus: teacher and healer 2   Robert Draycott

Tuesday 21 February

Mark 10:32–34

True greatness: sacrifice

This is an important day in the Christian calendar, the final day before the season of Lent begins, with its ending in Holy Week. Many Christians follow the discipline of some kind of fasting during these forty days. But before the fasting comes the feasting of Shrove Tuesday, as it is known in Britain. That name reminds us of the fundamental importance of being forgiven, of being 'shriven' of our sins, in preparation for the season of Lent. Food and forgiveness, provision for the body and the soul that reminds us how the spiritual and the physical aspects of the Christian life are intertwined. That is true of today's reading: physically Jesus is on the road to his final destination, spiritually he explains that his sacrifice will not be the last word:

> '[T]he Son of Man will be handed over to the chief priests and the scribes, and they will condemn him to death; then they will hand him over to the Gentiles; they will mock him, and spit upon him, and flog him, and kill him; and after three days he will rise again.'

> (part of verse 33, and verse 34)

These words point us straight to the heart of the Christian faith, to the sacrificial, self-giving love of the Son of God. And to the conviction that death does not have the last word.

Looking back at the last ten days' readings, they have shown us that Jesus offered physical healing which inevitably also transformed the inner spirit of those he healed. For him it was not a choice of either the 'outer' or the 'inner' – it was both. Health is a combination of both physical and spiritual well-being. For Christians, faith and action go together.

† Thank you, Lord, for the health and wholeness we enjoy, for feasting and forgiveness, for sacrifice and resurrection, for all your unconquerable love. Amen

For group discussion and personal thought

• Why is encouragement so important? Can you give examples from your own experience?

• Do we need to know, can we know, all the answers, or does faith help us to live with uncertainty?

Robert Draycott   Jesus: teacher and healer 2

Trees

Trees in the Old Testament (1)

Notes based on the *New Revised Standard Version* by

Marcel V. Măcelaru

Dr M.V. Măcelaru is a Romanian theologian. At the time of writing he is living in Osijek, Croatia, where he teaches the Old Testament and serves as the Executive Dean of Evanđeoski teološki fakultet (Evangelical Theological Seminary).

Introduction

Trees are very special. They are an important part of God's creation and life on our planet would be impossible without the oxygen they produce. Beyond this biological function, trees also play a major role in the story of God's dealings with humankind. According to the Bible, history itself begins and ends under two unique trees. In the Garden of Eden, Adam and Eve commence the sad human condition – sinful separation from God – by eating from the Tree of the Knowledge of Good and Evil. In the end, those who transcend this tragic state will partake from the Tree of Life in God's New Jerusalem.

Wednesday 22 February (Ash Wednesday): *Genesis 1:26-31*
A celebration of life

> *God said, 'See, I have given you . . . every tree with seed in its fruit.'*
>
> (part of verse 29)

The biblical account of the beginnings of the world and the destiny of humankind is an amazing story – a true celebration of life. In other creation stories the appearance of life is a random hostile happening, but in the Bible God is its designer, the Creator involved in its very emergence. Even more, today's reading shows that humankind is at the centre of all this divine activity. Everything God creates serves to fulfil our needs. What a theology of blessing! The message here is an assurance of love and care. Our Creator is also our preserver and provider. But we also need to remember the other face of the coin. We are not only beneficiaries of the creation. We are also to care for it.

† We thank you, Father, for the gift of life, for all that you have prepared for us!

Thursday 23 February

Genesis 18:1-8

The secret of a good life

'Let a little water be brought, and wash your feet, and rest yourselves under the tree.'

(verse 4)

Water and trees – what an idyllic picture of repose and peacefulness! Sadly, however, for many nowadays this is an unfamiliar vision. We live in a world where economic collapse, natural disasters and strife have increased the anxiety and discomfort we experience. Solutions to the problems we encounter seem to be rather scarce and much too often we find ourselves wanting. We know that this is not how God intended life to be and therefore freeze in perplexity when faced with such unexpected challenges.

The biblical story of Abraham reveals that life was not much different in the old days. Abraham faced estrangement, peril, war and, worst of all, childlessness. However, his actions described in today's reading show beautifully that he knew the secret of a good life. His practice of hospitality testifies to a basic understanding of common humanity that goes beyond established differences in order to embrace equally friend and foe, kinsfolk and stranger. This is how Abraham understands relating to others! He does not hesitate to provide for the needs of the neighbour and the foreigner, and by doing so he becomes a reflection of divine provision and embrace. Such practice of hospitality is, I believe, the alternative that changes lives. It brings back into our world kindness and compassion; and where kindness and compassion rule, indifference and selfishness are eliminated.

† Heavenly Father, we live in a world where the true practice of hospitality is often neglected. Fill our hearts with compassion and help us to address the needs of the other with kindness.

Marcel V. Măcelaru

Trees in the Old Testament 1

Friday 24 February

Leviticus 27:30-33

Worshipping God in a new way

All tithes from the land, whether the seed from the ground or the fruit from the tree, are the LORD's.

(part of verse 30)

Should we tithe? Does this odd law apply to us today? Responses to such questions vary. To some tithing is a ritual from ancient Israel's socio-religious system. To others it is a divine command that spans time and space and therefore must be practised by all. Some tithe because they believe this is a sure way to earn divine favour. For others tithing is a burden, one's duty as a believer. Interestingly, today's reading gives a different picture. Here tithing is placed alongside worship practices, in a context that establishes the parameters of proper devotion to God. The fact that there are limits and regulations to how one approaches God suggests that practising tithing brings order to one's life and makes a statement of reliance: not reliance on one's ability to survive but on God's provision and love. Furthermore, being holy (set apart) for the Lord, which is applied here to produce, reveals that God has a claim on every aspect of our life. It is an acknowledgement of God's lordship over the entire reality. Seen in this light, the practice of tithing teaches a few fundamental truths. First, it helps to set our priorities straight – that which belongs to God has primacy. Second, it announces that there are limits to what and how much one should accumulate. Third, it rightly defines our relationship with God as one of dependence on him. Fourth, and most importantly, tithing is an act of worship. Giving in this context means loving God with all that we have.

† Lord God, we devote ourselves to you with all that we have. May our giving be a real act of worship, pleasant in your sight.

Trees in the Old Testament 1   Marcel V. Măcelaru

Saturday 25 February

Deuteronomy 8:1-10

The two faces of love

*Know then in your heart that as a parent disciplines a child so the L*ORD *your God disciplines you . . . You shall eat your fill and bless the L*ORD *your God for the good land that he has given you.*

(verses 5 and 10)

The image of parenthood impressed on us in today's reading is one of the most reassuring ways to describe God and how he relates to the believer. In the book of Deuteronomy this is the second time that this metaphor is used and the two passages must be taken together. In the first instance (1:31), God's parenthood manifests as tender care and protection for his people. In today's passage the same parent-like love leads God to instructively chastise his people. Thus this is both a heartening and a cautioning metaphor. A parent's love, when complete, manifests itself in embrace as well as in discipline. This may sound to some scary, for ordinarily no one likes to be disciplined. However, in these two facets of God's love we see his immediate as well as long-term provision. God is near – he addresses all our day-to-day needs, be they physical, spiritual or emotional. But at the same time he is undertaking a life-long process of education, helping us to grow into the kind of people we ought to become. Such education sometimes requires correction, but God's discipline is not a random occurrence, but rather a well-planned instructional tool. This is both a message of comfort and one of hope. It tells us that although we may not always understand the circumstances of our lives, God is with us every step of the way and in the end his good work in our lives will come to a blessed fulfilment.

† Heavenly Father, my heart longs for you and my hope is in you. Thank you for caring and instructing me, for your blessing and discipline.

(The questions 'For group discussion and personal thought' can be found at the end of the first complete week of this theme, on p.63.)

Marcel V. Măcelaru   Trees in the Old Testament 1

Trees

Trees in the Old Testament (2)

Notes based on the *New Revised Standard Version* by

Marcel V. Măcelaru

For Marcel's biography see p.53.

Introduction

Those of us who live in cities or in wooded countryside can take trees for granted. But in more barren landscapes, trees are important features, acting as landmarks, meeting places, shade and welcome food. And trees can play a surprising part in the relationship between human beings and God.

Sunday 26 February: *Deuteronomy 20:19-20*
Save the planet!

> *Are trees in the field human beings that they should come under siege from you?*

> (part of verse 19)

We are all familiar with the phrase 'Save the planet!', which in recent decades has become the urgent cry of individuals and groups as concern with the state of our planet grows more pressing. As today's reading shows, care for our planet is very much a biblical teaching. Protecting trees is placed on an equal footing with showing compassion and humanity towards others in an armed conflict. Being asked to show compassion and care while at war may seem odd, but it is a message that we should all hear. It is first of all a call to temperance and restraint. No matter what our circumstances, no matter how justified we are in our undertaking, the ultimate goal is, and must always remain, care for God's creation. This implies a condemnation of all activities that destroy our planet, such as wars, the unwise use of resources, and any activity that pollutes the environment. This passage also teaches us that it is not only the end of the journey that counts, but also the journey itself. The Israelites should not cut down trees even when such action is necessary in order to accomplish their goal. The end does not justify the means.

† Lord God, you have created this wonderful world for us to live in, but we have not cared for it faithfully. We repent of all our abuses, of all the destruction we have brought, and ask for wisdom to correct our wrongs.

Monday 27 February

Deuteronomy 24:19-22

Efficient social care

When you beat your olive trees, do not strip what is left; it shall be for the alien, the orphan, and the widow.

(verse 20)

Many of the laws and teachings in the book of Deuteronomy deal with how the community should care and protect those that are weak, marginalised and powerless. Today's reading, for instance, describes a costless yet efficient system of social care. It has multiple advantages over some of our experiences. Firstly, it is available to all that are in need; no exceptions or distinctions are made. Secondly, it does not segregate, for it is not administered by some for the benefit of others. Rather, people in need are empowered by the fact that they can have direct access to resources. Thirdly, it is characterised by fairness, for the assumption is that people in need will take and use only as much as they need. Fourthly, it is free of political and ideological interests. Givers have no control over receivers, and receivers have no indebtedness to the givers. This prevents acts of charity being done for unethical gain. Fifthly, it acknowledges the fact that the regulator of any exchange is God. He rewards generosity (verse 19) and punishes parsimony (verse 15). But beyond all these, the passage is a wake-up call to those of us who have become forgetful or thoughtless. It draws attention to the needy in our societies and in so doing ought to stimulate our conscience and fuel our desire to act selflessly on behalf of the less fortunate and for their benefit.

† Heavenly Father, it is comforting to know that our wellbeing concerns you. Open our eyes to see the needs around us and help us to live according to your will, acting generously for the benefit of those in need.

Marcel V. Măcelaru   Trees in the Old Testament 2

Tuesday 28 February

Judges 9:8-15

Choosing wisely

'Shall I stop producing?'

(part of verses 9, 11 and 13)

Choices – we face them every day. Most are easy and therefore, we think, insignificant. Yet this is not always true, for even the smallest choice can lead to grave consequences. This is what in chaos theory physicists have called 'the butterfly effect' – given time, any action, no matter how small, has the potential to effect great changes. However, we can neither foresee consequences nor do we exercise conscious control over every gesture we make. In fact, when making 'insignificant' choices, most of the time we react instinctively rather than in accordance with a thought-out plan. But then there are choices we recognise as important, which may have the potential to redefine our lives. Today's reading teaches at least three things about acting wisely in such circumstances. Firstly, it shows the role that motivation plays in the process of decision-making, and implicitly calls for a sincere evaluation of our impulses. Secondly, it teaches the importance of weighing decisions before they are made. And thirdly, it gives criteria for making such evaluations based on more than the attraction that a particular course of action may hold for us. According to the olive, the fig, and the vine, becoming king of the trees would prevent them from acting for the benefit of all, producing fruit that made their lives meaningful. In other words, any decision that results in us being unproductive, or even worse, counterproductive, should give cause for alarm.

† Lord God, we are limited and cannot foresee consequences. Give us insight and help us to make wise choices.

Trees in the Old Testament 2   Marcel V. Măcelaru

Wednesday 29 February

1 Kings 19:1-8

A prelude to revelation

[H]e himself went a day's journey into the wilderness, and came and sat down under a solitary broom tree.

(part of verse 4)

Tiredness and disappointment, fear and despair – these are feelings confronting all of us. The reading for today talks about such circumstances in the life of Prophet Elijah. Having victoriously challenged the Israelites and their king on Mount Carmel, Elijah ends up running for his life. He is alone and weary, as desolate as the solitary tree he sits under, and he wants nothing else but to die. Such radical reversals of situation are surprising, unwelcome and confusing. It is during such times that unsettling questions regarding our worth, the value of our endeavours and ultimately the significance of our lives flood our minds. Of course, there is nothing wrong with reflecting on any of these; however, when such reflection is generated by exhaustion and accompanied by disillusion and self-pity, the outcomes are similar to Elijah's: a solitary, depressing journey in the wilderness of our thoughts. But thank God that that is not how this story ends! In the end Elijah's needs are comprehensively cared for. The nourishment and rest he gets provide his physical restoration. But more importantly, his dire circumstances are followed by him meeting God in a new way. In other words, despair becomes a prelude to greater revelation. There is a hopeful message for all of us here: sometimes in the midst of anguish the seeds for new blessings are sown.

† Heavenly Father, only in you and because of you have I hope. Help me keep my eyes on you and not on the dire circumstances of my life. Work in my life, I pray, and change desolation into joyful new revelation.

Marcel V. Măcelaru   Trees in the Old Testament 2

Thursday 1 March

Psalm 1

What trees and people have in common

*They are like trees
planted by streams of water . . .
In all that they do, they prosper.*

(part of verse 3)

According to this psalm, there are three things one should know about a righteous man: he does not do certain things, he does others, and he experiences prosperity. Firstly, he does not pursue evil thoughts, neither his own nor those of others. Also he does not knowingly choose to act wickedly, even if everyone else around him does so. And of course, when he learns that something is wrong in his life, he stops doing it; he will not persist in doing evil. Secondly, in stark contrast to the wicked, the righteous man roots himself in truth much as a tree spreads its roots until it gains access to life-bringing springs of water. Such rootedness is explained as the result of intentional and uninterrupted meditation on the word of God. This leads to the third characteristic of the righteous man: the blessed consequences of such living. It includes abundance in all aspects of one's existence; just as a tree is a non-discriminatory source of goods, available to all, so will the righteous one become a selfless resource, the person to whom those in need will turn. It also includes the promise of health and long life. As a tree with access to water remains green and lasts even in extreme conditions, so the righteous man remains standing in God's presence, in joy and sorrow, and in the hour of temptation. Finally, the promise of such a life is prosperity, that is, fulfilment and the successful completion of all that we do.

† Lord God, you have called us to righteousness and blessing, to living a life worthy of your holiness. Help us to avoid the path of the wicked and lead us through your word.

Trees in the Old Testament 2   Marcel V. Măcelaru

Friday 2 March

Psalm 92:12-15

What trees and people have in common

The righteous flourish like the palm tree,
and grow like a cedar in Lebanon.

(verse 12)

Today's reading continues the metaphorical link between trees and righteous people. Here those who know and truly worship the Lord are likened to the palm tree, which is a symbol for victory, abundance and peace, and the evergreen cedar of Lebanon, a symbol for endurance and strength. There are several implications resulting from such a comparison. Firstly, the righteous flourish and grow strong – clearly a reiteration of yesterday's statement regarding abundant life and steadfastness. This is, however, contingent on being planted in the house of the Lord. In other words, the blessedness of the righteous continues for as long as they walk with God. Secondly, the palm and cedar stay green and never cease to produce fruit, and in the same way the righteous are a fruitful source, productive individuals. They are people that God will use to draw non-believers to him. Finally, the righteous will testify to the fact that God is true to his promises, right in his judgements and reliable in his faithfulness. There is here (verse 15) a sense of wonder about who and what God is, and comparing God to a rock speaks of his permanence. No wonder that in rabbinical tradition this psalm is regarded as a suitable song for the era to come, the eschatological time when God's work will be complete and evil will be no more. I believe that only by reading the psalm in this way will we experience in the present the marvellous wonders of the future, the undisputable reign of God over the entire creation.

† Lord God, I praise you and worship you. You are the beginning and the end, my origin and my destiny. Make me like a palm tree and a cedar, fruitful and strong.

Marcel V. Măcelaru   Trees in the Old Testament 2

Saturday 3 March

Psalm 104:10-18

A celebration of life revisited

The trees of the LORD are watered abundantly,
the cedars of Lebanon that he planted.
In them the birds build their nests;
the stork has its home in the fir trees.

(verses 16 and 17)

These meditations end where they began on Ash Wednesday, at the creation and its significance. Psalm 104 begins as a celebratory hymn praising God for his marvellous acts that brought the universe into existence. As we saw earlier, the biblical understanding of creation is unique, for it is a celebration of life. It is seen as something entirely positive, a perfect divine accomplishment. In the creation account in the book of Genesis (1:31) God concludes his work by taking time to reflect on, and evaluate, what he has done. He looks at what he has created and declares that it is all very good. He finds pleasure and delight in the work he had undertaken. Today's reading recalls that image of the industrious Creator enjoying the conclusion of his work. If God had sung a hymn to celebrate what he had done, I don't think he could have found a more suitable song than this psalm. I believe the lesson for us is clear. We are to appreciate what God has done. That means at the least protecting and enjoying all that he has created.

† Lord God, the work of your hands is amazing! I thank you for your gifts, for everything you have created.

For group discussion and personal thought

• Do you enjoy God's creation? How do you abuse it and how do you care for it?

• How do you show care for the needy and the stranger, and practise hospitality?

• Do you think your life is a blessing to others? If not, what can you do about it?

Trees in the Old Testament 2   Marcel V. Măcelaru

Trees

Trees in the Old Testament (3)

Notes based on the *New Revised Standard Version* by

Tim Brooke

Tim Brooke is a priest in the Church of England. He is retired from parish ministry and works for a number of charities supporting homeless people and refugees. He has a passion for trees and was absolutely delighted, at a recent conference abroad, to take part in planting a grove of trees to reduce the carbon footprint of his flight.

Introduction

We continue our study of trees in the Old Testament, and this week some of our trees are symbols of new life, healing and salvation.

Sunday 4 March: *Isaiah 10:33 – 11:3*
What is a Messiah?

According to the gospels it was Peter who first came out with it. 'Who do you say that I am?' asks Jesus. 'You're the Messiah, the Christ', blurts out Peter (Matthew 16:15-16). And at the back of his mind may have been this picture from the Old Testament of a tree-stump and a shoot coming out of it which was David, the shepherd-boy son of Jesse, who became the greatest king Israel ever had. The Messiah, the ideal king, would be descended from David and would come to set his people free.

> *A shoot shall come out from the stump of Jesse,*
> *and a branch shall grow out of his roots.*
> *The spirit of the LORD shall rest upon him,*
> *the spirit of wisdom and understanding.*

(chapter 11, verse 1 and part of verse 2)

The Messiah would be filled with gifts of the Spirit and above all he will fear the Lord. This is not being terrified by an unpredictable, ruthless god. It is having a humble reverence for God and admitting we are dependent on God. There is a lot in the Bible about the need to fear God. Fearing God is not the opposite of the command to love God. It is an added dimension to how we approach God.

† Help me to understand how my delight too can be in 'the fear of the Lord'.

Monday 5 March

Isaiah 41:17-20

God will plant a desert with trees

African leaders have begun planning a 'Great Green Wall of Africa' stretching nearly 8,000 kilometres (5,000 miles) from Senegal on the Atlantic coast to Djibouti on the Red Sea. It will consist of a strip of trees fifteen kilometres (nine miles) thick and will be even more visible from space than the Great Wall of China. Its purpose is to create a green barrier which will stop the Sahara desert spreading any further south.

The Book of Isaiah has the same sort of vision. God says:

I will put in the wilderness the cedar,
the acacia, the myrtle, and the olive;
I will set in the desert the cypress,
the plane and the pine together.

(verse 19)

This passage shows two truths about God. The first is that we are to rejoice that God is the Lord of nature. The second is that he has a very special care for his human creatures when they are in distress.

How we do respond? Certainly we are to join him in his work in the natural world. If we have the opportunity, for example, why not plant trees? We have just had to have two trees in our garden cut down, but we have replaced them with two more. We see ourselves as stewards of his creation trying to enhance it for the next generation. But we still always have to take notice of the poor and needy. This passage makes us think of the need to bring water to people whose 'tongue is parched with thirst'. We need to be thankful and support those who do that.

† Let us rejoice in the work of trees in keeping soil in its place, giving shelter from fierce winds, bringing shade from hot sun, uplifting the human soul.

Trees in the Old Testament 3 — Tim Brooke

Tuesday 6 March

Isaiah 44:13-20

How ridiculous can you get!

Half of it he burns in the fire . . . The rest of it he makes into a god.

(parts of verses 16-17)

The ancient Roman general Pompey conquered Jerusalem in 63BC. He entered the Temple and what he found shocked him. It was different from all other temples. He had reached the Holy of Holies, the most sacred part of the Temple, the place where the presence of God dwells. It could only be entered by one person, the High Priest, on only one day of the year. But it contained no jewel-encrusted idols, no treasure. The sanctuary was empty.

Trees were the source of many pagan idols. One of the great Jewish gifts to the world was to show how ridiculous it was to treat a piece of wood as a god; religion does not have to have idols. God can be worshipped in spirit anywhere at any time. But the Old Testament shows that many people did not keep to that ideal. There was the constant temptation to set up idols and to believe that they had the power to help people in their lives.

Human beings have a great capacity for self-deception. It is easy today, too, to give things priority over God without realising it.

An American prison chaplain keeps his house unlocked. He finds the keys of the prison are so oppressive that it is a relief to be free of keys at home. He has plenty of things that are valuable to him but he says: 'If I become so attached to my belongings that I'm afraid of losing them, I shouldn't have them.'

† Lord, help us to see what idols there are in our lives.

Tim Brooke

Trees in the Old Testament 3

Wednesday 7 March
Isaiah 55:6-13

The hills are alive with the sound of music

You shall go out in joy,
and be led back in peace;
the mountains and the hills before you shall burst into song,
and all the trees of the field shall clap their hands.

(verse 12)

This is one of those moments in the Bible of sheer exuberance. The world bursts into song and the trees applaud, full of wonder at God's goodness and saving power.

St Francis and his friars walked along the Italian country lanes from village to village singing at the tops of their voices, praising God for the glory of his creation. Francis preached that the created world revealed the creative presence of God. He especially loved trees because they made him think of the cross of Christ. He loved all God's creatures and not just the attractive ones. He loved rats and bugs as much as fluffy lambs.

A good way of praying is to take a walk through woods or fields or along a country road looking for signs of God's love, beauty, power, wisdom, balance. Pick out for special attention some of the things you normally take for granted. Use each of your five senses in turn and perhaps feel some of the exhilaration of St Francis. Think too of some of the mysteries in God's creation that we find difficult to explain, like the problem of sin and evil in the world, and hand over your puzzlement and frustration to God for him to use.

† Let everything that has breath praise the Lord! (Psalm 150:6)

Trees in the Old Testament 3   Tim Brooke

Thursday 8 March

Jeremiah 11:14-20

Trees under threat

The LORD once called you, 'A green olive tree, fair with goodly fruit'; but with the roar of a great tempest he will set fire to it, and its branches will be consumed.

(verse 16)

In the first half of this passage the green olive tree, planted by God, is a symbol of God's chosen people. But everything has gone wrong. They have gone away from God and he now threatens to destroy them. In the second half, from verse 18, the prophet Jeremiah learns that there is a plot to murder him. He pictures himself as a fruit-tree about to be cut down. The point of both pictures is that human beings and trees, as living entities, are intensely vulnerable and can be destroyed in a moment.

The same threats can apply to us. We too can be tempted to turn away from God because we find other gods more attractive. We too can come under attack because we have stood up for what we believe to be true.

The answer, even before we meet these threats, is to admit that we are vulnerable and to offer our vulnerability up to God. We need to be honest with him, and ourselves, about how helpless we sometimes feel. In doing so a new and healing energy can be released.

Dame Cicely Saunders, who founded the hospice movement in Britain, spoke about how weak and inadequate friends and family of a dying person can feel: 'Your helplessness is what you have to offer. You have that in common with the ill person. So you are together with them in that experience. That is what they need.'

---

† Lord, I am no longer my own but yours. Here are my weaknesses. Please use them as you wish.

Tim Brooke   Trees in the Old Testament 3

Friday 9 March
Ezekiel 31:1-12

The story of the cedar

My favourite landscape tree is a cedar of Lebanon. One reaches out over the road near where I live, and it makes it a joy to walk along that road. It is so wide-spreading and majestic and stately, 'beautiful with its mass of branches, the envy of all the trees of Eden that were in the garden of God' (verse 9).

In the book of the prophet Ezekiel, what better symbol of a fine powerful country like ancient Egypt or Assyria! But then it all turns sour. The tree becomes too proud of itself and it ends up being cut down.

> *Because it towered high and set its top among the clouds and its heart was proud of its height, . . . I have cast it out.*
>
> (part of verses 10-11)

Pride in this sense is about being totally self-centred and self-sufficient, being able to do without God. Of course we don't need God to lead a good life. Many people do just that, but they miss out on so much. They miss out on being able to pray to God, being in touch with their maker, the creator of our whole universe, and being open to receive his grace in their lives. And they miss out on understanding something of what this world is about, what its meaning is and why we are here. Above all they miss out on the joy and excitement of knowing that they are joining in God's work of bringing in his kingdom in the place where they live.

† Lord, help us to have a sense of purpose in our lives and not to be afraid to share your values with others.

Trees in the Old Testament 3   Tim Brooke

Saturday 10 March
Ezekiel 47:7-12

Leaves for healing

Ezekiel here has a vision of an earthly Paradise. God's life-giving creative power brings fresh water to the Dead Sea and the previously bare banks of the river will be covered with trees. Fruit will be picked all the year round and leaves will be used for healing.

Their fruit will be for food, and their leaves for healing.

(part of verse 12)

The ancient Greeks used willow leaves to reduce fever and aches and pains. Willow trees contain the active ingredient to make aspirin. The Pacific Yew tree is the origin of tamoxifen, the main weapon in stopping breast cancer recurring. Rain-forest trees supply the ingredients of a quarter of the medicines used in western countries.

If we are seriously ill, we may pray to God for a miracle or have hands laid on us for healing. Sometimes nothing much happens to answer our prayers. We may feel disappointed. But that is to forget how God works – both through doctors and nurses and other medical staff, and through the natural creation supplying leaves and bark and roots to heal.

† Give thanks for the marvellous treatments, old and new, that come from God's creation.

For group discussion and personal thought
- Go outside and look for two trees: one which is like the sort of person you would like to be or your goal in life, the other which expresses the kind of person you are now. What do you need to do to change from how you are now to how you would like to be – or how you think God would like you to be?
- What can you learn from trees?
- Find some beautiful leaves and study them as part of God's creation. Share them with someone else.

Tim Brooke   Trees in the Old Testament 3

Trees

Trees in the Old Testament (4)

Notes based on the *Good News Bible* by

Iain Roy

Iain Roy is a retired Church of Scotland minister, a former moderator and clerk of Ardrossan Presbytery, still active in local ministry.

Introduction

For many years I lived near the sea. The sea is fascinating to most of us, ever-changing with the ebb and flow of the tide, the rise and fall of the wind. Living now in the country, I have discovered that trees have an equal fascination. They too are ever-changing as the seasons come and go. But the oldest of them, in particular, also have a reassuring presence. Their roots are firmly planted in the ground as our own lives need to be rooted in God's love.

Sunday 11 March: *Daniel 4:10-17*
I have a dream

Dreams, as Freud, Jung, and others have taught us, are rarely about the things that are seen but about the things that are unseen.

> *While I was asleep, I had a vision of a huge tree in the middle of the earth. It grew bigger and bigger until it reached the sky and could be seen by everyone in the world.*
>
> (verses 10-11)

To the outside observer, everything in Nebuchadnezzar's life seemed to be prospering. He had position, wealth, power. But, as his dream showed, change was imminent. The man who had everything was about to find that, through ill-health, he had nothing. It is a reminder to all of us of how swiftly and dramatically our lives can be changed, often by circumstances and events over which we have no control. It should also be a reminder to us that sometimes the reality of other folk's lives is very different from what we see on the surface. We need, as the Scots poet Robert Burns put it, 'To gently scan our brother man, still gentler, sister woman'.

† Lord, give us a kindlier eye, an eye of understanding that can see the hidden needs and struggles of the lives we meet.

Monday 12 March
Daniel 4:18-27

The interpreter of dreams

It can be dangerous to be an interpreter of dreams, especially if like Daniel you are called upon to shatter someone's delusions of grandeur.

> *'This is the dream I had,' said King Nebuchadnezzar. 'Now, Belteshazzar, tell me what it means. None of my royal advisers could tell me, but you can, because the spirit of the holy gods is in you.'*

(verse 18)

Thankfully for Daniel, Nebuchadnezzar had a hunger to hear not what people thought he would like to hear but what he really needed to hear. How often life would benefit in politics, industry and commerce, and even the church, if we were prepared to hear what we need to hear – spoken always, of course, in love as well as truth. It is Jesus himself who reminds us that we can only move on in life when the truth sets us free (John 8:31-32). Nebuchadnezzar's eventual salvation lay in coming to terms with the reality of his situation. It is often our salvation too.

† Lord, give us a glimpse of where we really are in our lives and bless us through the family, friends and others who help us to see what we need to see, and to hear what we need to hear, so that our lives can move on fruitfully, for Jesus' sake, Amen

Iain Roy   Trees in the Old Testament 4

Tuesday 13 March

Hosea 14:4-9

The sweet smell of cedar

My wife and I have a wooden chest which is a delight to open, because immediately we are greeted by the sweet smell of the cedar wood that lines the box. This is one of the metaphors Hosea used to describe God's promises to his people.

> The LORD says,
> 'I will bring my people back to me.
> I will love them with all my heart . . .
> They will blossom like flowers . . .
> They will be fragrant
> like the cedars of Lebanon.'

(part of verses 4-6)

Hosea shows us what a revelation faith can bring to a human life. It can open blind eyes to God's blessing; it can remind us of the promises he makes to fulfil our lives. What makes this revelation to Hosea so remarkable is that he believed he was richly blessed in spite of his wife's unfaithfulness to him, and his children's disregard of him. The cedar tree not only gives us a sweet smell, it is also a tree of magnificent stature and strength, just like the strength of God's love for us.

† Holy Spirit, come like a breath of fresh air into our lives, show us again how you bless our lives each day, and surround us with the strength of your love this day, for Jesus' sake, Amen

Trees in the Old Testament 4   Iain Roy

Wednesday 14 March

Joel 1:1-12

Under attack

I have a tree in my garden called *Cercidiphyllum japonica* (or Katsura). It has been much admired over the years, especially because of the glory of its autumn colour. A friend thought she would plant one in her garden too, but sadly an insect seems to have attacked it, weakening its growth. There is nothing so sad as a tree under attack.

> *An army of locusts has attacked our land;*
> *They are powerful and too many to count;*
> *their teeth are as sharp as those of a lion.*
> *They have destroyed our grapevines*
> *and chewed up our fig-trees.*
> *They have stripped off the bark,*
> *till the branches are white.*

(verses 6-7)

Joel saw the people of Israel as similarly under attack. But whereas my friend's tree is an innocent victim of infestation, Joel saw the people of Judah as makers of their own fate. What Joel is really describing here is not the devastation caused by locusts and drought but the spiritual barrenness of a people who have lost their way before God. In time, as Joel knew, the land would recover. His question was, would the people? Would they return to God? It is a question many faithful people ask today in the church. We have to answer it with the same positive belief as Joel – that young and old alike can have fresh vision and renewal through the grace of God.

† Revive your church, O Lord, and rekindle in us the desire to love you and serve you with all our heart and mind and spirit. Amen

Iain Roy   Trees in the Old Testament 4

Thursday 15 March
Micah 4:1-5

Prayers for the blessed

Our prayers of intercession are most often directed towards those who are in difficulty or need. We are less inclined to pray for those for whom life is good, in spite of the fact that Paul reminds us to 'Be happy with those who are happy, weep with those who weep' (Romans 12:15). Micah's vision, therefore, is a good corrective for us of this imbalance in our prayers.

> *In days to come . . .*
> *Everyone will live in peace*
> *among his own vineyards and fig-trees,*
> *and no one will make him afraid.*
> *The Lord Almighty has promised this.*

(part of verse 1, and verse 4)

Although Micah's image of peace is the Mediterranean one of tending vines and fig-trees, it is not far removed from the sentiment of the English poet Robert Browning: 'God's in His heaven – All's right with the world!' So often all is not well with the world, or even with that little part of it that we inhabit. But when it is, we have especial cause to rejoice, not least in other folk's happiness, success and achievements.

† Father, we pray for those who will be married today, have a child born to them, find a job, pass an exam, be discharged from hospital, be visited by someone who lifts their spirits. Help us to accentuate the positive today as well as be concerned about all that negates human living, for Christ's sake, Amen

Trees in the Old Testament 4   Iain Roy

Friday 16 March
Jonah 3:10 – 4:11

The servant of God

The writer of the book of Jonah has, I think, a wicked sense of humour. He places Jonah in the most awkward situations: with God, with the people of Nineveh, with a sea captain and ship's crew, and, most bizarrely of all, with a large fish or sea mammal – and then with a tree.

> The LORD God made a plant grow up over Jonah to give him some shade, so that he would be more comfortable. Jonah was extremely pleased with the plant. But at dawn the next day, at God's command, a worm attacked the plant, and it died. After the sun had risen, God sent a hot east wind, and Jonah was about to faint from the heat of the sun beating down on his head.

(verses 6-7, and part of verse 8)

The book of Jonah is a wonderful picture of one man's idea of the good life: doing his own thing – choosing his own word to preach rather than God's, being judgemental about others rather than himself, avoiding anything he personally did not want to do, taking his leisure even if everybody else was going to hell. It is exactly the opposite of the picture presented by some of the best role models for our own Christian discipleship: men and women who have put themselves about for God, because they realise how God in Christ has put himself about for them. It has made them not only more dedicated but also more compassionate than Jonah obviously was. The good thing is that eventually Jonah saw the kind of person he really needed to be, if he was to be the servant of God.

† Lord, show us how to be your obedient servants, to do not what we want to do, but what you want done, ever and always with love and compassion, Amen

Iain Roy   Trees in the Old Testament 4

Saturday 17 March

Habakkuk 3:16-19

Working things through

As gardeners we can easily be disappointed when a tree does not flourish, a plant withers, the yield of vegetables or fruit is poor. If it is not our livelihood, however, we can generally live with it. How different it must be for those who live by what they grow.

> *Even though the fig-trees have no fruit*
> *and no grapes grow on the vines,*
> *even though the olive-crop fails*
> *and the fields produce no corn . . .*
> *I will still be joyful and glad,*
> *because the LORD God is my saviour.*

(part of verse 17, and verse 18)

Here is a remarkable man of faith – no leisure gardener but a man of the soil, earning his living by the soil. The worst has happened, and yet he still retains his faith that God is and will be his saviour, that even if things temporarily go against us, over all God is with us, and his love and his provision will be our salvation. In the meantime he does what folk of faith will always do – gets back to work so that God can in time bless his labours.

† Christ, help us to endure when we cannot triumph, to keep on working at things when we cannot see our way through them. Help us with you to work things through, knowing that the alternative is to face life without you, your blessing and love.

For group discussion and personal thought
- Is there any tree in your life which has spoken to your pleasure or to your pain?
- We all need roots in life. What are the things that anchor your life and give you strength, and what do you see as God's part in all this?

Trees in the Old Testament 4   Iain Roy

Trees

Trees in the New Testament

Notes based on the *New Revised Standard Version* and (Friday) *Today's New International Version* by

Philip Wadham

Philip Wadham is a retired Anglican priest, living on Vancouver Island in western Canada. He has worked in England, Canada and South America and travelled extensively in Latin America and the Caribbean.

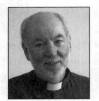

Introduction

Jesus told stories to teach his listeners about living as a child of God. He often drew on local scenes with which the people were familiar. In the province of British Columbia, western Canada, trees are an important part of the economy and many people's jobs are dependent on the forests. Bruce is a logger (lumberjack) with twenty years experience of working in the forests. These are some of his stories.

Sunday 18 March: *Matthew 7:15-20*

Growing strong

Bruce had 'fallen in love' (his words) with the forests in his early twenties, having spent a summer tree-planting with other young people. For these forests to continue to be healthy and provide jobs, saplings are planted where mature trees have already been cut down and harvested. Sometimes Bruce's job was thinning out these saplings. 'How do I select which should stay and which should be pulled?' he had asked his team boss. 'Look for good growth' was the reply.

> [Jesus said], 'Every good tree bears good fruit, but the bad tree bears bad fruit.'
>
> (part of verse 17)

Next day, in a section of forest that had been replanted some years previously, Bruce wondered which young trees should stay and which should go. Some were clearly doing well while others had already failed, but there were also those that showed small signs of progress. 'I'll leave them,' decided Bruce, 'they're doing well enough. There are some signs of growth and that's promising.'

† Lord, thank you for your patience with us. May your Holy Spirit help us to bring forth good growth.

Monday 19 March
Matthew 13:31-32

Faith-filled lives (1)

That evening, back at the camp with other forestry workers, the young people who, like Bruce, were working in the forest over the summer, swapped stories of their day. Bruce told how in the section where he had been working, the young trees were at different stages of growth. 'Some', he commented, 'were much more advanced than others. It's as though they had taken a growth pill,' he joked. The leader of the group, an experienced forester, laughed. 'It seems like that, Bruce, and in a way they have. These trees are being fed by an underground stream that feeds the roots and gives them an advantage over the others. The saplings all start off small but those being fed by the stream leap ahead of the others and reach maturity more quickly. Like us, they need good nourishment to thrive.'

'The kingdom of heaven is like a mustard seed . . . the smallest of all seeds, but when it has grown it is the greatest of shrubs and becomes a tree.'

(part of verses 31-32)

As a member of his local church, Bruce thought of those who fed him in his Christian life, particularly those whose lives were an example of a living faith. He thought of Joan, who each week visited the local hospital. She talked with patients, listening to their concerns and helping where she could. There was Leo who, though struggling with his own difficulties, served each week at a free lunch programme. And there was Jeannie, who regularly visited a care home for seniors. She played piano and helped with worship but mostly she just talked with the residents, 'her friends' she called them. Christians living faith-filled lives, feeding him like that underground stream.

† Nourishing God, continue to feed us with your word, written in the lives of all your faithful servants.

Trees in the New Testament   Philip Wadham

Tuesday 20 March

Matthew 21:18-22

Faith-filled lives (2)

Now in his forties, Bruce had seen many changes in forestry. When he had begun logging, a section of forest was clear cut – all the trees were cut down, even the smaller ones. This had scarred the forest for years to come. Now he and his crew selected only mature trees, leaving others to continue their growth. This change in logging showed greater care for the forest. David, Bruce's oldest son, was growing up in a world that, like forestry practices, had greatly changed. Since moving to the city David had drifted away from the church. 'How is David's faith now?' wondered Bruce. A conversation with a pastor some 20 years ago came to mind. 'Faith is about a way of living' she had told him, and Bruce thought about David's 'way of living'. Though he had little connection with church, David worked at a centre that cared for people disabled by a variety of personal and social issues. Alcohol and drug abuse were common. In his free time David had developed a good relationship with young people whose lives were, like the forest, scarred by past practices – young lives trying to cope with a mountain of painful experiences. David met with them, talked with them and hoped his presence might bring some healing to their scarred young lives.

> Jesus (said) 'Truly I tell you, if you have faith and do not doubt . . . even if you say to this mountain, "Be lifted up and thrown into the sea", it will be done.'

(part of verse 21)

Bruce smiled to himself: 'Though David's way may be different from mine, we live the same faith.'

† What does the Lord require of [me], but to do justice, and to love kindness and to walk humbly with [my] God (Micah 6:8).

Philip Wadham   Trees in the New Testament

Wednesday 21 March

Luke 19:1-10

March

A wise teacher

The work crew that Bruce led consisted of six men. The other members with less experience of logging respected his knowledge and generally followed his advice. On their homeward journey one commented to Bruce, 'You're different to some of the bosses I've had. One was a real pain to work for, shouting his orders and getting angry if we didn't follow them exactly. You guide us and listen to our ideas rather than order us and that's much better.' Bruce too had suffered in his early logging days from less than helpful crew bosses. He recognised that he had learned more and appreciated more those who listened to him, answered his questions and explained things clearly. Those had been the best teachers and most influenced him.

> [Seeing Zacchaeus in the sycamore tree, Jesus] said to him, 'Zacchaeus, hurry and come down; for I must stay at your house today' . . . Jesus said to him, 'Today salvation has come to this house.'

> (part of verses 5 and 9)

Bruce was thinking of leadership when he was at church the following Sunday. The Bible reading described Jesus teaching the disciples by example. He had taken a towel and washed his disciples' feet. He, their teacher, had taken on the role of a servant. He had made himself available to them (John 13:3-5). Bruce recognised that good leadership follows this pattern. It doesn't shout out orders and expect blind obedience. Rather, it is open to the ideas and concerns of others and by both word and example it teaches a way of living that is healthy and pleasing to God.

† Gracious God, as we serve others following the example of Jesus, may they hear the good news he both taught and lived.

Trees in the New Testament   Philip Wadham

Thursday 22 March

John 1:43 – 51 1

Love is the message

It had been a wet and cold morning in the forest. Bruce's work crew sheltered together as they ate lunch and hoped the weather would break for the afternoon. They talked about their small town. 'I hear there's a new pastor,' said James, directing his remark at Bruce. 'I don't go to church but word soon spreads. Is he okay?' Bruce was by nature a quiet man. He talked little about his faith except when asked directly, so he simply replied, 'He only arrived two weeks ago so it's too early to say, but I like what I've heard so far.' 'So has he scared you with judgement and hell fire yet?' joked Simon, whose experience of the church had been so negative that he had little regard for the church and preachers. 'No, on the contrary,' replied Bruce, 'he talked about how God, having created human beings, saw that it was good (Genesis 1:31) and that God looks for the good in everyone and rejoices in it.'

> When Jesus saw Nathanael coming toward him, he said of him, 'Here is truly an Israelite in whom there is no deceit!'

(verse 47)

'Well, that's a different message to the one I heard in church,' said Simon. 'It was like I was being judged every time my minister spoke. I couldn't stand it, so in the end I just left.' 'That's a shame', responded Bruce. 'The message I hear, and that I read in the gospels, is that God knows each one of us and loves us. And that knowing we are loved by God helps us to love each other.'

† Gracious God, as you embrace me in love, may I reach out and draw others into that same love.

Philip Wadham   Trees in the New Testament

Friday 23 March

Romans 11:17-24

Diversity is the key

Continuing yesterday's conversation, Simon said 'That's all very nice, to say that God loves all of us but some preachers seem to think that they're the only ones who are right. They spend a lot of time saying bad things about other Christians who don't believe exactly as they do. I don't see much love in this.' Bruce thought about Simon's comment. 'We've been working in the valley bottom this morning. What trees did we cut down?' he asked. 'Pine, Alder and Douglas Fir,' replied James, 'and Cottonwood and Red Cedar.' Simon said, 'And there was that magnificent Yellow Cedar. And they were all so healthy. I guess it's because of the river that runs through.' 'Yes,' continued Bruce, 'a variety of trees all depending on the one river for their health. It's really the ideal forest, it's diverse and when it's replanted we won't simply plant one type of sapling. We'll plant a diversity of trees so that the new forest will be as mixed as the old one. And because it's mixed, it will be healthier than if every tree was the same.

If some of the branches have been broken off, and you, though a wild olive shoot, have been grafted in among the others and now share in the nourishing sap from the olive root, do not consider yourself to be superior to those other branches.

(verse 17 and part of verse 18)

'Okay,' said James, 'I get your point. In order for the church to be healthy we shouldn't all be the same. Is that it?' 'That's right,' replied Bruce, 'and even though we are different, doesn't the same stream feeds us all?'

† God of all creation, may I always be open to hear your voice, from wherever it comes.

Trees in the New Testament   Philip Wadham

Saturday 24 March

Revelation 22:1-7

The kingdom is the goal

The afternoon after yesterday's conversation, the rain ceased, the clouds broke up and the sun broke through. The river, swollen by the rain, was running clear. Bruce looked around him. There was nowhere else he would rather be or any other job he would rather do. It was heavy manual labour and at the end of the day he was generally dirty and tired, but most days he felt fulfilled, in part because he saw his work as caring for the forest. The harvested trees would in time be replaced by new ones, the cycle of life, death and new life would be repeated. Next spring the river would be teeming with fish as salmon returned from their four-year sojourn in the ocean. They would swim upstream and lay eggs of future salmon that in their turn would carry on their cycle of birth, life, death and new life. Bruce was grateful to God for placing him here and silently offered up a prayer of thanksgiving.

Then the angel showed me the river of the water of life, bright as crystal, flowing from the throne of God and of the Lamb . . . On either side of the river is the tree of life . . . And the leaves of the tree are for the healing of the nations.

(part of verses 1-2)

† Praise be to God who gives birth, life and death.

For group discussion and personal thought

• Who has fed you in your Christian life (Monday)? Was it through their words or their actions?

• Jesus invited himself into Zacchaeus' home (Wednesday). Imagine/discuss a conversation between them.

• If Christians are diverse in their beliefs (Friday), what is central to our faith, without which we cease to be Christians?

Philip Wadham   Trees in the New Testament

Trees

The tree of shame is made the tree of glory

Notes based on the *New Jerusalem Bible* by

Anthea Dove

Anthea Dove is a great-grandmother, a retired teacher, retreat-giver and writer. She was married in Kerala, South India, where she lived for six years. She is a Roman Catholic with a strong commitment to social justice and ecumenism.

Introduction

When I first saw, in old writings, the cross on which Jesus died referred to as a tree, I was surprised. But when I thought about it, I realised that his cross was not the finely crafted and polished thing we usually see representing the crucifixion, but a rough piece of wood hacked from a living tree, perhaps as mutilated and disfigured as the body that was to be nailed to it. After the resurrection, that same piece of wood became the symbol of new life, the symbol of Jesus Christ, risen in glory.

Sunday 25 March: *Genesis 2:4b – 9, 15-17*

The first trees

In this story of the creation of the world, the planting of trees is very significant.

> *From the soil, Yahweh God caused to grow every kind of tree, enticing to look at and good to eat, with the tree of life in the middle of the garden, and the tree of the knowledge of good and evil.*

(verse 9)

There are trees growing in all the different countries of the world. They vary in size and leaf shape, but they are almost always beautiful and nearly all of them are fruitful and useful to human beings. But the trees of God's world are in danger, as those greedy for power and money cut down large swathes of rain forest, ruining not only the landscape but also the whole diversity of the region and the livelihoods of the people. We are like Adam and Eve in the garden, as we choose between good and evil.

† Lord, keep us steadfast as we have to face choices and make decisions. Help us to do your will in every situation. Help us to appreciate the wonder of your creation and to treat all people, all creatures and the whole of Nature, with humility and respect.

Monday 26 March

Genesis 3:1-13

Walking in the garden

There is a lovely image in this passage, showing how it was (and can be again) for those who are innocent and know themselves to be in a close relationship with God.

The man and his wife heard the sound of Yahweh God walking in the garden in the cool of the day, and they hid from Yahweh God among the trees of the garden.

(verse 8)

We can picture Adam and Eve behaving like naughty children, just before they realise what they have thrown away by their actions: their happy, intimate friendship with God. Many centuries later came Holy Saturday, when the crucified Jesus went down to hell to rescue them. There are graphic paintings showing Jesus beckoning to the chastened couple as they emerge from the place of punishment. The story of Adam and Eve is both delightful and sad, and whether or not we believe it literally, it teaches very clearly the doctrine of redemption, of the saving of sinners through the suffering of Jesus on the cross. Of course the world we live in today is a thousand times more complex than the world of the time of the Garden of Eden, but human nature is no different, and like Adam and Eve we have to choose between right and wrong, in our case every day and in every situation. But through Jesus we are redeemed and we can sometimes discover a glimpse of Paradise, in other words, the Kingdom of God. We can even walk among the trees in a garden in the cool of the day, and feel close to God in silence and peace!

† Lord, help us to know ourselves, so that we may see clearly the way we should go.
Lord, give us the strength to resist temptation.
Lord, teach us to see with the eyes of Christ, especially when we look at our brothers and sisters.
Lord, make us ever grateful for the life of Jesus and all the blessing he brings.

Anthea Dove   The tree of shame, the tree of glory

Tuesday 27 March

Genesis 3:22-24

Paradise lost

What do you long for most? If you are hungry, you long for food. If you are lonely, you long for friends. If you are in prison, you long for freedom. People who believe in God long for his kingdom to come. They long to be part of it, to live in peace and harmony and goodness. Adam and Eve did live in peace and harmony and goodness, but it was taken from them, or rather, they threw it away by disobeying God.

> *Then Yahweh God said, 'Now that man has become like one of us in knowing good from evil, he must not be allowed to reach out his hand and pick from the tree of life too, and eat and live for ever!*

(verse 22)

But the paradise lost through the sins of human beings is the likeness of the paradise to be regained through the grace of Jesus Christ, through forgiveness and reconciliation. This is what we hope to win, this is ultimately what we as Christians long for. Sadly, there are some people who think, or feel, that they can never be forgiven because their sin is so great. They cannot forgive themselves, they cannot believe that others will forgive them, most importantly they cannot imagine God ever forgiving them. But they are emphatically mistaken. He is always ready to forgive, no matter what. Indeed he longs to forgive people, as the Father in the story longed to embrace the prodigal son. And so we must remember that there is hope for everyone, even the most wretched of sinners, and that one day there may be a place for us in the eternal Garden of Eden, where we will be free to pick fruit from the tree of life.

† Lord, may I never lose trust in you, or the hope of happiness with you.
Lord, bless those who are fearful, and believe they can never be forgiven. Grant them faith in you and in themselves.
Lord, I ask your blessing on the hungry, the lonely and the imprisoned.

The tree of shame, the tree of glory   Anthea Dove

Wednesday 28 March

Galatians 3:6-14

People of faith

In this letter, St Paul urges the Galatians to imitate Abraham, the man of faith. God will consider us upright in his sight if we live, not in obedience to the Law, but in faith, trusting in God completely, always and everywhere, as Abraham did. Paul writes:

Christ redeemed us from the curse by being cursed for our sake since Scripture says: 'Anyone hanged is accursed', so that the blessing of Abraham might come to the gentiles in Christ Jesus and so that they might receive the promised Spirit through faith.

(verses 13-14)

It is amazing that through Abraham and, most especially, through Jesus, who were both Jews, we Gentiles received the promised Spirit. It was the apostles Peter and Paul who first understood that this was what Jesus himself wanted: that everyone, no matter where in the world they lived, could be a believer, a person of faith, someone especially blessed. That is why missionaries, sometimes priests or ministers, sometimes laypeople, travel from countries all over the world to teach people about God and encourage them to have faith. I have a friend who comes from Ireland. He became a priest in order to become a missionary in Africa, and for some years he brought the good news of Jesus to people in Liberia. Then he went to the Philippines, where he taught other men to become missionaries and go to other countries to preach. After this, he lived in India, again teaching men to work in the missions in different lands. And now he is in America. So the word of God is spread among the Gentiles, and many men and women are drawn to become people of faith.

† Lord, fill me with the Holy Spirit and deepen my faith in you.
Lord, I ask your blessings on all those who work as missionaries. Give them the courage to face difficulties and help them to persevere if they feel discouraged.
Lord, as we hope to draw others to have faith in you, keep us open and sensitive to cultures different from our own.

Anthea Dove   The tree of shame, the tree of glory

Thursday 29 March

1 Peter 2:18-25

Straying sheep

In this letter St Peter tells us that through the bruises of Jesus as he was crucified, we have been healed. It is wonderful to imagine this, and perhaps equally marvellous to understand that when we are suffering, in whatever way, still our Lord Jesus is with us in the heart of that suffering, bearing it with us. Peter wants us to imitate Jesus in everything, which is a tremendous challenge and very hard to do. He left us an example to follow: of courage and compassion, understanding and humility, and all the virtues we can think of! Of course we fall short, over and over again, but it is good to keep on hoping and struggling and holding on to our faith in God. Peter tells us that because Jesus suffered so cruelly for our sake,

You had gone astray like sheep, but now you have returned to the shepherd and guardian of your souls.

(verse 25)

Sheep are notoriously silly, and when we come to think about it, so are we – at least some of us, some of the time! In St John's Gospel, Jesus tells the story of the good shepherd who lays down his life for his sheep, who knows his own flock and cares for them. He goes on to say that there are other sheep who are 'not of this fold' which he must lead too, perhaps referring here to us, the Gentiles. The good shepherd leads his flock with tenderness, carrying the lambs in his arms and seeking tirelessly for any sheep that are lost. So it is with Jesus; he never drives or forces us, or makes impossible demands. He leads us gently and draws us to him by his love.

† Lord Jesus, thank you for your patience and long-suffering love.
Lord Jesus, I would love to be like you in all things but I know it is impossible. Teach me to accept myself and my shortcomings.
Lord, lead me back to you whenever I stray and help me to look out for those who are lost.

The tree of shame, the tree of glory   Anthea Dove

Friday 30 March

Song of Solomon 2:1-7

Jesus Christ the apple tree

The Song of Solomon is unlike any other book in the Bible: it is an expression of love depicted in beautiful poetry. It can be interpreted as showing the love between Christ and his church, the love we feel for Jesus and he for us. All through the ages, poets have tried to show their love through their imagination. For example, Shakespeare compared his lover 'to a summer's day'. The writer of the Song of Solomon uses a different but equally unusual comparison:

> *As an apple tree among the trees of the wood,*
> *so is my love among young men.*
> *In his delightful shade I sit,*
> *and his fruit is sweet to my taste.*

(verse 3)

In the eighteenth century, or possibly much earlier, an anonymous writer composed the carol known as 'Jesus Christ the Apple Tree', which may have been inspired by the Song of Solomon. I wonder why or how this writer saw Jesus as an apple tree. We can't know, for all the imaginings of painters through the centuries, what Jesus looked like, but we do know that in mind and spirit he was beautiful. We know also that he was indeed fruitful, that his words have inspired millions of people all over the world, often changing their lives. So the carol celebrates the beauty and fruitfulness of Jesus, and as we ponder this image we may like to ponder on the depth of his love for us and of our love for him.

† Lord Jesus, I thank you for your great love for me, and ask you to deepen my love for you.

Anthea Dove   The tree of shame, the tree of glory

Saturday 31 March

Matthew 21:1-11

Gifts of homage

Great crowds of people spread their cloaks on the road, while others were cutting branches from the trees and spreading them in his path.

(verse 8)

We may ask why the people cut down branches from the trees. I think it was because they wanted to honour Jesus and show him their love. Trees and flowers are beautiful and precious in our eyes, and there is a human instinct to give them in homage to those we respect. So in many countries, people give garlands of flowers as a mark of reverence. When Princess Diana died in Britain, thousands of people laid flowers in her memory, and flowers are often placed at a spot where someone has died. We planted a weeping cherry tree over the grave of our little son. All these are instances of the way we are moved to demonstrate our powerful feelings for someone, and so it must have been natural for the people of Jerusalem to show their joy in what seemed the triumph of Jesus, by their spontaneous gestures of giving.

† Lord, give us the warmth of heart to rejoice with those who are joyful and grieve with those who sorrow.

For group discussion and personal thought

• What is the significance of the 'tree of life' for you?

• If you have a favourite tree, can you explain is significance for you?

• How do you react to the idea of Jesus Christ the Apple Tree?

The tree of shame, the tree of glory   Anthea Dove

IBRA International Appeal

Imagine the only book you have to help you read the Bible is in French (or if you're a French speaker, try Tagalog!). Maybe you can understand bits of it, but imagine your joy when you discover someone has translated it into English for you!

Hundreds of thousands of people around the world experience similar joy when they discover the IBRA books and readings lists have been translated into their language. And this is all through the generosity of IBRA readers.

Each year, the IBRA International Fund provides funds for local groups to translate, print and distribute IBRA Bible notes and reading lists. Last year more than 68000 people in eleven different countries received copies of the IBRA books which had been translated, printed and distributed by IBRA partners. The reading list was also translated into French, Spanish, Telugu (India), Tokelau (Samaoa) and several Congolese languages, enabling 250000 people to receive them in a language useful to them.

The funds are given exclusively by IBRA readers like you, who give generously towards the fund, raising over £20000 each year. With your gift, more people will be able to experience the joy of reading the Bible using notes or a list of readings in a familiar language.

Please consider either giving for the first time, or increasing your donation this year. You can donate using the envelope which is part of the leaflet insert that came with this book, or add your donation to your order for next year's books.

Thank you!

International Bible Reading Association
1020 Bristol Road
Selly Oak
Birmingham
B29 6LB
Tel. 0121 472 4242

Readings in Mark

3 Holy Week

Notes based on the *New Revised Standard Version* by

Terry Lester

Terry Lester is an Anglican priest working at St George's Cathedral in the Diocese of Cape Town, South Africa. He has a great interest in the way people of faith in Africa respond to the challenges facing them, and in building and strengthening common bonds across faith divides.

Introduction

In the readings for this week we walk alongside Jesus as the story of his passion unfolds. Mark sets the events against the backdrop of the Jewish Passover, which re-enacts God's saving acts, freedom from slavery, and setting off to the land of promise. Mark tells the story lest the faithful forget, and also to remind them that the Father's work continues through them. In the busyness of life, we too need to remember the cost and the calling.

Sunday 1 April: *Mark 14:17-31*
The Last Supper

> *While they were eating, Jesus took a loaf of bread, and after blessing it he broke it, gave it to them and said, 'Take, this is my body.'*

(verse 23)

The events related in this passage coincide with 'the day the lambs for the Passover meal were killed' (verse 12). The Passover meal not only reminded Jews of God's past action on their behalf, it also looked forward to the day when God's people would be a blessing to the nations. The Passover meal began with the eating of the bread of affliction and ended with the drinking of the cup of blessing. Its fourfold action of taking, blessing, breaking and giving describes both how God acts on his people – and how God acted through his Son, taking him, without blemish, breaking him and giving him as expiation for our sin. As those who say 'yes' to this generosity of God, the followers of Jesus are reminded that their life too will follow this pattern.

† Lord Jesus, thank you that you have taken me and blessed me. Break and bend me to your will so that it conforms to your way, and bring me to the knowledge of your grace and love, for your mercy's sake. Amen

Monday 2 April

Mark 14:32-52

The Garden of Gethsemane

Abba, Father, for you all things are possible; remove this cup from me; yet, not what I want, but what you want.

(verse 36)

The first Adam hid from God in the garden because he was ashamed of his nakedness; the second Adam goes to the garden to talk to his Father. His nakedness will be forced on him, as too will the suffering and death that will follow. For the first Adam nakedness was the consequence of greed and disobedience; for the second Adam, Jesus, it is the consequence of self-emptying and obedience to the Father's will. He cannot face it alone and asks his closest disciples to pray for him as he reasons with his Father. Abraham, the father of the Jewish nation, engaged with God to save Sodom if only five righteous people could be found, when God had a larger figure in mind. So here, the father of the new community of God, Jesus, is the one righteous person who will give his life in order that all of humanity will live.

† We thank you, Jesus, that we are saved by your righteousness alone and that your love and grace have made us right with the Father. Amen

Holy Week

Terry Lester

Tuesday 3 April

Mark 14:53-72

Jesus before Caiaphas, and Peter's denial

Peter had followed him at a distance, right into the courtyard of the high priest and he was sitting with the guards, warming himself at the fire.

(verse 54)

The disciples had been called to follow Jesus so that they could hear his words and witness to his actions. The place of the disciple is to follow closely and to be watchful. Peter is representative of all the disciples who, as the pressure intensifies on Jesus, are either falling asleep at crucial moments or lagging behind and following at a distance. There appears to be far greater intimacy with the enemy – Peter warms himself at the fire and sits in the courtyard with the guards – while Jesus is abandoned by his followers who should be remaining close to him. Yet a few days later, Jesus will reaffirm that Peter is the rock and foundation on which God's church will be built. The story serves as warning to the early church to be more alert to the ways they abandon Jesus and see their tardiness as akin to cosying-up to the enemy. Whether this is out of fear or expediency, the effect is the same: they miss God's 'hour which has come'. We, as followers, also miss moments that call for alertness, so making ourselves complicit in the death of the innocent. Speaking truth to power is not an optional extra to discipleship.

† Lord, keep me close to you so that I can hear you whisper, and alert to you so that I can recognise when your hour is at hand. Amen.

Terry Lester   Holy Week

Wednesday 4 April

Mark 15:1-15

Jesus before Pilate

As soon as it was morning, the chief priests held a consultation with the elders and scribes and the whole council. They bound Jesus, led him away, and handed him over to Pilate.

(verse 1)

What is striking in these accounts of Jesus' trial is both the speed with which it happens and the various powers that co-operate for it to happen. Sworn enemies make common cause with one another and power speaks to power to guard the vested interests of each. The Scribes and Pharisees had autonomy to administer and enforce their laws according to their jurisprudence. Breaking down the Temple, as witnesses attested Jesus had said, was as ludicrous as forcing a camel to go through the eye of a needle, but he was not charged for cruelty to animals! Instead of seeing the humour in his saying about the Temple, they became deadly serious and would not let go of it. Pilate wanted to make sure he was not dealing with someone who had nationalistic designs on power or who was about to proclaim himself king. He was not convinced that this was the case with Jesus but he saw the determination of the Jews too and so he decided on a middle way – have Jesus the lover of people killed but release the killer of people, Barabbas. One ethnic group was not more – or less – culpable or complicit than the other in their contribution to the death of Jesus. All fell short and each allowed their arrogance and fear to blind them to truth and justice. We can do the same.

† For all the times when I have made swift judgements and pronounced harshly on others, when I have failed to see my own arrogance, or allowed my fear to stifle truth and justice: Father, forgive. Amen

Thursday 5 April

Mark 15:16-24

Jesus is mocked

They began saluting him, 'Hail, King of the Jews!' They struck his head with a reed, spat upon him, and knelt down in homage to him.

(verse 18)

Noise and activity are the terminal conditions of our time! They deafen our ears and blind our eyes to the presence of life and truth and love in our midst. It contrasts with the silence of the Son of God in the midst of the madness of the activity going on around him. In my most self-righteous moments I feel contemptuous of those who were in the presence of the source of all life and were too busy snuffing out that life to notice! I'm sure I would have noticed! But would I really have? Am I any better than my forebears in these passages, who had set their course and planned their actions and would not stop for a moment to listen and ask if they were still following the right promptings or acting in accordance with truth? Elijah had to concede that God was not in the wind, nor in the earthquake, nor in the fire but, rather, in the still sound of silence. Our obsession with doing can amount to mere mockery of the one whose essence is to be found in just being with him. Talk is cheap and often our flowery language can sound as hollow as the salutations of the soldiers.

† Lord, help me to hear your voice in the sound of sheer stillness. Amen.

Terry Lester

Holy Week

Friday 6 April (Good Friday)

Mark 15:25-39

The crucifixion

Now the centurion, who stood facing Jesus, saw that in this way he
breathed his last, he said, 'Truly this man was God's Son!'

(verse 39)

In my country, Pretoria Central Prison was where the gallows were. In June 1989, mere months before Nelson Mandela's release, over 33 people were hanged. Society has never been short of ideas on how to discard those it deems to be a menace, or those whose continued existence on this earth will neither serve justice nor be of further use to society, for whom the only option left seems to be to execute them. Fewer and fewer countries have death as the ultimate penalty. And with each execution the words of the centurion are hard to refute: This is God's son or God's daughter. The discarding of a human life made in the image of God, bought by the blood of Christ, and endowed with Jesus' Spirit so that each person is a child of God, has no place in God's plan for his children. What Jesus does, he does once and he does it for all. Jesus' death on a cross at the place of execution outside the city walls marks humanity's darkest moment and God's clearest identification with those our society discards. And a Roman soldier alerts the church to this truth.

† Lord Jesus, your gift is life, abundant life for all, and to give it, you let us snatch yours. Forgive our foolishness. Amen

Holy Week   Terry Lester

Saturday 7 April

Mark 15:40-47

Jesus is buried

Joseph of Arimathea, a respected member of the council, who was also himself waiting expectantly for the kingdom of God, went boldly to Pilate and asked for the body of Jesus.

(verse 43)

Mark ends his gospel in suspended animation, leaving the outcome of these events shrouded in uncertainty, even though we know that Jesus' efforts didn't end in burial, fear and failure but rather in triumph over death and despair and in hope and life. Our presence today is the ongoing witness to that fact. And what of those who wait expectantly for the kingdom? Well, there is a place for all in it – rich, poor, Jew, Gentile, those of much faith and those of little, men and women, children, the sick, the widow, the orphan, the discarded and the indispensable – it is only our fear that can hold back the dawn of the Kingdom of God and its breaking into our world. That breaking in of God's kingdom relies on the boldness of those who have waited with expectancy. Now is a time to be bold – God's hour has come.

† Lord, when I feel overwhelmed by fear and faint in spirit, help me to be bold like Joseph of Arimathea. Amen

For group discussion and personal thought

• What are the fears that hold us back from following closely behind the crucified Christ?

• How does the community of the cross also live the eucharistic life of faith?

Terry Lester   Holy Week

1 Corinthians

1 The wisdom of God

Notes based on the *New International Version* by

Yordan Kalev Zhekov

Yordan Kalev Zhekov is an Evangelical Christian born in Bulgaria who studied at the University of Ljubljana, Slovenia. He currently works in the field of addiction and homelessness in Watford, UK, and is the author of *Defining the New Testament Logia on Divorce and Remarriage in a Pluralistic Context.*

April

Introduction

It is not only lack of wisdom that produces negative outcomes but also where we look for our wisdom. This week's theme, the wisdom of God, shapes Paul's message to the Corinthians as the power needed in every sphere of their lives. Following the biblical message, we look at the impact of divine wisdom on our Christian living.

Sunday 8 April (Easter Day): *1 Corinthians 15:50-58*

Eternal life – divine wisdom for Christian living

In our secular world death signifies the end. Its impact on the living is enormous. The dilemma about what comes after has been denied, or managed through imagination and philosophy. The Corinthians, under differing influences, struggled with the issue. The mystery of life after death is revealed through Christ's resurrection. It pronounces victory over sin, which has lost its power over believers' lives, and also the defeat of death. This defeat will be realised at Jesus' return, when all believers will experience transformation according to Christ's resurrection. The dead will be raised and together with the living will be transformed for eternal life.

> *When the perishable has been clothed with the imperishable, and the mortal with immortality, then the saying that is written will come true: 'Death has been swallowed up in victory.'*

(verse 54)

This coming future promised by divine wisdom was not only an inspiration for the Corinthians but can also inspire us as Christ's followers to invest our lives in the Lord's work.

† Please help us, Lord, to be empowered by the hope of eternal life.

1 Corinthians 1:1-17

Disunity approached with divine wisdom

Our contemporary society is characterised by political, social, economic, racial and religious divisions. Stereotypical thinking and prejudice encourage us to differentiate and even reject others in order to promote ourselves. The Corinthian church seems to have had a problem of internal divisions at variance with the ideal of church unity proclaimed by Paul in the gospel of Christ. These divisions were linked to who administered baptism, as well as other issues of social status, knowledge, wisdom and spirituality. The divisions even led to challenging Paul's authority in relation to the church. Hence Paul stresses his apostolic authority, urges the Corinthian believers to unity, and underlines his attitude towards them. He focuses on their qualities as Christians formed through their faith in Christ and firmly grounded in the gospel. Paul also points to their mutual hope in the coming of Christ and their common effort in building up their faith in the meantime. Even though the Corinthians are shaken by various problems and struggles, Paul still believes that Christ's work in them will be successfully accomplished.

He will keep you strong to the end, so that you will be blameless on the day of our Lord Jesus Christ.

(verse 8)

In our daily struggles and our various battles throughout life, we have failed many times to share Paul's positive view even towards those who questioned his authority. Our view as Christians about ourselves and our fellow believers should be underlined by God's grace, Christ's faithfulness and the work of Holy Spirit in us.

† Please help us, Lord, to see ourselves and our brothers and sisters in Christ through your eyes!

Yordan Zhekov   The wisdom of God

Tuesday 10 April

1 Corinthians 1:18 -2.5

The wisdom of God experienced

In our contemporary society, dominated as it is by the imitation of celebrities, boasting appears to be a virtue. This attitude is underlined by people's efforts to gain popularity by promoting themselves above others. The relationships between different groups in the Corinthian church were characterised by boasting. This arrogant self-exaltation over others derived from human wisdom. Paul deals with the problem by contrasting human wisdom with the gospel. The so-called wise have rejected it as foolishness, but it is the way God has chosen to express his wisdom and to humiliate the wisdom of human beings. Paul provides three pieces of evidence to support his claim: the cross, the Corinthians' status, and his own preaching. The death of Christ on the cross, a dreadful humiliation and defeat in terms of human wisdom, provides salvation to those who believe. The low social status and insignificant origins of the Corinthians are an embarrassment in the eyes of the wise, and yet they have been chosen by God for salvation.

It is because of him that you are in Christ Jesus, who has become for us wisdom from God – that is, our righteousness, holiness and redemption.

(verse 30)

Paul's preaching did not comply with human wisdom and its standards but with God's power, which was the foundation of the Corinthians' faith.

Pressured to conform to the social dynamics of the competitive world, we may often have ended in the Corinthians' situation ourselves, following human wisdom and exalting ourselves over others. The solution to detaching ourselves from human wisdom and opposing its arrogance lies in understanding the nature of Christ's death on the cross, remembering God's choice of us, and knowing that our faith is based on his power revealed in the gospel.

† Please help us, Lord, to shape our thinking and behaviour according to your wisdom.

The wisdom of God   Yordan Zhekov

Wednesday 11 April
1 Corinthians 2:6-16

The wisdom of God revealed

Political power touches every dimension of our lives, national, social, religious and domestic; so we have all tasted the bitterness of political games shaped and executed through a selfish, arrogant, self-centred wisdom which eradicates all virtue and altruism. The Corinthians' embrace of human wisdom is contrary to their faith in Christ. Paul demonstrates that by following this wisdom they have gone against the wisdom of God. The mysterious character and timeless nature of the latter is established by divine formulation of salvation. Its fulfilment in Christ has been completely ignored by the bearers of worldly wisdom. The secrecy of God's wisdom has been revealed to believers through the Spirit of God.

We have not received the spirit of the world but the Spirit who is from God, that we may understand what God has freely given us.

(verse 12)

Therefore believers have become the bearers of God's wisdom through the Spirit of God whom they have received through faith in Jesus. This spirituality has no relation to worldly wisdom. On the contrary, true spirituality is defined by the work of God's Spirit in the believer. Thus the believer is able to understand God's thinking and perceive reality in a spiritual way. The Corinthians needed to be reminded that they had the mind of Christ and that they should act accordingly.

Many times we have become entangled in political games and have allowed worldly wisdom to define our decisions and guide our actions. As Christians we also need to be reminded that we have the mind of Christ through the Holy Spirit who lives in us and that we need to shape our understanding and form our behaviour accordingly.

† O Lord, lead us through your Spirit always to think, see and act spiritually.

The wisdom of God in the church

April

Leadership and hierarchical structures in the churches have a significant impact on Christians. Our secular ambitions have led us to become more interested in the power dynamics of our church structures then in our own spiritual growth. For Corinthian believers the fascination of worldly wisdom and loyalty to different leaders led to divisions in the church. Paul addresses the problem by revealing the spiritual stature of the Corinthians and the role of leaders in their life as a church. He builds on his previous argument about the contrast between true spirituality and human wisdom. Embracing the latter had led the Corinthians to spiritual stagnation, in spite of having the potential to grow through God's Spirit. Hence they acted in a worldly way that kept their spiritual development – and their spiritual nourishment – at the level of infants. But still they did not change their worldly behaviour, in spite of the availability of God's wisdom. This distorted their perception of the role of leaders such as Paul and Apollos and fragmented the church and their personal relationships. So Paul clarifies the status of the leaders as servants who are fulfilling God's important purpose: the Corinthians' faith. Paul uses the metaphor of the field to show the equality of the leaders and emphasise God's role:

I planted the seed, Apollos watered it, but God made it grow.

(verse 6)

In the light of Paul's argument, we need to examine our own attitude to the church and its hierarchy, and our relationships to our leaders. This should lead to our spiritual growth.

† Lord, please help us to understand and live your wisdom with regard to the church.

The wisdom of God   Yordan Zhekov

The wisdom of God in the ministry

Ministry is an important part of Christian life and it takes various forms. Knowing that all services are important for the Kingdom of God, we sometimes tend to value and promote our own ministry over others in our local church. This becomes even more obvious when it happens on the larger scale of Christian denominations and traditions. Are we not all members of God's church, with a common goal? Paul tackled a similar problem with the Corinthian church by using the metaphor of a building. He emphasises that he had laid the proper foundation and everyone who builds on it should build with solid materials.

> *For no-one can lay any foundation other than the one already laid, which is Jesus Christ.*

(verse 11)

But the Corinthians were following worldly wisdom, not using the right materials, and so erecting a very fragile construction, which would not survive the judgement fire of God at the time of Christ's return. The Corinthians had to turn to the wisdom of God and use solid materials to build on the good foundation. To further emphasise his point, Paul uses the image of God's temple to stress the importance of the church and its moral stature in the midst of an immoral society. The fact that Holy Spirit dwells in the church and that judgement is coming to those who seek to destroy it underlines the importance of having a ministry based on God's wisdom. This ministry is a stewardship, because everything belongs to God and he will reward such service. So let us strive to practise our ministry as good stewards of God's church, valuing the work of our fellow Christians.

† Lord, please help us to do your work equipped with your wisdom.

Saturday 14 April

1 Corinthians 4:1-13

The wisdom of God in faithful living

Living in the busy and demanding world requires from us discipline, organisation and determination to maintain a high standard of life. We strive for perfect order in our daily existence. When challenges occur in spite of our efforts, we tend to question God and judge things prematurely. The Corinthians, fascinated by worldly wisdom, shaped their lives accordingly and pronounced judgement on Paul's authority, life and ministry. The apostle dismissed their judgement as insignificant in the light of God's truly accurate and comprehensive judgement at the time of Christ's return.

Therefore judge nothing before the appointed time; wait till the Lord comes. He will bring to light what is hidden in darkness and will expose the motives of men's hearts. At that time each will receive his praise from God.

(verse 5)

Paul presents his life and the lives of the other apostles as faithful to Christ in all difficulties, unlike the flashy, worldly lives of the Corinthians. Using sarcasm and irony, Paul paints a picture of the Corinthians ruling from their exalted positions and the apostles exposed to misery and suffering. It is a humiliating image for Paul, but its truthful reality stems from God's wisdom. The life of the apostles may be defined as faithfulness to God in imitation of Christ's life and sufferings. Hence the Corinthians are challenged to change their perspective and live faithfully according to God's wisdom. And so are we.

† O Lord, help us to go through life's difficulties guided by your wisdom.

For group discussion and personal thought

• What characterises a spiritual man or woman?
• Create a profile of God's wisdom. What are its distinctive features?

The wisdom of God   Yordan Zhekov

1 Corinthians

2   Disorder in Corinth

Notes based on the *New Revised Standard Version* by

Alec Gilmore

Alec Gilmore is a Baptist minister, Senior Research Fellow at the International Baptist Theological Seminary in Prague, and author of *A Concise Dictionary of Bible Origins and Interpretation* (Continuum).

Introduction

Because the issues in these chapters are still with us, we need to remember that, despite Paul's eminence today, he was one leader dealing with one particular church at one particular moment in time, long before there was any widely established Christian tradition. He was also a pastor, not a lawyer; and at times Paul is clearly struggling with the issues himself. It is therefore inappropriate to universalise what he says and apply it to all other situations, however similar. Better to see the specifics as symptomatic of a church in turmoil and reflect on how Paul handles it overall, rather than the details.

Sunday 15 April: *1 Corinthians 4:14-21*
Listening to the wider tradition

In Corinth Paul founded a Christian community of some 50 members in a prosperous, cosmopolitan, maritime and commercial city with a steadily widening gap between rich and poor, and a constant influx of immigrants. He left after two years, and not surprisingly there were problems. Infighting, perhaps; one or two trying to rule the roost; or newcomers from other churches questioning what Paul had left behind. Paul, perhaps over-protective and a bit heavy-handed, says,

> For though you might have ten thousand guardians in Christ, you do not have many fathers.

(verse 15)

Naturally he wants them to maintain what he established, but in time they will also need to listen to others and discover the faith and the church for themselves.

† Father, keep me ever alert to the wider church, to see, to listen, to understand and to hear your voice in all the mayhem.

1 Corinthians 5:1-13

Expecting something better

Paul is clearly shocked and angry at what is going on, but why? It seems to be with the church rather than the man. Paul is aware he is dealing with hearsay and an extreme case, and does not necessarily buy the idea that it was a case of incest. That would have been offensive to the Jews and the whole Graeco-Roman world. The man's father may have been dead, and his father's widow may have been his stepmother and not even a believer. Paul therefore uses it as a timely reminder to the reader to see the life of the church in relation to the customs of the world they are living in and to avoid any signs of isolation or separatism.

I wrote to you in my letter not to associate with sexually immoral persons – not at all meaning the immoral of this world, or the greedy and robbers, or idolaters, since you would then need to go out of the world.

(verses 9-10)

This is realistic. Many of the Christians worked in businesses owned by non-believers and many were slaves in pagan households. Detachment from the world, any world, was not an option. It is also good missiology, because if the world around them is to be changed, it needs the church to provide the new yeast as leaven for the lump. So why are they so gossipy and fractious instead of creating the yeast? Could they not agree? Was the offender too big a fish to be handled? Either way, they were missing an opportunity to demonstrate a different way of life.

† Father, keep me ever alert to the need not to cut myself off but to present to the world I live in a different set of attitudes and a healthier way of solving problems and treating people.

Disorder in Corinth   Alec Gilmore

Tuesday 17 April

1 Corinthians 6:1-8

Meet and talk

The very fact of going to court gives some insight into the composition of the Corinthian church, because in most societies you need a certain level of income before you can even consider it. But what was it all about? In the light of your own church experience, consider what might have been going on. Verse 7 suggests it was fraud, or 'being wronged', but what did that mean? Someone with money, perhaps, trying to get their way in the courts when they could not get what they wanted through the fellowship; or someone with an over-inflated view of their own importance feeling they had been overlooked or getting uptight about something of minor consequence. Other possibilities are a crucial doctrinal issue dividing Jews and Gentiles, or devotees of Paul in conflict with newcomers from other places who have never even heard of him but are so sure they are right and so determined to establish their line that they will stop at nothing (not even a public appearance in the courts) to prove their point. All these scenarios are familiar and too many churches have known splits in the fellowship as a result.

Whatever it was, Paul's advice is clear:

> I say this to your shame. Can it be that there is no one among you wise enough to decide between one believer and another, but a believer goes to court against a believer – and before unbelievers at that?

(verses 5-6)

† Father, never let personal strife and differences destroy the fellowship or convey a bad impression of the faith to others; and when personal conflict and divergent views threaten, enable us always to talk to one another, with a third party or (if necessary) even with someone from another church or a totally different community.

Alec Gilmore   Disorder in Corinth

Wednesday 18 April
1 Corinthians 6:9-20

What is beneficial

Corinth, a city of depravity, was a mixture of tribes and races resulting in a variety of behaviour, beliefs and attitudes, and members of the Corinthian church had obviously been part of it before embracing Christianity (verse 11). In an attempt to deliver them from all that held them to a traditional way of life, Paul's emphasis on freedom in Christ was sometimes (mis)interpreted as freedom to do what they wanted. Hence the reminder that not everything lawful is beneficial, followed by an invitation to see the body as God's sanctuary.

Paul had probably never heard of body language but might well approve of it. Our body language speaks volumes, in ways we may never imagine or even be aware of. Older churchgoers may remember the days when smoking and alcohol were rejected on the grounds that they damaged the body that God had given them, and today we all know how right they were.

Paul's major concern is sexual relations. He makes a distinction between using the body as a means of sharing and giving, and using it as a means of receiving and finding satisfaction – a fundamental element of Christianity much underplayed and until recently largely ignored. Reflect on his reasons.

Do you not know that your body is a temple of the Holy Spirit within you, which you have from God, and that you are not your own?

(verse 19)

Not right and wrong, but what is beneficial and harmful. Not the wrong use of the body but the need to care for it and preserve it for what is right. Not because of what the fathers (or the last generation) taught, but because our body is a gift from God.

† Father, may I never forget that what I do with my body speaks volumes about what I am.

Disorder in Corinth   Alec Gilmore

Thursday 19 April

1 Corinthians 7:1-16

Weigh before you buy

In a few short verses Paul gives general pastoral guidance on four crucial topics that are still with us: sexual relations within marriage, sexual desires in single people, divorce and remarriage, and marriages with unbelievers. Two points stand out: firstly, unlike the traditions of historic Judaism and many other groups, Paul recognises the equality of the sexes.

> *For the wife does not have authority over her own body, but the husband does; likewise the husband does not have authority over his own body, but the wife does.*

(verse 4)

Secondly, he makes a useful distinction between 'the teaching of the church' with its ring of certainty (what 'the Lord says', verse 10) and his personal opinion (with a strong pastoral undertone, verse 12), and the verses that follow demonstrate Paul's ambivalence and uncertainty on a number of issues.

In a time of individualism and charismatic leadership such as today, it is useful to be reminded to always distinguish personal opinions from widely accepted positions, whoever holds them, however strongly, and whatever the evidence. 'Bad science', with under-researched conclusions and loaded promotion, is not unknown in religious circles. It is always good to evaluate anything carefully before taking it on board.

Readers with a high regard for Paul might do well to ponder his uncertainties and modesty, rather than capitalise on some of his opinions (especially when they naturally agree with our own). Some of Paul's views carried limited weight and recognition even among believers in his own society and are even more questionable today. Better to study Paul where he differs from us rather than where he upholds our prejudices.

---

† Father, teach me in my prayer life to ask questions rather than seek answers, to examine my doubts rather than reinforce my certainties, and genuinely to seek your will and hear your voice rather than my own.

Alec Gilmore   Disorder in Corinth

Friday 20 April

1 Corinthians 7:25-40

Keep things in proportion

Paul's reluctance to lay down hard and fast rules continues and these verses show an openness of understanding for the way in which we are all different and have different needs. Much of what he says is based on the assumption that 'the end is nigh', which may not be where we are today despite global warming, problems of the environment and one catastrophe after another, but it gives Paul a not unwelcome sense of urgency and to that extent is a plea to all of us to stick to what matters and avoid trivial pursuits.

> *I say this for your own benefit, not to put any restraint upon you, but to promote good order and unhindered devotion to the Lord.*

(verse 35)

What favours and creates 'good order and unhindered devotion' should be actively promoted. What hinders it need not necessarily be rejected but can conveniently be put to one side.

In times of crisis or turmoil, when nothing seems certain, everything seems to be up for grabs, and you have no idea what tomorrow will bring, it is often the case that what we were brought up to believe and do no longer seems to work. As with Job, experience leads us to question what we have always taken for granted. To change or not to change?

Such moments may not be the time for change, or big decisions. Arguments, differences of opinion and divisions may only hinder. Better to stick to where we are and leave God to handle the rest. In this way Paul keeps faith with his own convictions while at the same time demonstrating strength, tolerance and understanding to others, and above all he strives to keep things in proportion.

† Thank you, God, for Paul's word of assurance, comfort and hope in a time of need.

Disorder in Corinth   Alec Gilmore

Saturday 21 April

1 Corinthians 8:1-13

Love before creed

When the choice is between Greek knowledge and Christian love, Paul is in no doubt. Knowledge is inevitably limited and finite. Love knows no bounds and is infinite.

> *Now concerning food sacrificed to idols: we know that 'all of us possess knowledge'. Knowledge puffs up, but love builds up.*
>
> (verse 1)

We need to identify our own 'food for idols', which could be any issue that arouses strong feelings, creates sharply defined positions, and threatens good personal relationships. We are all at different stages of spiritual growth and development. What once seemed crucial, and to some still is, may no longer worry us. In this, we may be leading the way long before everyone else can go with us – or feeling superior or practising pure licence. Hence the call to remember 'the weaker brother'. This is usually a plea for one-way tolerance: A must refrain until B is ready. But this is not always practical and may appear hypocritical. Better perhaps to see it as a plea for human understanding of the 'other', with love taking precedence over conviction – on both sides. Results may vary according to people, place and time, once again reflecting Paul's pastoral openness over legalistic exactitude.

† Father, give me the courage to be myself in order to be loyal to you, but also help me to be ever mindful of the sensitivities of others.

For group discussion and personal thought

- How does your body language send out messages, create impressions and convey moods? How much is your body in touch with your faith? What does it convey and conceal?
- Find two issues where you want to say Amen to Paul and two where he makes your hackles rise. Work out why in both cases, and then try discussing it with your Christian friends.

Alec Gilmore   Disorder in Corinth

1 Corinthians

3 Baptism and the Lord's Supper

Notes based on the *New Revised Standard Version* by

Catherine Williams

Catherine Williams is an Anglican priest working as the National Adviser for Vocations for the Ministry Division of the Archbishops' Council, in the Church of England. Her role is to enable and encourage Christians to discern God's call. Catherine is married to the Vicar of Tewkesbury Abbey.

Introduction

As we continue to explore Paul's first letter to the Corinthians, we encounter some of the issues that faced this young church. Paul offers support and advice to enable the Corinthian Christians to grow in faith and develop their worshipping life together. Underpinning all his comments are the importance of baptism into the death and resurrection of Christ and continued incorporation into Christ's body through the regular sharing of the Lord's Supper. Paul's wise reflections, read and interpreted in context, continue to speak to the church's concerns today.

Sunday 22 April: *1 Corinthians 9:1-14*

'My rights!'

Some of the Christians in Corinth were asserting their 'right' to enjoy freedom in Christ by living outside the traditional food laws. Paul introduces a passage on 'rights' by explaining the rights he has as an apostle and why he has chosen not to exercise them. He and Barnabas have chosen not to accept payment for the work of founding the Corinthian church.

> *[W]e have not made use of this right, but we endure anything rather than put an obstacle in the way of the gospel of Christ.*
>
> (part of verse 12)

Paul is not saying that people should not be paid for their work, whether as a soldier, farmer or apostle. Rather, the task of proclaiming the good news of Jesus Christ should come before all other considerations.

† Lord, help me to put your 'good news' before 'my rights'!

Monday 23 April

1 Corinthians 9:15-27

Reaching out to all

Paul continues his discussion of rights by showing that freedom in Christ comes with responsibilities attached. There is an obligation to preach the gospel placed on him as an apostle. He recognises that it is necessary for him to curtail his freedom in order to reach out with the gospel to all. This means reaching into people's lives, understanding their contexts and finding common ground. The message of Jesus Christ remains constant but the way in which that message is delivered must be flexible if all are to be reached. So Paul is prepared to embrace other cultures and traditions, to go back to his roots, to become weak, to do whatever it takes to connect with people where they are, with the saving message of Jesus Christ.

I have become all things to all people, that I might by all means save some. I do it all for the sake of the gospel, so that I may share in its blessings.

(part of verse 22, and verse 23)

Paul goes on to use the analogy of the athlete to illustrate how the life of the Christian needs to be disciplined, self-controlled and focused in order that Christ may be proclaimed to all. Often we can become comfortable and certain about our own faith, while losing sight of the need to get alongside others with the news of Christ. What is the message of Christ you carry? How are you doing at reaching out to all? What more could you do?

† Lord, make me a flexible bearer of your good news. Show me who needs to hear your message of love and give me the courage to reach out to them.

Catherine Williams   Baptism and the Lord's Supper

Tuesday 24 April

1 Corinthians 10:1-13

Watch out!

History repeats itself. Wherever we live in the world we will be aware of incidents in our local or national history where we seem not to have learned the lessons from the past. Paul is at pains to remind the Corinthian Christians that looking back will help them move forward. Retelling the story of the Exodus, Paul draws parallels between Israel's history and the life of the early church. He shows how the Israelites being 'baptised' into Moses in the cloud and the sea prefigures the Christian baptism into Jesus the Messiah by the Spirit and with water. However, despite being God's people, the Israelites in the wilderness strayed from the truth and ran into all sorts of error. Paul warns against complacency:

So if you think you are standing, watch out that you do not fall.

(verse 12)

It's a warning as much for us today as for those first followers of Christ. Being baptised into the body of Christ is no insurance policy against sin. Human beings are capable of all sorts of unkind, wicked and evil acts and believing in God doesn't mean we are immune from such behaviour. 'Watch out!' warns Paul. However, with his warning comes comfort. While we may struggle to live good and holy lives, God is constant and remains faithful. Being in Christ means that we will not be tested beyond what is bearable. Though the Israelites in the wilderness received many spiritual blessings from God, they complained, chased after other 'gods', were immoral and put God to the test. Standing today in Christ, where are you in danger of 'falling'? Pray that Jesus will show you the path into holiness.

† Lord Jesus, as I stand before you and walk in your ways, keep me from falling.

Baptism and the Lord's Supper

Catherine Williams

Wednesday 25 April

1 Corinthians 10:14 – 11:1

The big picture

Paul continues his advice to the Corinthians. Living a new life in an old order, it's hard for these new Christians to work out which things are allowable and which are not.

'All things are lawful', but not all things are beneficial. 'All things are lawful', but not all things build up.

(verse 23)

Being in Christ has brought a new freedom, which has to be exercised with responsibility and maturity. This requires some 'growing into'. The Corinthians are struggling with the nitty-gritty detail of what they can and can't eat when they go out. Paul reminds them of the importance of the eucharist which builds them up as the body of Christ. From this position of strength they can make informed decisions about what they should and shouldn't do when they eat in the homes of non-believers and buy food in the marketplace. The bottom line for Paul is that everything should be done for the glory of God, so that those who do not yet know Christ may be saved through the generosity and acceptance of the believers.

When we're faced with difficult decisions about how to live as Christians in a world where different values prevail, it is helpful to be reminded of the big picture. God loves everyone and longs for all to know him in Christ. Do our words and actions help people along the road towards that goal? Is the message we bring one of love and reconciliation? Are we building one another up in Christ to the glory of God? Today, be aware of how your decisions impact on others and bring them closer to God – or not.

† Lord, help me to build up the body of Christ through my words and actions. Keep me faithful to your big picture.

Catherine Williams   Baptism and the Lord's Supper

Thursday 26 April
1 Corinthians 11:2-16

All in order

Another day, another issue for Paul from the Corinthian church. This time, it is appropriate behaviour in worship for men and women. Freedom in Christ has brought challenges for the Corinthians. Traditionally men have worshipped God with their heads uncovered, while women covered their heads for worship. Now that in Christ all are equal, both men and women are disregarding the traditions regarding their heads and expressing their freedom in worship. Paul reminds the Corinthians of the ordering of creation and that gender differences are to be celebrated, not confused. In Christ men and women need one another for the body to be whole:

> Nevertheless, in the LORD woman is not independent of man or man independent of woman. For just as woman came from man, so man comes through woman; but all things come from God.

(verses 11-12)

Moreover, the way in which worship is conducted impacts on those outside the body of Christ. In the culture of the time prostitutes wore their hair down and their heads uncovered. Anyone looking in on the Corinthians at worship might easily get the wrong idea about this new faith. Keeping order in worship and abiding by the conventions of the culture not only honour God but also speak volumes to those on the edges of believing. It's important that we don't simply lift Paul's strictures from this passage and apply them directly to our own situations. Rather, we need to think about what will attract or repel others when they witness us in church, and how we can honour God's creation through our ordering of worship.

† Lord, teach me to be interdependent on those around me and on you.

Baptism and the Lord's Supper   Catherine Williams

1 Corinthians 11:17-34

Table manners

Next, Paul tackles with the Corinthian Christians their celebration of the Lord's Supper. It seems they have allowed the social divisions that exist in Corinth to extend into their gatherings. Instead of practising equality at the Lord's table, there is no sharing of food. Each member brings their own meal, and some go hungry while others have too much. Paul, using the most ancient words we have from the Last Supper, reiterates the words and actions of Jesus:

'This is my body that is for you. Do this in remembrance of me'. . .
'This cup is the new covenant in my blood. Do this, as often as you drink it, in remembrance of me'.

(part of verses 24-25)

When the Corinthians celebrate the eucharist Christ is amongst them, bringing together the past, the present and the future. By not practising equality and unity in the body of Christ they dishonour Jesus and bring judgement on themselves. Paul even suggests that this judgement can be seen in the way various members are suffering.

Today we share the bread and wine of the eucharist equally amongst those who partake. Yet there are still subtle ways in which we make distinctions between church members. Race, gender, age, social class, and patterns of belief still divide Christians. What more could you be doing to ensure all are equal in your local expression of church? What could you do to begin to heal some of the divisions that exist between denominations? Pray for wisdom, patience and courage.

† Lord, help me play my part in encouraging unity in your body, the church.

Catherine Williams   Baptism and the Lord's Supper

Saturday 28 April

1 Corinthians 12:1-11

Giftedness

April

Along with the other divisions in the body of Christ at Corinth was an emerging hierarchy of gifts. Some Christians thought that certain spiritual gifts were more important than others. Paul reminds his hearers again of the equality to be found and practised in the body of Christ:

> *Now there are varieties of gifts, but the same Spirit; and there are varieties of services, but the same LORD; and there are varieties of activities, but it is the same God who activates all of them in everyone.*

(verses 4-6)

The Spirit gifts each person who has been brought into Christ through baptism and who remains in Christ through the eucharist. The gifts given together build up the body of Christ in order to witness to the world. Sometimes we can be worried that we haven't received the Spirit because our experience of the Spirit's work in us is not the same as someone else's. Paul's words at the beginning of this passage are vitally important here. It is only through the power of the Holy Spirit that anyone can proclaim 'Jesus is Lord'.

† Lord, thank you for your Holy Spirit. Help me discover and use the gifts you have given me.

For group discussion and personal thought

- Spend time thinking and praying through what the Lord's Supper means for you and your church.
- What divisions exist in your fellowship? How can you help address them?
- Who needs to hear the good news of Jesus Christ most in your locality? What steps can you take to make that happen?

Baptism and the Lord's Supper   Catherine Williams

1 Corinthians

4   Gifts of the Spirit

Notes based on the *New Revised Standard Version* by

Sister Christopher Godden OSB

Sister Christopher is a Benedictine nun living the enclosed life in a monastery in Chester, England. Here she tries to integrate her spiritual life and daily domestic monastic duties within the monastery and become a Christian.

Introduction

From Acts we learn that the church at Corinth was made up mainly of Gentiles who had not received the formation in Old Testament scripture given to Jews. As a result their faith was based not on the fulfilment of Old Testament prophecy but on dramatic manifestations associated with the outpouring of the Spirit (1 Corinthians 2:4). In his letter Paul seeks to redress this balance by teaching them not to give up what they have, but to enrich their faith by accepting the full range of Christian doctrine and charisma.

Sunday 29 April: *1 Corinthians 12:12-31*
All for one and one for all

> *[B]ut the members may have the same care for one another. If one member suffers, all suffer together with it; if one member is honoured, all rejoice together with it.*

(part of verse 25, and verse 26)

By choosing to use the body and its parts as an example of the church, Paul teaches the Corinthians that they belong to something both united and diverse. Each church is important to the entire Christian community, just as each individual member is equally important to their own church. Reminding the Corinthians of their place in this structure will help them to remember their responsibilities towards themselves, each other and the entire movement. Exciting and encouraging as manifestations and experiences of the Holy Spirit are, we must be cautious, as they are only part of what we, as Christians, are about.

---

† Speak clearly, O Lord, so that all whose lives are bound in pain or worry in this world of noise and hurry may hear you and find your peace and your presence in their lives.

Monday 30 April

1 Corinthians 13:1-13

The heart of the matter

Love never ends.

(part of verse 8)

To like is not to love, in fact, liking can get in the way. When we like someone it is too easy to put our liking first and then make allowances that are not wise for fear of hurting a relationship. In his book *The Road Less Travelled*, author M. Scott Peck defines love as 'the will to extend one's self for the purpose of nurturing one's own or another's spiritual growth' (Century Hutchinson, 1976, p.81). Love is a deliberate choice and involves effort: an attitude of mind translated into action physical, mental or spiritual, or a combination of any of the three.

In today's reading Paul gives us a list of some of the positives and negatives of loving (verses 4-7), all of which require a deliberate choice of attitude followed by action that can be very difficult to make. Changing a feeling of anger into understanding; a desire to express one's own view into trying to hear another's (equally valid) point; accepting others for what they are now and not trying to change them into how we think they should be: all these (and more) require deliberate effort that is not always easy to make.

But with prayer, discipline and self-forgetfulness, love can become the shaping force of our lives, drawing us ever nearer to God and our neighbour. Love is literally putting your self out.

† Father, on those days when effort is hard, help us to remember to ask for your grace that we may truly and deeply come to love and serve you and our neighbour. Thank you for the times, on good days or bad, when we succeed.

Gifts of the Spirit   Christopher Godden

Tuesday 1 May

1 Corinthians 14:1-12

A time to keep silence, and a time to speak (Ecclesiastes 3:7)

So with yourselves; since you are eager for spiritual gifts, strive to excel in them for building up the church.

(verse 12)

'I think Bob Geldof is a prophet.' This statement by my brother startled me to say the least. How could the lead singer of the Boomtown Rats possibly be called a prophet? Long hair, weird clothes, yes – but surely there the similarity ended? The word 'prophet' comes from the Greek *prophētēs*, which means one who speaks before others (either in time, or in front of them); one who speaks out. The message of a prophet is usually clear to those who hear it, although they may choose to ignore it.

Concentrating on speaking in tongues was not helping the Corinthians to build up their church into a community. Community is an ongoing process which needs continual input and careful maintenance, and somehow the young church in Corinth had lost this focus.

Very carefully and gently Paul tries to get them to re-focus – not away from God but towards God and each other and in that way increase their sense of church and community.

Maybe I could not understand the words the Boomtown Rats sang, but the effect of the words sung later by Live Aid to help some of the poorest people of the world speaks for itself.

† Send your prophets into this needful world, dear Lord, and open ears, hearts and minds so their message may be heard and acted upon.

Christopher Godden

Gifts of the Spirit

Wednesday 2 May

1 Corinthians 15:1-11

Centre point

Now I would remind you, brothers and sisters, of the good news that I proclaimed to you, which you in turn received, in which also you stand.

(verse 1)

Paul has now come to the heart of his message: the resurrection of Jesus. The poetic language and imagery of the previous days' passages is gone, replaced by an introductory paragraph (verses 1-2) followed by a list of six resurrection appearances that had actually taken place, to which witnesses might still be alive. Next, verses 3-4 describe the death and resurrection of Jesus, bringing in the authority of Scripture.

Paul does not mince words or spare himself embarrassment when he goes on to acknowledge his own background of persecution of the early church, calling himself unfit to even be called an apostle. There is something immensely humbling and self-effacing in his description of himself and his call to preach after his previous actions, and his recognition that this is the reason behind his enthusiasm for the gospel and all that it means. He freely acknowledges that it is only through 'grace' that he is now able to do what he does and be who he is. Grace alone has brought him to this point and the Corinthians must remember this, for it is not who preaches the message that is important, it is the message itself that must be heard, believed and acted upon, and that can only be done by, with and through grace.

† We pray for all in this troubled world who are searching for a faith to believe in. We remember also all whose faith is fragile and all who resist faith.

Gifts of the Spirit   Christopher Godden

May

Looking at both sides of the argument

[H]ow can some of you say there is no resurrection of the dead? . . . in fact Christ has been raised from the dead, the first fruits of those who have died.

(part of verses 12 and 20)

There is a certain sort of person who can see, and is able to hold , both sides of an argument in their mind at the same time, and in today's passage we have a supreme example of just that.

Some of the members of the church in Corinth are having doubts. Yesterday Paul cited witnesses to the validity of the resurrection; today he stands that argument on its head by examining the idea that resurrection of the dead is impossible – and what this means in practice. For him the resurrection of Jesus is the key, heart and start of the Christian faith, and he wants to remind the members of the young church of the care he took when teaching them that faith and all it includes, and how important it is that they should remain true to the message and teaching they received knowingly and accepted at that time.

Doubts are a way of strengthening faith, although confronting them and dealing with them can be difficult and painful. Our faith is not something static, a gift given and that is that; it is more like a journey of discovery and exploration as one delves deeper and deeper into all of its mysteries and implications and encounters the living God in every aspect of our lives.

† Lord, help all your children to increase in faith as we progress through life, until we finally come to know, love and be with you for ever.

Christopher Godden   Gifts of the Spirit

1 Corinthians 15:35-49

From common sense to poetry

So it is with the resurrection of the dead. What is sown is perishable, what is raised is imperishable. It is sown in dishonour, it is raised in glory. It is sown in weakness, it is raised in power.

(verses 42-43)

The sharp rebuke in verse 36 is a timely warning to us all. We live in the present moment – in the 'now' – and living that present as well as we possibly can is what matters in this life. We believe that death is not 'The End' of life; it will come to us all eventually, but how, when and where is not for us to know yet. No matter how long we may think or speculate about the hereafter we cannot find out about it until we reach there. Such discussions may be interesting but need to be limited, otherwise things can get out of balance and the essentials of life ignored. This is obviously what has happened to some degree to the young church at Corinth and Paul is trying to nip the problem in the bud.

Verses 37-44 describes what is sown, what we have to deal with in this life: a bare seed, an earthly human body that is perishable, dishonourable, weak, needing to die in order for the spiritual body to come to life. That is where the Corinthians need to put their focus and their priorities.

In the monastery we daily try to maintain a balance between our prayer time, work time and study time. It can be a juggle to get priorities right but perhaps this is best, because it cuts down time wasted on useless speculation, no matter how interesting it may seem.

† Lord, today many people will be too busy to think of you and many unable to think of you; stretch our prayers over them that they may be protected.

Gifts of the Spirit   Christopher Godden

Final words

Keep alert, stand firm in your faith, be courageous, be strong. Let all that you do be done in love.

(verse 13)

In Corinthians 4:14 Paul describes himself as 'father' of the young church in Corinth. This week we have seen how as a father he has advised, pleaded, corrected, taught and encouraged. Now, as his letter draws to its conclusion, like a parent seeing a child off from home to make their own way in the world, he issues a few last instructions, explanations, warnings and advice.

There is practical advice about tithing for a gift to the church in Jerusalem, an explanation for his continued absence in case it is misconstrued, encouragement for a warm welcome for Timothy when he arrives, and an explanation for the absence of Apollos, who had been one of the church's co-founders (1 Corinthians 1:12).

Finally there are two short verses – staccato phrases of encouragement ending with the reminder that love is the key to real life and living.

† O Lord, watch over and protect all those leaving home soon to make their way in the world, and also those who have recently left home, especially because of unhappiness or to escape an intolerable situation.

For group discussion and personal thought

- A member of your church confides in you that they are having doubts about their faith. How would you react ? What could you suggest ?
- Does you church bear a prophetic witness to the Christian faith? How? Are you called to be a prophet? What does that mean ? Who are today's prophets?
- Looking at the issues raised and dealt with by St Paul in 1 Corinthians, what would be your last instructions for young Christians having to be responsible for their own lives ('leaving home') for the first time?

Christopher Godden   Gifts of the Spirit

Jerusalem

1 Jerusalem: city of David

Notes based on the *New Revised Standard Version* by

John Holder

John Holder was born in Barbados and is Archbishop of the Anglican Province of the West Indies. He is married with one son.

Introduction

During the time of David Jerusalem emerged as Yahweh's elected dwelling place. Much theology and an extensive eschatology developed around Jerusalem. Starting out as the site of a pre-Israelite shrine, it became the dwelling of the ark and the site of the Temple. It developed into the symbol of salvation and the ground of hope for Jews and Christians.

Sunday 6 May: *2 Samuel 6:12-15*
Restoring the symbol of God's presence

> *So David and all the house of Israel brought up the ark of the LORD with shouting, and with the sound of the trumpet.*
>
> (verse 15)

Celebrating the presence of God with song and dance goes very far back in the history of religion. It was an affirmation of the presence of God and an act of thanksgiving. As leader of the people David is also the leader in worship. The bonds created here between David and the ark link him to two of Israel's pillars of salvation. The house of David, and the ark that will eventually rest in the house of Yahweh, constitute the bedrock of salvation in the Old Testament. This passage highlights the element of joy; is this central element present in our worship? Worship should always be a joyous response to the goodness of God. Is this reflected in your worship? What can you do to create and sustain this central element of worship?

† O God, give us joyful hearts to worship you in thanksgiving. Amen

Monday 7 May

2 Chronicles 6:12-21

God's uncontainable presence

Even heaven and the highest heaven cannot contain you; how much less this house that I have built!

(part of verse 18)

One of the central themes in any discussion of worship, one that is very prominent in the Bible, is the theme of God's uncontainable presence. Although we create symbols of his presence, whether it is the ark or the temple, the Bible or the cross, we must at all times be aware of the danger of restricting his presence to our symbols. This important point about worship was very critical for those who wrote the books of Chronicles. They were in exile, without the Temple or Jerusalem. But they had to affirm God's presence in their community. The words of Solomon already present in 1 Kings 8:27 spoke directly to the time of the Chronicler. God's presence could not be confined to the Temple or any other building. He was as present with his people in exile as he was with them in the Temple in Jerusalem.

Some three hundred years later St Matthew tells us in chapter 27:51 of his gospel that on the day of Christ's death the temple veil was torn in two. The symbol of God being confined to the Temple was destroyed. Here is one of the pillars upon which the church has been built. We believe in a God who cannot be contained. He is a God who is far bigger and far more extensive than any symbol of his presence can ever convey. We worship a great and loving God whose power is far greater than we can ever imagine. Share this understanding of God with someone today. Tell them that he is stronger than all the challenges they may face today. Be God's presence of love and compassion and understanding for them.

† O God, whom heaven cannot contain, grant us the vision of your presence and power today. Amen

John Holder   Jerusalem: city of David

Psalm 122

The joy of being in God's presence

I was glad when they said to me,
'Let us go up to the house of the LORD!'

(verse1)

Have you ever wondered what our world would be like without its cathedrals, churches, temples, shrines and other places of worship? What many consider a significant strand of human experience would be missing. The world would be poorer. Places of worship are far more than the materials we use to construct them. They represent for us the symbol of God's presence. They evoke in us a range of emotions: joy, humility, contrition, peace, and a deep sense of God's love and protection. We understand why the psalmist would be glad to go to the house of the Lord. For him it was an exceptional experience. It encompassed the years of hope that his people had linked to Jerusalem and its Temple. It was a reminder that God was available to them at the best of times and the worst of times. This psalm was probably sung on the occasion of a pilgrimage to the Temple in Jerusalem. It captures a sense of moving nearer to God.

All life is a pilgrimage. The Christian life is a special pilgrimage as we follow the way of Our Lord day by day, making our journey through this world to the heavenly Jerusalem.

† Lord, give us your grace to live each day as pilgrims on our way to your kingdom. Amen

Jerusalem: city of David

John Holder

Wednesday 9 May

2 Kings 25:8-21

The destruction of the symbols of God's presence

[H]e burned the house of the Lord.

(part of verse 9)

At this period, however, the 'house of the Lord' in Jerusalem could no longer be treated as the exclusive presence of Yahweh. Some time earlier the prophet Jeremiah had sent a message to the exiles encouraging them to settle down and assuring them that God was with them in Babylon (Jeremiah 29:1-9). Their distance from the Temple could not be interpreted as distance from God. He was as near to them in exile as he was when they were in the Temple in Jerusalem. The destruction of the Temple undoubtedly created some great challenges to the faith of those who saw it as the place where the community encountered God in a special way. Its long history and traditions created a foundation for the faith of Israel that few other things were able to match.

Its absence did not, however, lead to the destruction of this faith but only to its adjustment. The destruction of the Temple did not mean the destruction of Yahweh. The power of Babylon was limited. It was under the constraints of time in a way that Yahweh could never be.

Sometimes in this life we too lose symbols of our faith, such as a charismatic and beloved leader. Our faith, like that of the worshippers in the Jerusalem Temple, can be shaken and tested. At such times the faith of the prophet Habakkuk can come to our help. In a time of a crisis of faith he declared: 'Though the fig tree does not blossom, and no fruit is on the vines . . . yet I will rejoice in the Lord; I will exult in the God of my salvation' (Habakkuk 3:17-18). There can hardly be a stronger expression of faith. Let us make it our own.

† O God, in time of trial give us the faith of Habakkuk.

John Holder   Jerusalem: city of David

Ezra 3:8-13

The joys of rebuilding and restoring

[T]he people shouted so loudly that the sound was heard far away.

(part of verse 13)

The experience of joy has returned. The Temple that was destroyed nearly one hundred and fifty years before is about to be rebuilt. The need for the symbol of God's presence is as strong as ever. The time in Babylon without the Temple was not, however, a time of loss. It was indeed one of preparation for the time when there would be a temple. That time is now. The efforts to rebuild have been harnessed and put to work. Thanks to the benevolence of the Persians and the leadership of Nehemiah, the project is on its way. There could be no greater occasion for joy and celebration.

All the old traditions that were attached to the pre-exilic Temple are revived. The worship is conducted according to the directions of David, and a powerful theme of hope is reflected in the words of their hymn of praise and thanks:

'For [the Lord] is good,
for his steadfast love endures forever toward Israel.'

(part of verse 11)

It was a time of rejoicing. With the beginning of the construction of the new Temple, God was indeed good, and his mercies did extend through the exile and were now being experienced in this new effort. The ability to get going again after a setback is one of the essential qualities of life. It is a quality that Christians treasure. The cornerstone of our faith is the resurrection of Our Lord. The experience of Our Lord's resurrection got the disciples going again after the experiences of Good Friday. Ours is a resurrection faith. Let us today help someone to keep going along the Christian path.

† O God, thank you for the power to pick up the pieces and start afresh. Amen

Jerusalem: city of David   John Holder

Friday 11 May

Nehemiah 2:11-18

Rebuilding the walls

'Come, let us rebuild the wall of Jerusalem, that we may no longer suffer disgrace.'

(part of verse 17)

The invitation to rebuild the walls of Jerusalem is also an invitation to repair the cracks in the faith of the community that had been created by the destruction of Jerusalem in 587BC. Nehemiah is responding to the kind of community despair described in the psalms: 'O God, the nations have come into your inheritance; they have defiled your holy temple; they have laid Jerusalem in ruins' (Psalm 79:1). By the days of Nehemiah, Jerusalem was embedded in Israelite theology as a place with an indestructible link to God, but now the physical appearance just did not match the theology. There was a massive divide between the two, and the rebuilding of Jerusalem could bridge the gap. A restored city and Temple would make it far easier to believe again in God's presence in them. The theology needed to be maintained, but the returning Jews also desperately needed to experience God's goodness and his favour in a tangible and physical way that only a rebuilt city and a rebuilt Temple could provide.

There will always be discussions on how much we need buildings and other physical symbols to affirm God's presence. The history of religion has shown that there is really no substitute for these symbols. Let us thank God for those we have inherited. Let us do our bit to ensure their upkeep and preservation. Later generations will need these symbols of God's presence even as we need them today.

† O God, we thank you for all that we have inherited that helps us to grasp your presence. Amen

John Holder   Jerusalem: city of David

Saturday 12 May

Zechariah 1:16-17

The return to Jerusalem

[T]hus says the LORD, I have returned to Jerusalem with compassion; my house shall be built in it, says the LORD of hosts.

(part of verse 16)

Like Ezra and Nehemiah, the prophet Zechariah provided the encouragement and the rationale for the rebuilding of the Temple. It must have taken a great effort to rekindle the fire and passion that were once part of the response to Jerusalem and the Temple, after seventy years of neglect had reduced them to insignificance. However, some, including Zechariah, held passionately to the Jerusalem traditions and never gave up hope that city and temple would one day be rebuilt. The prophet's encouragement came, typically, in the form of a vision direct from Yahweh that renewed the link between Jerusalem and Yahweh's presence. By insisting that Yahweh was part of the rebuilding process, the prophet presented the work in a form that few in the community could resist. Part of the struggle that gripped the community of Zechariah's day was for survival. In the face of hostility from those who probably regarded the returning exiles as intruders to be resisted, the prophet placed Yahweh firmly on their side. Their rebuilding of the Temple, that restored and preserved the treasures of the past, would be further evidence of where the presence and support of Yahweh were to be found.

† O God, we thank you for the treasures of the past. Help us to appreciate and preserve them.

For group discussion and personal thought

• What are the important symbols in your relationship with God and the church?

• What objects, places and actions particularly remind you of God's presence?

• 'The ability to get going again after a setback is . . . a quality that Christians treasure.' How have you experienced this quality in your own life?

Jerusalem: city of David   John Holder

Jerusalem

2   Jerusalem: the holy city

Notes based on the *Good News Bible* by

Iain Roy

See Iain's biography on p.71.

Introduction

The city of Jerusalem seems to have drawn Jesus like a magnet. It was, of course, for him, as for all Jews, the holy city, the focal point of faith, its Temple the supreme place of worship. It was also for Christ both the place of greatest danger and the place where he could most fully reveal his Father's love for us, which was why he was there.

Sunday 13 May: *Luke 2:27-32*

Devotion rewarded

There are some things about Mary and Joseph we would like to know and never shall. One thing, however, is clear: they were both devout people. They observed their religion faithfully and the Temple in Jerusalem was at the heart of it.

> *When the parents brought the child Jesus into the Temple to do for him what the Law required, Simeon took the child in his arms and gave thanks to God.*

(part of verse 27, and verse 28)

For devout Simeon too, the Temple was the focus of faith. He reminds me of all those faithful men and women who slip into churches all over the world to deepen their faith through a quiet moment of prayer. Simeon's devotion was rewarded by an extraordinary insight. He looked on a child and saw in his face God's love for him and for his people. The gospel invites us to do the same: to look on Jesus, the child, the growing boy, the man, especially the man on the cross, and see in him not only our own saviour but the saviour of the world.

† Lord, help us to keep our gaze firmly fixed on you so that we may see your Father's love for us and walk trustingly in his presence.

Monday 14 May

Luke 2:41-51

Faith as growth

There is no episode in the gospels that shows more clearly the humanity of Jesus than this incident of him as a boy in the Temple.

> *On the third day they found him in the Temple, sitting with the Jewish teachers, listening to them and asking questions . . . His parents were astonished when they saw him, and his mother said to him, 'My son, why have you done this to us?' . . . He answered them, 'Why did you have to look for me? Didn't you know that I had to be in my Father's house?'*

(verse 46, part of verse 48, and verse 49)

Jesus could be one of the young people we know ourselves: inquisitive and trying to make sense of life, sceptical of our worry for them, still conforming in part to our wishes, largely because of their material dependence on us. His parents did not understand him, any more than we sometimes understand our own children. But for Jesus this visit to the Temple was another necessary step in the process of growth towards the fulfilment of his calling. Our faith and commitment too must never be static, but always dynamic. We are never too old, nor too young, to learn, especially in faith!

† Lord, help us to keep on growing our faith by listening, learning, thinking and praying, for your sake, Amen

Jerusalem: the holy city

Iain Roy

Tuesday 15 May

John 5:1-18

The demand of need

Jesus may have lived the greater part of his life in the relative obscurity of Nazareth, and even sought out the quiet place that was the desert to think, but the city of Jerusalem was largely the place where his mission was revealed and tested.

After this, Jesus went to Jerusalem for a religious festival. Near the Sheep Gate in Jerusalem there is a pool with five porches . . . A large crowd of sick people were lying in the porches . . . A man was there who had been ill for 38 years. Jesus saw him lying there, and he knew that the man had been ill for such a long time.

(verses 4-6)

The testing of Jesus took many forms. Here specifically his testing is a direct result of his own compassion. It was this compassion which drew Jesus to this place where hopes were often raised and often dashed. In particular, however, Jesus was drawn to this man, ill for so long. It is not that Jesus was indifferent to all the other sick and handicapped people lying there. It is rather that Jesus saw human need, as we should see it too, in personal terms. Behind all the generalities we use to describe what befalls humanity: famine, flood, earthquake, poverty, illness, war, violence, is always an individual like ourselves, a child of God.

† Lord Jesus, help us to see the situations of others as you see them: as burdens to be shared, needs to be answered as if they were our own. For your sake, Amen

Wednesday 16 May

Luke 24:44-53

In the beginning

Every great enterprise has a place where it begins. For the Christian faith this place is Jerusalem. Here Christ died and God's love for humankind was revealed; here the church had its beginning and here too it began its task of bringing the good news to every soul and every land.

> *Then he opened their minds to understand the Scriptures, and said to them, 'This is what is written: the Messiah must suffer and must rise from death three days later, and in his name the message about repentance and the forgiveness of sins must be preached to all nations, beginning in Jerusalem. You are witnesses of these things.*

(verses 45-48)

This message was addressed to the first disciples, but it is equally a message for us. The words 'evangelical' and 'evangelism' are sometimes appropriated by the few. They are, however, words to be taken seriously by all who profess to be Christians. After all, our own faith would not exist if others had not imparted it to us and taken seriously Jesus' instruction to be his witnesses. The faith we keep to ourselves and do not share is a selfish faith, indeed, perhaps not faith at all.

---

† Keep us, Lord, from the selfishness that can keep faith as a personal possession. Remind us that it is only *our* faith when we are eager to make it *theirs*.

Jerusalem: the holy city

Iain Roy

Thursday 17 May

Acts 1:10-14

Spiritual success

We are often tempted, even in the church, to measure success in material terms: how many members, how large the worshipping community, how great the offerings. The Upper Room in Jerusalem, the smallness of the group assembled there, the vulnerability and powerlessness of those first disciples, ought to remind us to resist this temptation.

They gathered frequently to pray as a group, together with the women and with Mary, the mother of Jesus and with his brothers.

(verse 14)

The very naming of the disciples one by one in this passage reminds us not only of each of them as individuals but also of their weaknesses and faults. Yet, despite all this baggage they carried with them, the holy catholic or universal church comes from their efforts under God. As we face up to the problems of spreading the gospel today, we need to take heart from their achievements and remember the source of them: their prayer and their devotion, and their trust in Christ's continuing presence with them.

† Lord, when we feel daunted by the task of spreading the good news, help us to remember that your worldwide church began with a small group in a small room in Jerusalem.

Iain Roy   Jerusalem: the holy city

Friday 18 May

Acts 3:1-10

Lowered expectations

This is the story of a man who settled for less than he needed, and of another who had more to give than he knew.

> *There at the Beautiful Gate, as it was called, was a man who had been lame all his life . . . When he saw Peter and John going in, he begged them to give him something . . . But Peter said to him, 'I have no money at all, but I give you what I have: in the name of Jesus Christ of Nazareth I order you to get up and walk!'*

(part of verse 2, and verses 3 and 6)

Money is not the answer to every problem in life. What this lame man needed was healing, not a hand-out; only with that could he gain his independence of others. The truth is that his condition had eroded his expectations. In any case, Peter had no money to give him. Probably Peter felt as inadequate as we so often do ourselves in the face of another's need. But Peter had more to give than he knew. He had God's love and his own compassion for this man. This is where all we do for others must start: with a remembrance of the worth Christ has placed on each of us.

† Christ, our Lord, help us not to promise others what we cannot deliver, or to raise false expectations in their hearts, but rather to give and do what we can for them, always with a glad heart and a sensitive spirit. Amen

Jerusalem: the holy city

Iain Roy

Revelation 21:1-7

The eye of the beholder

My nearest city is Glasgow. It is often perceived from afar as a city of crime and violence. But the city which many of us love is very different from that perception, a city of warm-hearted, humorous citizens, and great commercial, industrial, spiritual and cultural resources.

Then I saw a new heaven and a new earth . . . And I saw the Holy City, the new Jerusalem, coming down out of heaven from God.

(verses 1-2)

The city John saw was not the earthly city of Jerusalem with all its faults, nor a place of buildings, but a place of people whose lives had been transformed by the coming of Christ. It was not a static community of a particular place and time, but rather a community of faith spanning the generations, spanning eternity. Many of the folk John addressed faced persecution and martyrdom, and his message was one of reassurance to them and to us that Christ is with us in the places where we live, calling us to change these very places to reflect God's love.

† Give us the assurance, Lord, that where we are, you are also, and help us to make where we live a fit place for your presence, Amen

For group discussion and personal thought

• How important to you are the act of public worship, and private devotion? How much do the sacraments contribute to your spiritual life?

• The healing of the man at Bethesda is only one of many incidents in which Jesus answered someone's need. Look at some other incidents in Doctor Luke's Gospel (4:31ff; 5:12ff; 5:17ff; 6:6ff; 7:1ff); what insights do they give on how to care for others?

• Take a good hard look at the place where you live. What would you change in it to make it a better place for you and others to live?

Iain Roy

Jerusalem: the holy city

Readings in 1 Samuel

1 The calling of Samuel

Notes based on the *New Revised Standard Version* by

Lesley George Anderson

Lesley G Anderson is a Christian who is committed to Christ and dedicated to his church. He is a theologian who lives and works in Trinidad and Tobago as Superintendent of the North Trinidad Methodist Circuit.

Introduction

Samuel was one of the most important prophets of Israel, with great political as well as religious influence. This week's readings cover his birth, consecration and call, the loss and recovery of the Ark of the Covenant during battles with the Philistines, and their final defeat with the help of Samuel's prayers. The week ends with the Israelites demanding a king, which Samuel initially views with foreboding but then accepts.

Sunday 20 May: *1 Samuel 1:1-20*

Make the leap of faith

Hannah, Elkanah's much-loved but childless wife, was in severe pain and distress because of her childlessness. Elkanah's other wife, Peninnah (the Arabic name means a rival or fellow-wife) bore him many children. In biblical literature, 'fertility' is a sign of divine favour, while 'infertility' is regarded as a sign of divine judgement, the closing of a woman's womb by God, and childlessness was a disgrace. Peninnah's constant torment caused Hannah much suffering, and Elkanah was unable to comfort her. In the darkness of her nightmare, Hannah boldly makes the leap of faith, cries out to the Lord in prayer and makes this vow:

> *'O Lᴏʀᴅ . . . give to your servant a male child, then I will set him before you as a nazirite until the day of his death.'*

> (part of verse 11)

Note that a nazirite was someone separated or consecrated to God by means of a special vow. Like Hannah, when we are in distress or downtrodden, with a broken heart and weeping bitterly, let us remember to whom we belong and to whom we can go!

† Lord, in our days of trouble and struggle, help us to make the leap of faith and pray. Amen

Monday 21 May

1 Samuel 1:21 – 2:11, 18-21

Turn to God in trust

God heard Hannah's powerful, penetrating, inspirational prayer, responded positively to her need, and provided her with a son, Samuel. The impossible was made possible with God. In keeping with her vow to God, she made the journey to Shiloh to offer Samuel in trust to Eli, the priest. This is what she said:

> *'For this child I prayed; and the Lord has granted me the petition that I made to him. Therefore I have lent him to the Lord; as long as he lives, he is given to the Lord.'*

(verses 27-28)

It was an unforgettable day when at the age of fourteen I became lost in the woods adjacent to Rainbow City, Canal Zone, Panama. I took what I thought was a shortcut to go and meet some friends. I was alone and suddenly I was trapped by quicksand. I struggled to stay alive. I was in a dilemma because no one knew where I was. In fear and trembling I cried out to the Lord Jesus. He heard my cry and saved me from the horror, terror and sting of death. Somehow, I got out of the woods alive.

In the darkness of our pain, trials, despair and the taunting problems of life, we can turn to God. He is there for us. Sometimes it is a prayer, a psalm, a song or a cry that we lift up to God that will make the difference between life and death. We need to trust God more!

† O Lord, our guide and protector, in the darkness of our distress and suffering, deliver us. Amen

Lesley Anderson   The calling of Samuel

1 Samuel 3:1 – 4:1a

God is calling, are you listening?

God is always calling but we are not always listening. Sometimes God's call is through his Word proclaimed, a prayer said on our behalf, a hymn that touches our heart, a saintly life which inspires us to holiness and service.

At the age of fifteen I responded to the call of God to enter the full time ministry. This was a momentous event in my life! I was warmly supported by my parents, enthusiastically guided by my minister, encouraged by my youth counsellors and received the prayers of the church. Young Samuel needed the assistance of Eli to recognise that God was calling him:

> *Now the Lord came and stood there, calling as before, 'Samuel! Samuel!' And Samuel said, 'Speak, for your servant is listening.'*

(verse 10)

When we listen and respond positively to the call of God, he forgives, cleanses, prepares and sends us out to participate in his mission. The ministry is not a profession. It is a vocation, a calling to follow Christ in service to and for others. Be on the alert for God's call to service. If you hear his call, pray and then act on it. Let God know that you, his servant, are listening!

† O Lord, teach us how to discern your voice and dedicate our lives to your service. Amen

The calling of Samuel   Lesley Anderson

May

Wednesday 23 May

1 Samuel 4:1b-18

God alone is able

Israel is at war with the Philistines. Four thousand Israelite men are dead. In their anxiety and desperation the elders said:

> 'Let us bring the ark of the covenant of the LORD here from Shiloh, so that he may come among us and save us from the power of our enemies.'

(part of verse 3)

Tragically, a total of 30,000 men are killed and the Ark of the Covenant is taken into exile. In the books of Samuel, the Ark of the Covenant is the visible sign and symbol of the dwelling-place of the Lord. Where the ark is located, the Lord himself is present (see Joshua 3, 4 and 6). It was placed in Shiloh, the centre of worship, the venue of the sacred tent ('temple', 1 Samuel 1:9). At one time the ark was carried through the wilderness. It contained the tables of the Jewish law (the Ten Commandments). It was a box about the size of a chest covered with gold. On the top of it were two cherubs with their wings outstretched. The top was called the mercy seat, because the blood of the sacrifice to atone for sin was sprinkled on it. Within the temple the ark was hidden from sight by a curtain and only the high priest had access to this box. Taking the ark into battle did not save the Israelites. Sometimes in our troubles we turn to a friend; we hurriedly give to a charity; we go to church for consolation; but God is not worshipped. God alone is able to meet all your needs!

† O Lord, you alone are able to meet our needs in times of trouble or disaster. Amen

Lesley Anderson   The calling of Samuel

1 Samuel 5:1-12

God is mighty

Hophni and Phinehas, Eli's two sons, are dead and the Israelites have been slaughtered. There was great sorrow in the land. The ark, symbol of the Lord's presence, was captured by the Philistines, and Eli died on hearing the news. Now his pregnant daughter-in-law, the wife of Phinehas, gives birth to a son and names him Ichabod before she dies. Ichabod means, 'The glory has departed from Israel.' God himself is the glory and the glory is now in exile.

The Philistines placed the ark in the temple of one of their deities, Dagon. Dag means corn, hence Dagon was the god of crops or vegetation. Dagon was dethroned by God. His head and hands were separated from the rest of his body.

This is why the priests of Dagon and all who enter the house of Dagon do not step on the threshold of Dagon in Ashdod to this day.

(verse 5)

There is a difference between God and idolatry. God is greater than all other gods and idols of this world. Some people make power, money, honours and popularity their gods. Others make idols of their fame, knowledge and social standing, but none of these is lasting. God alone remains on the throne. He is greater than Dagon or any other god or idol!

† O Lord, our God, you are a mighty God, you alone are sovereign in our lives. Amen

The calling of Samuel

Lesley Anderson

May

God is holy!

When John Wesley wrote about his conversion experience, he noted that his 'heart was strangely warmed'. He felt that he did trust in Christ alone for his salvation and that he was cleansed from the law of sin and death. His legacy was a call to all Methodists to spread scriptural holiness throughout the land. With violence pervading the world in which we live, and ungodliness, corruption, terrorism and crime invading our towns and cities, we are reminded of the question raised by the people of Beth-shemesh:

'Who is able to stand before the Lord, this holy God?'

(part of verse 20)

God calls us to live holy lives.

God loves us but hates our sins.

God sends his son, Jesus, to die on Calvary's cross as a gift for our salvation.

He suffered, died and rose from the dead in order that we can be free of sin. His victory on the cross is our victory. Let us live in that victory!

† O God of holiness, embrace us with your love, and teach us to live and walk in paths of righteousness. Amen

Lesley Anderson

The calling of Samuel

Saturday 26 May

1 Samuel 8:4-22

God is love

God is the invisible king of Israel, but the elders were determined to have a kingly government. They rejected God by requesting a king like other nations:

'You are old and your sons do not follow in your ways; appoint us, then, a king to govern us, like other nations.'

(part of verse 5)

Four reasons lay behind this demand: Samuel was old and found it difficult to let go of his life-long vocation as a judge; Samuel's sons were unfit and unsuitable to replace him; the people wanted to be like other nations; and they wanted a leader capable of fighting their battles (see verse 20). Samuel was not pleased with the demand of the elders, but he turned to God in prayer and received the guidance he needed (verse 7). In this passage we glimpse the heart of God who, motivated by love, takes the initiative and reaches out to his people to nurture a strong relationship with them. Driven to sorrow by people like us who demand, forget and betray, nevertheless God loves us.

† O Lord, you are sovereign over all nations of the earth; remove every evil, injustice and oppression from us; grant us your peace, love and joy. Amen

For group discussion and personal thought

- Is it difficult for people to turn away from idols like Dagon and towards God? Are you holding on to an idol? If so, what is it, and what are you doing to get rid of it? Where could you find help?
- Samuel was a man of prayer. How important is prayer in your life? Do you know the power of prayer? What experience are you able to share about the power of prayer? What is the place of prayer in your life, home and church?

The calling of Samuel   Lesley Anderson

Readings in 1 Samuel

2 King Saul

Notes based on the *New Revised Standard Version* by

Sham Thomas

Revd Dr Sham P Thomas is an ordained priest of the Mar Thoma Syrian Church of Malabar. Formerly a professor at the United Theological College, Bangalore, he is now ministering in the Mar Thoma Syrian Church, Secunderabad-Hyderabad, India, where he lives with his wife Jolly and daughter Shyama.

Introduction

The call, rise and rejection of Saul as the first-ever king of Israel form this week's readings. Saul was chosen by God and empowered by God's spirit. He did not aspire to power nor play games to grab it. In that sense, he had a wonderful beginning. However, for various reasons he failed to build on this good beginning and ended up on a tragic note. This is a warning for us to stay on course so that, as Paul said, we too will be able to say we have finished the race and kept the faith (2 Timothy 4:7).

Sunday 27 May (Pentecost): *1 Samuel 9:1-21*
How God works

How God uses unexpected or even insignificant circumstances to intervene for great purposes in people's lives is graphically portrayed in today's reading. Saul went in search of his lost donkeys and turned out to be the answer to the search for a king for Israel. It was God's choice and even Prophet Samuel had no role except to be a messenger. When Samuel informed Saul of the impending leadership role, the latter responded humbly:

> *'I am only a Benjaminite, from the least of the tribes of Israel, and my family is the humblest of all the families of the tribe of Benjamin. Why then have you spoken to me in this way?'*

(verse 21)

In a world where people move around with credentials seeking leadership, Saul's humility is noteworthy and challenges the contemporary culture of self-marketing and manoeuvering for power.

† Thank you, Lord, for the example of Saul: leadership is your call and gift, not our seeking or decision.

1 Samuel 9:22 – 10:16

A leader with another heart

Saul's choice as the first king of Israel was conveyed to him by Prophet Samuel in a variety of ways, verbal, non-verbal and ritual. Samuel anointed Saul in private and informed him of his primary responsibility as king, which was to save the people from their enemies, especially the Philistines. Kingship or power is not given in order to overpower, but to serve and to save its subjects. In order to do this, the leader has to function with a distinct perspective.

As he turned away to leave Samuel, God gave him another heart.

(part of chapter 10, verse 9)

Saul assumed leadership as a new person – with a new heart and with the spirit of God. It meant a radically new orientation, perception and commitment. When people are elevated as leaders they can pose as renewed and reformed characters, but in practice they alienate friends, become overbearing, and act arrogantly. On the contrary, the portrayal of Saul prophesying with others offers us the challenge to perform secular functions as a sacred responsibility. Saul needed to be transformed by the spirit of God to be the ruler of Israel. It is not only the job of priest or catechist that requires the spirit of God. People assuming power and office also need to be under the influence of the spirit of God, if they are to use their power and position for the glory of God and the good of the people.

† Sovereign God, help us to be God-chosen and spirit-filled people. May the Holy Spirit dwell in us so that we may be transformed to serve and save others in our homes, church and society. Amen

King Saul   Sham Thomas

Tuesday 29 May

1 Samuel 10:17-27

Ensuring accountability

In today's reading we see how Saul was publicly selected as king of Israel and acclaimed by Samuel and the people of Israel. Even though Samuel had suggested that the desire to have a king of their own was a rejection of Yahweh's rule over them, Yahweh chooses a king for Israel as an act of divine grace. God's choice was made known through the process of lot-taking. Once Saul was selected as king, they had to bring him from among the baggage where he had gone into hiding. Saul seems to have been reluctant to assume leadership responsibility, as were many other great leaders of Israel like Moses. Like them, we too can be reluctant to respond to God's call or partake in God's mission. Once the king was selected,

Samuel told the people the rights and duties of the kingship; he wrote them in a book and laid it up before the Lord.

(part of verse 25)

By writing the rules of governance, Samuel was attempting to hold the king to account for his actions. Leaders need to work within a given framework. Leadership without accountability is menacingly threatening in the world today, including in the realm of religion. Many such leaders break or circumvent rules for partisan ends and eventually become a rule unto themselves. Assuming power without responsibility is the modern virus eating into the peace and health of the world.

† Sovereign God, help us not to turn away from your choice of us, and make us accountable in everything that we do. Amen

Sham Thomas   King Saul

Wednesday 30 May

1 Samuel 11

The saving king

Saul was anointed privately and then acclaimed publicly, and in today's reading we see the heroic and charismatic leadership that cemented Saul's kingship. As in the case of earlier judges, Saul emerged as a leader at a time of political crisis. In his first act as a king, Saul goes about rescuing people from the cruel and oppressive rulers who wanted to shame and rule over vulnerable people.

And the spirit of God came upon Saul in power when he heard these words, and his anger was greatly kindled.

(verse 6)

The function of the spirit for leaders is to empower them to unite vulnerable people and act for justice and peace. The leader also needs to share a divine anger in the face of oppression and cruelty. Passivity or resignation in the face of oppression amounts to support for it. By defeating the enemy, Saul's position as king was further strengthened and there was immense pressure on him to annihilate his detractors within the country. Sycophants always try to protect the leader by crushing the opposition. Saul refused to do so and saved the lives of his detractors who had ridiculed him in the past. By doing this, Saul ensured a space for dissent in his country. Our world is becoming increasingly intolerant of differing or dissenting voices, but it is only by providing such a space that a strong and healthy family, church and society will emerge in the world.

† Lord, help us to respect even those who differ from us in ideas and ideals. Help rulers not to become authoritarian autocrats, but to work for the good of their people. Amen

King Saul   Sham Thomas

Thursday 31 May

1 Samuel 12

An impeccable leader

Today's reading provides a model for any leader who has to make a farewell speech to his people. Samuel possessed the integrity and moral courage to challenge the people to present any charges of misrule during his tenure as leader. He described five possible charges against a corrupt leader and subjected himself to their scrutiny. However, there were no charges against Samuel, a testimony to his upright and value-based leadership. It is only on the basis of such impeccable leadership that Samuel presents the history of God's redemption of Israel as a framework for their continued devotion to God. The major thrust of Samuel's speech is the need for the king and his people to be loyal to God and the dire consequences of any aberration in their behaviour.

> If you will fear the Lord and serve him and heed his voice and not rebel against the commandment of the Lord, and if both you and the king who reigns over you will follow the Lord your God, it will be well.

(verse 14)

The only way to protect the king and the nation, according to Samuel, is to follow the commandments of God. No leadership on earth is perfect and it needs to be subjected to the will of God. Even religious leaders sometimes forget that they and the people over whom they exercise authority are equally under the sovereign God. It is at their peril that such leaders forget God as they climb the ladder of power.

† Help us, Lord, not to use our leadership roles for personal gain and not to harbour the notion that leadership is a licence to abuse power and privilege. Amen

Sham Thomas   King Saul

Friday 1 June
1 Samuel 13:5-15a

The rejected king

The main focus of today's reading is Saul's rejection from the kingship. Saul had to face hostilities from external as well as internal forces. He did not have the manpower or sophisticated weaponry to match the Philistines. Samuel, who was a stalwart of faith in such terrifying situations, was conspicuously absent; he did not appear to offer the sacrifices seeking God's word and the people missed his reassuring presence. Was the sudden appearance of Samuel just after Saul had offered the sacrifice simply a coincidence? The dynamics between Saul and Samuel need to be taken into account in evaluating the kingship of Saul. Samuel appears to overreact and ignore the crisis situation which had prompted Saul to perform the role of priest and prophet. It is surprising that on the basis of one such act, Saul had to be removed from his position of leadership.

> Samuel said to Saul, 'You have done foolishly; you have not kept the commandment of the LORD your God, which he commanded you. The LORD would have established your kingdom over Israel for ever, but now your kingdom will not continue.'

> (verse 13 and part of verse 14)

Samuel may have been guarding the different roles of king and prophet in the context of the emergence of kingship in Israel. Emergency situations had been used by leaders in history to grab other offices, transgress boundaries and establish their power even more firmly than before. When power is divided between different people, there is a potential for conflict which may become reality if leaders start enjoying power without realising why and how it should be shared.

† Lord, make us vigilant when religious symbols are appropriated for political purposes and political interests influence decision-making in religious affairs. Amen

King Saul   Sham Thomas

Faith-filled action

In today's reading, Jonathan is portrayed as a better leader than his father. In facing a crisis, Saul seems to be passive and uses God as an excuse. In contrast, Jonathan takes bold and imaginative steps in faith.

> *Come, let us go over to the garrison of these uncircumcised; it may be that the LORD will act for us; for nothing can hinder the LORD from saving by many or by few.*

(part of verse 6)

Leadership requires decision-making, which is often a cumbersome process. However, refraining from decision-making, or only acting after ensuring an easy victory, is not good leadership. Unlike his father, Jonathan and his assistant went into the enemy camp and God acted for them. Many a time we cannot fathom what God wants or how God will act, and this uncertainty can lead us into passivity. Faith-filled people will, however, place each situation in God's hands and act believing that if our actions are in accordance with God's will, God will bless them, and if not, God will transform them.

† Lord, help us not to count on the few or many, but to entrust ourselves totally to your will and do our part, however small. Amen

For group discussion and personal thought

• What can we learn from King Saul for our leadership in various areas?
• How do you understand the use of power by Prophet Samuel?

Sham Thomas

King Saul

Readings in 1 Samuel

3 David

Notes based on the *Revised Standard Version* by

Emmanuel Borlabi Bortey

Emmanuel Borlabi Bortey is a minister of the Methodist Church Ghana based in the capital city of Accra. He is currently a Superintendent Minister responsible for the Adabraka Circuit of the church. He lives with his wife Abigail, and their four adult children.

Introduction

This week's readings take us through a very critical transitional period in the history of Israel. Saul's disobedience led to his rejection as king and the anointing of David as his successor. David's spectacular victory over Goliath led to his introduction to Saul's court. While Saul's son Jonathan became David's friend, King Saul felt so insecure that he frantically sought to eliminate David.

Sunday 3 June: *1 Samuel 14:24-36*
Do not hastily make a vow

Saul's main task was to deal with the menace of frequent attacks from the Philistines. It was in the midst of one of these battles for supremacy that Saul vowed:

> *'Cursed be the man who eats food until it is evening and I am avenged on my enemies.'*

(part of verse 24)

Saul would not allow even a little break for refreshment. Unfortunately, a natural source of nourishing refreshment (honey) presented itself to the troops (verse 26). Jonathan, who had not heard his father's vow, tasted a little of the honey and immediately felt refreshed. When he was told of his father's vow, he tried to be loyal but had to point out that it had been a foolish action (verses 29-30). That single hastily pronounced vow of King Saul denied Israel a great victory over their arch-enemies, the Philistines, the very purpose for which Saul had been made king.

† Father, spare me the pain of being too quick to make a vow or promise that may not fulfil your purposes for my life, family and nation. Amen

Monday 4 June

1 Samuel 15:7-23

Obedience is better than sacrifice

Saul received divine instructions, through the prophet Samuel, to utterly destroy the Amalekites for being an impediment to Israel during their journey to the Promised Land of Canaan. Mosaic Law required an irrevocable destruction of persons or things placed under a ban (see, for instance, Deuteronomy 20:16-18).

Saul, however, in his own wisdom, chose to spare Agag, the king of Amalek, and 'the best of the things devoted to destruction' (verse 21), 'the best of the sheep and of the oxen to sacrifice to the Lord' (verse 15). Samuel responded to Saul's failure to adhere strictly to the terms of the ban placed on Amalek, in words which have become one of the best-known verses in the Bible:

'Has the Lord as great delight in burnt offerings and sacrifices,
as in obeying the voice of the Lord ?
Behold, to obey is better than sacrifice,
and to hearken than the fat of rams . . .
Because you have rejected the word of the Lord,
he has also rejected you from being king.'

(part of verses 22-23)

The real essence of worship is obedience. Saul got it all wrong when he thought God would be pleased with sacrifices of the animals he had disobediently preserved from the flock of the Amalekites. The ban placed on the Amalekites may seem too harsh to us; but the Lord knows why he made this order. Our obedience to God's commands must be total, not selective. So we cannot, for instance, acquire wealth through fraudulent means and then give an offering to God from such illegally acquired wealth.

† Father, grant us grace to worship you in truth through wholehearted obedience to all your commands. Amen

Borlabi Bortey   David

1 Samuel 16:1-23

Do not assess people by their outward looks

The Lord directed Samuel to go to the house of Jesse and to anoint one of Jesse's sons as a successor to Saul's throne. So Samuel invited Jesse's children to a sacrifice.

When they came, he looked on Eliab and thought, 'Surely the Lord's anointed is before him.' But the Lord said to Samuel, 'Do not look on his appearance or on the height of his stature, because I have rejected him; for the Lord sees not as man sees: man looks on the outward appearance, but the Lord looks on the heart.'

(verses 6-7)

Indeed, outward appearance can be deceptive. As human beings we often tend to esteem people with good looks, those who are handsome or beautiful, well-dressed, of good stature, and so on. A shabbily dressed person is likely to be overlooked as someone of no account. Samuel's experience in Jesse's house should constantly remind us never to assess people's stature or worth by their outward appearance. Above all, as human beings, we have no skill to determine people's real worth – their true inner qualities and capabilities. We must therefore refrain from passing judgement on our fellow human beings. In the words of our Lord Jesus Christ, 'Judge not, that you be not judged' (Matthew 7:1). Whenever we are required, for instance in a business environment, to assess colleagues or subordinates, we should do so with utmost humility and caution, knowing that we cannot wholly decipher another person's true inner character or ability.

† Heavenly Father, save me from the danger of judging people on the basis of their outward looks. Amen

David

Borlabi Bortey

Wednesday 6 June

1 Samuel 17:31-50

Depend on God in all things

The encounter between David and Goliath is one of the best known and loved historical accounts in the Bible. Here was a poor young shepherd boy with no military experience stepping out to engage in a one-on-one encounter with a huge giant who was a seasoned military man of war. Nobody would give David even a dog's chance against Goliath. You might even wonder why King Saul agreed to sponsor this mismatch. But perhaps David's assurances were too convincing:

'The LORD who delivered me from the paw of the lion and from the paw of the bear, will deliver me from the hand of this Philistine.'

(part of verse 37)

David's confidence and assurance stemmed from his personal experience of the workings of God in his own life in the field as a shepherd boy. And his unwavering faith was rewarded:

So David prevailed over the Philistine with a sling and with a stone, and struck the Philistine, and killed him; there was no sword in the hand of David.

(verse 50)

When in life we are confronted with challenges which seem well beyond our human capabilities, we need to learn to call on and depend on the limitless resources of God. There is no part of our human existence that is outside the sphere of God's influence and intervention. And we need to count our blessings; even the 'small mercies' (safety in journeys, healings etc.) received in the past should make us, like David, confident in God's never failing provision for newer challenges in our everyday lives.

† Heavenly Father, grant me the grace to know that you are actively concerned with every aspect of my life in your world. May I therefore learn to depend on you in all things. Amen

Borlabi Bortey   David

Do not be jealous of the success of others

The celebration of David's success by the women of Israel ignited in King Saul a deep sense of jealousy and even animosity against David.

The women sang to one another as they made merry,
'Saul has struck down his thousands,
and David his ten thousands.'
And Saul was very angry, and this saying displeased him.

(verses 7 and part of verse 8)

Saul feared that David's growing popularity might lead to him assuming the throne. He 'eyed David from that day on' (verse 9) and was attacked by an evil spirit (verse 10). The effects of jealousy can be disastrous. In the case of King Saul his jealousy made him lose his focus: he diverted his attention from dealing with the Philistine menace and instead fought David. He dissipated his energies hunting David and in the end lost both wars: he failed to eliminate David and ended up losing his life in a battle against the Philistines.

God our maker has given us human beings different endowments. We need to be content with whatever God's grace enables us to achieve, and to appreciate, and even be glad for, what others are also able to achieve. Indeed, we need each other to make living in God's world possible. Our gifts and abilities complement each other to deliver the services we need for our survival, such as water, food and electricity. To be envious or jealous of a neighbour simply denies us the peace of mind we need to be able to succeed in our own endeavours.

† Father, grant me grace to be appreciative of others and glad for the success of my neighbour. Amen

David   Borlabi Bortey

Friday 8 June

1 Samuel 19:1-18

True friendship is selfless

While David's success over Goliath evoked hatred and jealousy in King Saul, it evoked a totally different response from Jonathan, Saul's son. When David was introduced to Saul after the encounter with Goliath, 'as soon as [David] had finished speaking to Saul, the soul of Jonathan was knit to the soul of David, and Jonathan loved him as his own soul' (18:1). When Saul revealed his desire to kill David to his son,

> Jonathan spoke well of David to Saul his father, and said to him, 'Let not the king sin against his servant David . . . for he took his life in his hand and he slew the Philistine, and the LORD wrought a great victory for all Israel.'

(part of verses 4-5)

While Saul saw David as a threat to his rule, his son Jonathan saw David as a God-sent ally and an asset to the king. While Saul's response to David's success was dominated by a selfish ambition to secure his throne, Jonathan's response was dominated by a selfless love which placed the interest of the nation above a personal interest of securing his position as the heir apparent to the throne. Jonathan's persuasive argument against Saul's intention to kill David achieved a temporary success until David recorded another success against the Philistines. Then 'a harmful spirit from the LORD came upon Saul' and he pursued David right down to his home, where he narrowly escaped death (verses 11-18). While Saul's response to David's success was dominated by selfish ambition, Jonathan displayed the elements of true friendship: a selfless spirit which refused to see David as a threat to his political future.

† Heavenly Father, grant us the selfless spirit that can place the well-being of others above our personal ambitions and aspirations. Amen

Borlabi Bortey

David

1 Samuel 20:1-23

True friendship is based on true love

After Saul's attempt to kill him in his own house, David escaped to Samuel at Ramah; but Saul kept pursuing him. So David returned to report the threat on his life to Jonathan, his friend. Jonathan then undertook to cross-check on Saul's disposition towards David.

> *'But should it please my father to do you harm, the LORD do so to Jonathan and more also if I do not disclose it to you, and send you away, that you may go in safety'* . . . *And Jonathan made David swear again by his love for him, for he loved him as he loved his own soul.*

(part of verse 13, and verse 17)

Later events will prove how enduring was the love between David and Jonathan. If Jonathan had joined forces with his father King Saul, they could easily have plotted David's death; the alliance between David and Jonathan would have made it easy for Jonathan to know David's whereabouts and effectively attack and assassinate him. But what a friendship! Jonathan's love for David was so sincere that he remained faithful to David to the very end.

† Dear heavenly Father, grant us grace to remain faithful to our friends in all circumstances of life. Amen

For group discussion and personal thought

- Was David being unrealistic when he dared to face Goliath in personal combat? In what circumstances would it be right for us to undertake a task as a venture in faith? And when can such a venture not be justified?

- What were the factors that caused Saul to become jealous of David? Was Saul's jealousy justified? What factors do you think normally arouse jealousy among friends? How best can we deal with the problem of unhealthy jealousies?

June

David   Borlabi Bortey

Readings in 1 Samuel

4 The death of Saul

Notes based on the *New Revised Standard Version* by

David Huggett

For David's biography see p.29.

Introduction

Don't write Saul off as completely bad. Like all of us he was a complex character, with good and bad points, strengths and weaknesses. A tall and handsome young man, he came from a relatively wealthy and distinguished family. He showed considerable skill and courage as a leader, but his last days were shrouded in shame and failure: he could not cope with the pressures of his life, especially living in the shadow of someone who was usurping his own position of power and influence. Maybe we shall see something of ourselves in this man, and learn from his mistakes.

Sunday 10 June: *1 Samuel 20:24-42*

Two angry men

Saul knew, because Samuel had told him (15:26), that he had lost God's favour through his own foolishness. Saul also believed that the only way to ensure that his name and reputation did not die with him was to guarantee his son's inheritance. The custom was for a new king to eliminate all those who might pose a threat to the new dynasty (2 Samuel 3 and 4). So Saul was furious, not only with David for his absence from the royal table without permission, but also because his own son seemed to care nothing for the succession, accepting and even supporting David.

Then Saul's anger was kindled against Jonathan.

(part of verse 30)

Jonathan was angry too (verse 34), but his rage was justified. He could not accept his father's blind injustice.

† Lord, whenever I see injustice help me, like Jonathan, to have a 'fierce anger'.

1 Samuel 21:1 – 22:5

The dangers of hunger

Hunger, according to the United Nations, is the number one health problem afflicting our world today. Bigger than AIDS, malaria and tuberculosis combined, the situation continues to worsen. Almost a billion people (or 1 in 7) have insufficient food to keep them healthy and active. Stunted physical and mental development, and sometimes death, are the results. Maybe David's hunger was not that severe, yet he and his men were in serious danger. It does not excuse his lying (verse 2) or his subterfuge (verse 13), although it does make them understandable. I'm sure most of us have done similar things to get ourselves out of a tight spot. But there is guilt of another kind here – Saul's. By now he must have been aware of what people were saying about David. Even the Philistine ruler of Gath seems to assume that Saul is no longer in power:

'Is this not David the king of the land?'

(part of verse 11)

Saul is hungry too – not for food but for the power that he feels slipping away from him, and he reacts with hatred and malice. The problem was then, as it is now, that, as John Donne famously put it, 'No man is an island'. Our actions are seldom entirely private. They influence other people in ways that may surprise us. Saul's bitterness brought out David's fallibility, caused Ahimelech's fear, and encouraged Doeg's betrayal. Didn't Jesus have something to say about the responsibility we have for the effect our actions and words have on others (Mark 9:42)?

† Generous God, help me to become more aware of the different kinds of hunger in the world today and to play my part in feeding those in need.

The death of Saul   David Huggett

Tuesday 12 June

1 Samuel 22:6-23

A sorry indulgence

There is of course no justification for Saul's actions in this chapter. Certainly this was a brutal age but his jealousy, rage, bitterness and cruelty are ugly emotions resulting in evil actions. Yet underlying these there seems to be an attitude with which we may be all too familiar. Saul indulges in self-pity. You can hear the whine in his voice:

> *'Is that why all of you have conspired against me? . . . none of you is sorry for me.'*

(part of verse 8)

David's power is growing by the day: so is his popularity. Saul's own son seems to have turned against him, and he suspects that the members of his own tribe are ready to change sides when the time seems right. Even his closest supporters refuse to carry out his orders (verse 17). A soldier, recently returned from the war in Afghanistan and struggling to recover some semblance of a normal life after having been badly maimed by an exploding mine, made the comment, 'It's no use giving in to self-pity.' Yet we do. Saul hadn't learned that self-pity is unattractive and self-defeating. When we indulge in it we do ourselves no good. We repel the very people whose support and care we need. We admire the brave soldier, but when someone indulges in self-pity we find our own pity for them dries up. What is more, psychologists tell us that feeling sorry for ourselves 'generates the inability to do anything'. As Saul felt his own power dwindling, the very thing he needed to avoid he indulged.

† Patient and compassionate God, forgive me for the many times I indulge my selfishness by feeling sorry for myself. Give me grace to face suffering in myself with courage, and suffering in others with compassion.

David Huggett   The death of Saul

1 Samuel 24

Roles reversed

David is in grave danger. In chapter 23 we learn that he had about 600 men with him. Saul on the other hand was closing in on him with an army of 3,000 crack troops (verse 2). In addition, David appears to be trapped in the back of a cave. Then quite suddenly a simple call of nature, and their roles are reversed. Who says the Bible doesn't have a sense of humour? Now David the hunted outlaw has the king of Israel in his power. At a stroke, literally, he can grasp the throne for himself. Who can blame his men for suggesting that God must have provided this golden opportunity? But David shows admirable self-control, and perhaps a hint of the diplomatic gifts that he would later require as king. He will not carry out an act of treachery against an anointed king which in later years could be seen as a precedent that others might follow against him. He also sees the advantage of putting psychological and spiritual pressure on Saul. God can be relied on to be the judge between them:

> 'May the Lord judge between me and you! . . . my hand shall not be against you.'

(part of verse 12)

Now, with his greatly superior force Saul would have found little difficulty in blockading the cave and forcing David and his men to surrender. Instead, his life spared, Saul appears sincere as he admits his fault and asks for David's forgiveness. David, however, is cautious. Doubtless remembering his past experiences of Saul's double dealings, he knows he cannot trust him completely.

---

† Gracious Lord, may the spirit of mercy which David showed inspire me to show mercy when I am wronged.

The death of Saul   David Huggett

June

Thursday 14 June

1 Samuel 26

Sorry again?

Although this story has many similarities to the one we read yesterday in chapter 24, there are clearly some different lessons the writer wants us to learn. Saul has not learned from his experiences: he seems to be continuing on his downward spiral. Roles are reversed. Saul, in spite of his vast numerical advantage, is the vulnerable one. Once more it is David who has the upper hand. But this time it is not a call of nature that is Saul's undoing but a lack of discipline in his army, and evidence that his own authority is slipping further away. Although Abner admits his own guilt in allowing the guards to sleep who should have been defending their sleeping king, it is of course the man at the top – Saul – who bears the ultimate responsibility. David's compassion and his faith in God's ultimate purposes come across clearly as he reminds the king,

> 'The LORD rewards everyone for his righteousness and his faithfulness; for the LORD gave you into my hand today, but I would not raise my hand against the LORD's anointed.'

(verse 23)

Compare Saul's admission of guilt (verse 21) with the way he confessed it in chapter 24. Here it seems half-hearted. He acknowledges that he has been a 'fool', but he uses a rather weak word. It could almost be translated, 'Silly me'. He admits that he's made a mistake – no more than that. On the previous occasion he had been willing to acknowledge that David would be his successor: now all that he will concede is that David will enjoy success (verse 25).

† Merciful God, keep me from blaming others when things go wrong, and give me the courage to be responsible for what I do.

David Huggett   The death of Saul

Friday 15 June

1 Samuel 28:3-25

Listening

I have sometimes sat in an examination wishing that I had listened more attentively to my teacher. Listening is important, not only for learning but also for building relationships. No marriage will find it easy to survive if the partners are not prepared to listen to one another. Many wars could be avoided if nations listened to one another. Saul wouldn't listen – to Samuel, to David, to his son Jonathan, and to his own men. Worst of all he failed to pay attention to what God was saying. Now he faces the ultimate crisis. The Philistines are massing superior forces in the north for a final showdown. His suspicion of David's treason is confirmed as his rival joins forces with the enemy. Samuel, to whom he has always turned for advice in the past, is dead. As for God –

the Lord did not answer him.

(part of verse 6)

It was of course Saul's own fault. God had given him clear instructions through Samuel. God had spoken to him through various circumstances. Saul had not listened, so there was little point in repeating himself. Most of us I guess have had the kind of experience when God seems to be silent and unresponsive. As Isaiah exclaimed, 'Truly, you are a God who hides himself' (Isaiah 45:15). Before we start complaining, perhaps we should ask ourselves if God has already spoken in some way – and we just didn't hear or understand. Or perhaps, like Saul, we were so busy looking for help from some other source that God's voice was crowded out.

† Lord, help me to recognise your voice however it comes to me, and when I hear it give me wisdom to understand what you are saying, and grace to obey your will.

The death of Saul   David Huggett

Saturday 16 June

1 Samuel 31

Last rights

So Saul and his three sons and his armour-bearer and all his men died together on the same day.

(verse 6)

A sad epitaph for a man mainly remembered for his failures. True, he was frequently cruel, jealous, proud and power-hungry. But the people of Jabesh-gilead remembered his courage on their behalf (chapter 11). So before we leave Saul it is good to take account of some of the challenges with which he had to grapple. For example, he pioneered monarchy in Israel, exposing himself to pressures that highlighted some of his weaknesses. He faced hostility from many opposed to monarchy on religious grounds. Even Samuel, upon whom he relied heavily, gave him somewhat ambiguous support. He failed to turn up at Gilgal when expected (chapter 13), leading to Saul's stupid mistake. Samuel then anointed his successor behind his back. Saul's reign was also constantly threatened by the Philistines, who knew how to smelt iron and so were equipped with superior weapons. None of this excuses Saul, but it should help us to understand him.

† Merciful God, grant that I may always look for the best in others.

For group discussion and personal thought

• What unexpected ways could God use to speak to us today?

• Death can be a lonely and a bitter experience for some in our communities. In what ways could the local church help to prepare those at the end of their lives so that they may have 'a good death'?

• If you have been happily and effectively fulfilling a particular role in your church or community, what signs would you look for that might tell you that it is time to allow someone else to take over?

David Huggett   The death of Saul

Fathers

1   Fathers and children

Notes based on the *New Revised Standard Version* by

Philip G O'B Robinson

Philip Robinson is a former President of the Jamaica District of the Methodist Church in the Caribbean and the Americas (MCCA) and of the Jamaica Council of Churches. He is Methodist Chaplain to the University of the West Indies (Mona Campus) and to the Excelsior Education Centre, the largest educational institution of the MCCA. He also teaches at Excelsior.

Introduction

There are fathers who have good intentions but fail to address the critical needs of their children; there are the 'deadbeat dads' who do not care for their children and deny paternity. On the other hand, there are fathers who raise their children with careful discipline, sure guidance and loving care. We shall be looking at both kinds of fathers in this week's readings.

Sunday 17 June: *Job 1:1-5*
A father of faith

> *Job would send and sanctify them, and he would rise early in the morning and offer burnt offering according to the number of them all . . . this is what Job always did.*

(part of verse 5)

Job understood well that fatherhood was not a 'nine to five' job; nor was it a duty of care exercised only in respect of children below the age of majority. He obviously believed that there was a spiritual dimension to that duty of care, so although his children were married and independent he maintained a constant interest in their spiritual wellbeing.

The power of prayer is real and there are stories of miraculous changes in the circumstances of people who have been the subject of the unrelenting prayers of their parents. Unlike some other parents, Job did not pray only for the successful child, or only for the child who had strayed from the paths of piety. Job, the exemplary father, treated them all as equally important.

† Our Father in heaven, on this Father's Day we thank you for God-fearing fathers. Give power to their prayers so that they may be effective in the lives of their children.

Monday 18 June

Genesis 21:1-14

Torn between two loves

So she said to Abraham, 'Cast out this slave woman with her son' . . .
The matter was very distressing to Abraham on account of his son.

(part of verse 10, and verse 11)

Requiring a father to choose between a son and a spouse is a most difficult decision. Abraham was in such a position. Customarily, a barren wife could give a slave girl to her husband and any child they had would be the wife's, but now that the promised son, Isaac, was born it created a dilemma for Sarah and Abraham. Abraham's predicament was that he was being required to choose between keeping his son, Ishmael, the son of the slave girl, and preserving the unity and happiness of his marriage by satisfying the desire of his wife. He was a good father. He loved his son, but now he was faced with the challenge of being separated from him. He was torn between two loves. It was at this point that God intervened again and set Abraham's mind at ease (see verses 12-13).

Two things should not be missed. First, Abraham did not run away from his challenges, or pretend that they did not exist. He put family first and sought to find a solution that would be in everybody's interest, even if it caused him pain. Good fathers put the interest of family above personal desires. Secondly, he was sensitive and obedient to God's word of advice and comfort. It was only after putting his faith in the promise of God that Abraham was able to carry out a difficult decision with confidence. Good fathers trust and obey God.

† Loving God, hear the prayers that rise from the hearts of fathers today. Guide and direct those who have to make difficult decisions in the interest of their family.

Philip Robinson

Fathers and children

Tuesday 19 June

Psalm 127:3-5

Children: a father's heritage

Sons are indeed a heritage from the LORD,
the fruit of the womb a reward.

(verse 3)

Many fathers are prepared to do anything to avoid taking responsibility for their children. Such children are often seen as a burden rather than a blessing; an inconvenience instead of a God-given heritage. This position is often taken when the children are the unwanted results of a fleeting relationship, rather than the joyous privilege resulting from a committed and loving relationship between husband and wife.

Psalm 127 makes it abundantly clear that God values children and their place in human society. Therefore we ought to treat them with great respect and care. The psalmist declares that children are 'a heritage from the Lord'. They are not just the result of human activity; they are evidence of God's favour. They are God's gift to us and we answer to God for the way in which we receive and take care of this gift.

The psalm begins by declaring our total dependence on God in family and civic affairs, and the success and security that accrue when we build these on a foundation of faith, obedience and godly living. In later years, sons ensure the continuance of the family name through having children of their own. Good sons and daughters also give protection and care to the parents who have cared for them. These are other ways in which children become a heritage from the Lord.

† Lord, bless the homes in which our children live and bless those who give parental care. Enable fathers to accept this wonderful heritage and the awesome responsibility of sacred duty, that they may bring up their children in the Lord, surrounding them with things that are pure, lovely and of good report in your sight.

June

Fathers and children

Philip Robinson

Wednesday 20 June
Genesis 27:30-40

Good father, bad judgement

[Esau] said to his father, 'Bless me, me also, father!' But he said, 'Your brother came deceitfully, and he has taken away your blessing.'

(part of verse 34, and verse 35)

Today's reading relates one of the most painful experiences a father can be made to endure. The meltdown in Isaac's family was always a tragedy waiting to happen. The moment father and mother chose favourites from among their children (Genesis 25:28) the family was put into possible self-destruct mode. Children know when parents engage in favouritism because it is not easy to conceal. Unfortunately, it very often results in a build-up of jealousy and resentment among siblings that may persist way into their adult years.

Isaac would have known and must have remembered that God had told Rebekah that the descendants of the older boy would serve the descendants of the younger (see Genesis 25:23). Yet he still sought to divert the blessing to his favourite son. It was this misjudgement of a father that set off a chain reaction of intrigue, deceit, anger, hatred, alienation, contemplation of murder, and the threat of disintegration of the family (verses 41-42).

Isaac was not a bad father; he was a father who made a bad judgement. Fathers, or others who carry out fatherly duties towards children, should note two things. First, it is not only their personal desires and wishes for these children that matter. Secondly, there are moral and spiritual norms, such as those set by God, which must take precedence.

† Lord and God, give to fathers wisdom in the exercise of their authority and balance in their dealings with their spouse and children. May justice, equanimity and humility be the hallmark of their leadership. To this end, may your divine will and purpose supersede all their desires and underlie all their decisions.

Philip Robinson   Fathers and children

Thursday 21 June

Judges 13:1-24

A good father

Then Manoah said, 'Now when your words come true, what is to be the boy's rule of life; what is he to do?'

(verse 12)

This was the question of a man ready to take orders and to follow them. In stark contrast to Isaac (see yesterday's notes), here was a father ready to cooperate with God and with his wife in bringing up their child.

Manoah appreciated the demands made by being responsible to God for the bringing up of a child, so he sought divine guidance. There is great need for the proper ordering of home and family life. It is as much the responsibility of fathers as it is of mothers. That is why God has wisely placed us in families. Every good book store has books giving a variety of perspectives on parenting. Nevertheless, the effective father is aware that God's manual, the Bible, gives guidance and emphasises aspects of parenting, and fatherhood in particular, that he cannot afford to ignore.

We know now that Samson made some terrible decisions in his life, for which he paid the price. However, a good father cannot always be blamed for the decisions made and actions taken by adult children. The Lord was able to use Samson as he had planned because his father, along with his mother, had paid attention to the boy's rule of life as set out by God. This is a worthwhile model for fathers and a word of encouragement for them: if they obey the rules of God for the life of their children, they will have done their duty, and done it well.

† Lord, give to fathers the listening ear, the obedient disposition and the cooperative spirit of Manoah. May your word be the rule of life for them and their children.

Fathers and children

Philip Robinson

Friday 22 June

1 Samuel 2:12-17

Failed fatherhood

Now the sons of Eli were scoundrels; they had no regard for the LORD or for the duties of the priests to the people.

(verse 12, and part of verse 13)

Eli the priest failed to discipline his sons Hophni and Phineas, and when they became adults and were serving as priests they did much evil in the sight of God (1 Samuel 4:11-13). The father did speak to them then but it was too late; they would not listen to him and God had already pronounced judgement against them. They died at the hands of the Philistines (1 Samuel 4:12-18).

One is left to wonder how different the story of this family might have been if the children had been disciplined; how different the story would read if they had learnt to obey God and their father. They had not learnt the moral limits that God has set for all humanity. To give a child freedom without restraint is like giving that child a lighted stick of dynamite for a lollipop. It is a recipe for self-destruction. Fathers should teach their children, by word and example, to recognise the moral limits to their rights, freedoms, and authority. This lesson is necessary, not only for church, home and school, but also for the world of work and for life in general. To ignore this lesson is to court disaster. Solomon's wise word holds true: 'Train up a child in the way he should go, and when he is old he will not depart from it' (Proverbs 22:6).

† Today we ask forgiveness for fathers who grieve because they have not guided their children in the right way. We pray for those children, that by the grace and providence of God they may find fatherly care and be guided along the paths of righteousness.

Philip Robinson   Fathers and children

Saturday 23 June

Proverbs 4:1-4

Father as mentor

When I was a son with my father,
tender, and my mother's favourite,
he taught me , and said to me,
'Let your heart hold fast my words;
keep my commandments, and live . . .'

(verses 3-4)

A staff member at school was walking across the courtyard. Immediately behind him was his five-year-old son. Unknown to the father, the son was imitating him: swinging his arms as his father did and trying to walk in his father's exact footsteps. Solomon remembered how his father David encouraged his son to walk in his footsteps, as he sought to walk with God.

On Father's Day every year children, young and old, remember in a special way the fathers who have made an impact on their lives, as David did for Solomon. These may include men who are not biological fathers but who are father figures in the lives of these children. Fathers have a tremendous and inescapable duty to mentor children towards a successful and purposeful life: to give good advice and set good examples; to encourage children to embrace wisdom and point them in the right direction.

† Thank you God, for good fathers; we pray that all fathers may become even better fathers.

For group discussion and personal thought
The readings and notes make it clear that fatherhood is both a challenge and a glorious opportunity for human partnership.

• Is fatherhood something that you would choose and why? If you are already a father, what would you do differently?

• Prepare a simple guideline for fathers that could be valuable for anyone contemplating fatherhood.

• How do you think men could be helped to recognise that ultimately they must account to God for the children they bring into God's world?

Fathers and children   Philip Robinson

Fathers

2 Perplexities of fatherhood

Notes based on the *New International Version* by

Deborah Dunn

Deborah Dunn is a licensed marriage and family therapist in private practice in the US. She is also a professional writer and speaker. She occasionally teaches trauma counselling techniques to pastors and community leaders in disaster-prone areas across the globe. If you would like to know more about her work you can visit her website: www.deborahdunn.com/.

Introduction

Being a good father can be challenging under the best of circumstances. We are not born knowing how to parent; someone has to teach us. Unfortunately, a good number of us these days were never taught how to be a good father (or mother) to our children. But God is the ultimate good father and his Word is full of teaching about how to parent our children. We reflect together this week on what the Bible says about the sometimes perplexing and challenging role of fatherhood.

Sunday 24 June: *2 Samuel 18:24-33*
Dying so we may live

> *The king was shaken. He went up to the room over the gateway and wept. As he went, he said: 'O my son Absalom! My son, my son Absalom! If only I had died instead of you – O Absalom, my son, my son!'*

(verse 33)

There is no greater pain than losing a child, especially when their loss comes as a result of their disobedience to God. Such was the case of the king, whose son Absalom turned against him and died a horrible death as a result. Yet even so, the king declared he would rather have died himself if it would have spared the life of his son. He loved his son that much. Our Father in heaven did choose to die rather than giving us the death we all deserve. Christ is the king – yet he died so we could be spared, even while 'we were yet sinners' (Romans 5:8). He is the ultimate loving father. For that alone he deserves our total allegiance.

† Father God, thank you that you love us so much that you would die in our place, even when we are disobedient. Teach us to love our children as you love us. Amen

A father with great courage

Joseph did what the angel of the Lord had commanded him and took Mary home as his wife.

(part of verse 24)

There is no doubt that Joseph is one of the greatest heroes in the Bible, even though he never fought a great battle, became a great king, or amassed great wealth and power. But in one quiet act of amazing courage and humility, Joseph changed the world for ever. Under Jewish law, Joseph had every right to have Mary stoned to death. A more proud man less grounded in faith probably would have, for no doubt the village would blame him unfairly for her condition. But not Joseph; he chose to obey God in spite of the ridicule and shaming he must have endured. What courageous love!

One of the greatest ways a man can demonstrate his love for God or his wife is by being a good father, not only to those children that are biologically his, but to all children in the world. We are called to look after orphans and stand in as parents for them. A good father also loves the mother of his children, just as Christ loves us.

† Father, please forgive us when we forget that all children belong to you, no matter where they live, who they are, or what religion their parents practise. Give us the courage of Joseph, that we may protect children from harm.

June

Perplexities of fatherhood   Deborah Dunn

Tuesday 26 June

Matthew 21:28-31

Be quick to obey

'Which of the two did what his father wanted?'

(part of verse 31)

One son said yes, but did nothing; the other son said no, but then did it anyway. If you are a parent, you already know the answer to the query here. We all prefer a child who ultimately obeys us, even if it takes awhile. We are delighted when we see our children make good choices, even if they struggle in doing so. But we are sad when they lie to us, tell us what we want to hear, then knowingly do the opposite of what we have asked. We become fearful that they have no character. But how often do we do the same to God? God nudges us to pray for someone, but the minute they are out of our sight we forget them altogether. We know we are being called to a certain task, but we talk ourselves out of it because we are too busy or there is no real earthly gain. We tell God we will do it 'someday' but that day never comes. God knows our hearts. He knows when we are lying to him and to ourselves. But the good news in this parable is that God is patient and understanding. He knows how we struggle with obedience. Even so, we can always change our minds and obey. Is there something God has asked you to do but you disobeyed? There is still time to change your mind.

† Father God, we thank you for being a God of 'second chances'. Forgive us for our failure to listen and obey, and give us the strength to change our hearts and minds. Amen

Deborah Dunn   Perplexities of fatherhood

Luke 8:40-56

The demands of parenting

Jesus said, 'Someone touched me; I know that power has gone out from me' . . . Then he said to her, 'Daughter, your faith has healed you. Go in peace.'

(verses 46 and 48)

It's difficult to work all day, serve in our church and community, and have enough time for our children too. It sometimes seems there is just not enough of us to go around. Jesus must have felt the same way, especially once the miracles he performed became public knowledge. One can only imagine the horrors of the sickness, dust, heat, body odours, flies, and desperation on the faces of the afflicted crushing up against him, trying to get his attention. Nevertheless, Jesus stopped and made time for a woman who was not even supposed to be in the crowd. For a Jewish man, even having his garment touched by such a person was akin to being touched by a leper. Yet her faith was so strong that she caught his attention and he responded in love and grace as the patient and kind father he knew she needed.

Are you beset by the demands on your life? Do you handle interruptions, distractions, and improprieties with the grace and love he did? Be patient with your children. Perhaps they too, like the woman in the crowd, are desperate for the attention of their father.

† Father, please grant us the patience not only to deal with all the demands on our time and energy, but also to seek you out and touch you, knowing you will heal us if our faith in you is strong. Amen

Perplexities of fatherhood   Deborah Dunn

The father that lies

'[The devil] was a murderer from the beginning, not holding to the truth, for there is no truth in him. When he lies, he speaks his native language, for he is a liar and the father of lies!'

(part of verse 44)

Life is complicated, especially when it comes to parenting. There are times when we struggle to be honest, especially when we know the truth will hurt our children. We keep secrets from them about our mistakes, failures, or addictions. We sugarcoat truth out of fear of their reaction. Even so, children have an uncanny ability to sense when we are not being honest with them, and that confuses them. Confusion breeds contempt. No wonder they disrespect and rebel against us! In the long run, honesty *is* the best policy, especially when it comes to marriage and parenting. Of course, we must be judicious and wise about how much and when to tell the truth. But as spiritual leaders in our homes, it is the responsibility of fathers to set an example for their children. They must be able to trust that we are who we say we are. It is only then that they will respect us and want to be like us, and, hopefully, like their Father in heaven.

† Father in heaven, you are righteousness and truth. Help us to live our lives in such a manner that our children are not confused by our hypocrisy or secrecy, and will know that, as their parents, we stand for righteousness and truth as well. Help fathers to be spiritual leaders in their homes, leading in truth, honesty, and love.

Deborah Dunn   Perplexities of fatherhood

The paradox of doubt

[Jesus said] 'Everything is possible for him who believes.' Immediately the boy's father exclaimed, 'I do believe; help me overcome my unbelief!'

(part of verse 23, and verse 24)

This scripture passage contains one of the most dramatic and explicit descriptions of demonic possession in the Bible. A father brings his son to Jesus because of a violent and sadistic spirit that had tormented his child from birth. Can you imagine the pain the father suffered, watching his son all those years? It must have been horrible. No wonder the father questioned 'if' Jesus could heal his son. It is easy to doubt when we've lived for many years under terrible circumstances that seem insurmountable.

These days the spirits that torment our children are more than likely promiscuity, drugs, alcohol, and mental illness. There is no doubt that the demonic realm uses any weapon it can to defeat us. But Jesus makes it clear that our faith is what heals us, and what saves our children in the long run, either here on earth or on the other side. Faith will lead us to pray, and prayer always defeats the enemy.

† Father God, help us in our unbelief. You know the doubts that beset us and how the enemy would have us believe that our children are beyond your saving reach. Renew our faith so that we can pray for our sons and daughters. Amen

June

Perplexities of fatherhood
Deborah Dunn

Saturday 30 June

Luke 15:11-32

Taking God for granted

'My son,' the father said, 'you are always with me, and everything I have is yours. But we had to celebrate and be glad, because this brother of yours was dead and is alive again; he was lost and is found.'

(verses 31-32)

The parable of the prodigal son is comforting because it reassures us that our rebellious children will eventually come home. But what about the 'good son'? If we have children, we know how often they take us for granted. However hard we work for them, they complain or accuse us of favouring another child. But adults can be ungrateful children too! How often do we grumble about the way God deals with us? When we see others living the 'good life', calling themselves Christians but doing little to serve God, how often do we complain, reminding God that, unlike those 'prodigals', we have served him for years, often with little material reward or tangible blessing? But as the parable reminds us, we should never take our relationship with God for granted. After all, everything he has is ours. Everything! And, best of all, he is always with us.

† Father, strengthen us in our weariness and empower us to serve you with grateful hearts. Help us to teach our children that service to God is the greatest and most rewarding job in the world. Amen

For group discussion and personal thought

- What do the fathers you have met this week tell you about what makes a good father?
- Each father faced a dilemma in parenting. How did each of them deal with their dilemma in a way that pleased God?
- Sometimes we are guilty of paying more attention to our children's bad behaviour, and failing to notice when they do good. How can we praise and reward children for good behaviour?

Deborah Dunn   Perplexities of fatherhood

Fathers

3 Care and counsel

Notes based on the *New Revised Standard Version* by
Christian Glasgow

Christian E Glasgow is an Anglican priest in the Diocese of the Windward Islands, Province of the West Indies. He is the Archdeacon of Grenada, Rector of St George, Grenada, and the Provincial representative to the Anglican Peace and Justice Network. Eleanor, his wife (soon to be ordained) currently shares ministry with him as Director of Lay Ministries at St George.

Introduction
The readings for this week consist of a mixture of Old and New Testament passages which highlight the ideal father–child relationship with respect to care and counsel, as exemplified in the God–man experiences of humankind.

Sunday 1 July: *Hosea 11:1-4*
Unconditional love
Two friends who hadn't seen each other for a very long time were sharing their life's experiences. The first, Winston, spoke in glowing terms about his successes and was particularly proud of his relationship with his children. The other, John, had moderate success in life and also spoke about his children. He provided for them as best as he could, and would give his life for them. Yet they never appreciated him. They were more concerned about their friends and even now, grown up and on their own, the only time they seem to remember him is to satisfy their material needs. John ended by saying 'Yet I love them dearly.' Winston, with a puzzled frown, asked 'How can you?'

> 'The more I called them,
> the more they went from me . . .
> Yet it was I who . . . healed them.'

(part of verses 2-3)

A father's love is unconditional. God loves us even when we do not love him.

† Help us, Lord, daily to love others as you love us. Amen

Monday 2 July

Exodus 18:18-23

Foolishness is not sense

The story is told of a young minister, Charles, who was keen and eager to do well when he took charge of his first parish. He was full of zeal and energy and therefore plunged into the task of transforming his parish from its dormant state to a vibrant and active one. Charles was always busy. If he was not attending a meeting, he was occupied in building maintenance or some other task. He was involved in absolutely everything and it seemed to him that he needed more than 24 hours in a day. One day a gentleman, Robert, who had been observing Charles for some time went to visit him. As usual the minister was busy with a project but took time out to speak with Robert. After the exchange of pleasantries, Robert said, 'Sir, I hope you don't mind me getting straight to the point. "Foolishness is not sense!" I have been observing you running yourself into the ground doing things that others can do, while some crucial and pertinent areas of your ministry are suffering. You must be sensible about managing your affairs lest your efforts are fruitless.'

'You will surely wear yourself out, both you and these people with you; you cannot do it alone.'

(verse 18)

Like Jethro with Moses, Robert gave Charles fatherly counsel. Those of us who are in leadership positions need to be prudent in the delegation of duties and the use of our skills and talents for the benefit of the whole.

† Lord, help us to remember that you give us a variety of gifts for the benefit of all; may we never hinder others, knowingly or unknowingly, from using their gift to your honour and glory. Amen

Hebrews 12:7-12

Endurance the pathway to perfection

I once knew a young lady who felt called to the ordained ministry. However, she couldn't understand the trials that beset her once she had answered the call to test her vocation. She found herself vilified and castigated for patterning her daily life according to her training. She was the target of much unfounded slander, trials and tribulations. She would ask herself 'Why, why should I put up with all of this?' Totally disillusioned, she sought the advice of her spiritual adviser. Her adviser listened to her carefully without interrupting, as she poured out her soul to him. Then after much thought he said 'Do you know the process for making steel? Do you know that among other things it requires placing iron ore with all its impurities in a furnace? And do you know that the finest steel stays in the furnace the longest? Have you ever observed what happens when a fully inflated ball which was held under water is released? And, do you know that the deeper the ball is sunk, the higher it shoots when released?'

[D]iscipline always seems painful ... but later it yields the peaceful fruit of righteousness to those who have been trained by it.

(part of verse 11)

Suffering is not necessarily punitive. As a discipline, it is a tool for education, character formation and growth. Discipline is a component of parental love. Consider Jesus' path to glory as recorded in Philippians 2:5-11.

† Lord, teach us that in all things that may befall us you are in control and you always work for our good. Give us the strength to endure relying on your grace. Amen

Care and counsel

Christian Glasgow

Wednesday 4 July

Psalm 103:13-14

He needs help

Jimmy, a young offender who had broken a rule of a correctional facility for the 'umpteenth' time, stood before the disciplinary officer quaking in his boots. He was certain he was going to be severely punished. The officer looked at him, shook his head and with an understanding smile dismissed the youngster with a light punishment. His fellow officers looked at him puzzled. After the youngster left the room the officer said to his colleagues: 'Having done a comprehensive study of Jimmy I learnt some interesting facts about his background; he can't help it, he needs help.'

For he knows how we were made;
he remembers that we are dust.

(verse 14)

God our father knows our frailty. Even though his justice demands judgement, he dispenses it with compassion. We are challenged to see the reality beneath a person's appearance and to temper justice with mercy.

† Lord, open our ears to hear the unspoken truths of those around us; open our eyes to see beyond the façade of their appearance; and grant us the fortitude to exercise compassion in their daily encounter with us. Amen

Thursday 5 July

1 Kings 2:1-4

Faithfulness to God's way

A group of business students were interviewing a very successful businessman. They asked him many questions about the intricacies of his business operation, questions about staffing and a whole host of issues, in order to determine his secret of success. Then finally a student asked: 'Sir, what advice would you give to someone who wishes to venture into the world of business?' The businessman silently reflected on his road to success. He recalled the many experiences he had had: the good, the bad; the successes, the failures; the pain and the joy. He noted, however, that throughout it all there had always been a God reference in his life; even when he made mistakes, and he had made some terrible ones, he would always turn to God. Then he replied pensively, in much the same words as David used for his final advice to his son Solomon, 'My advice would be to put God first in all things. It is essential to have a God reference in our lives; faithfulness to God's way is absolutely important to lasting success.'

> '[K]eep the charge of the LORD your God, walking in his ways and keeping his statutes, his commandments, his ordinances, and his testimonies . . . so that you may prosper in all that you do and wherever you turn.'

(part of verse 3)

We are reminded that obedience to God's commands is faithfulness, and faithfulness to God's way is rewarded with everlasting blessing.

† O God, teach us in our daily existence, at all times and in every place, always to acknowledge you as our master so that you may direct our path to eternal bliss. Amen

Care and counsel

Christian Glasgow

Friday 6 July

Ephesians 6:1-4

Action speaks louder than words

Some recently graduated seminarians were reflecting on the years they had spent at seminary. They were recalling the many experiences shared and lessons learnt. Suddenly Joel, very animated and with great excitement, said 'Fellers, do you remember this one? It was in our second year; we were breaking all kinds of rules and we thought we were clever, we were really "pushing the envelope" and seemingly getting away with it. Remember?' 'Yeah, until it was our week to lead worship,' answered Richard. He remembered clearly as if it were yesterday. They had planned every detail of worship, hymns and theme to match the scripture readings. They collaborated in producing top class homilies extolling the benefits and virtues of Christian discipline and morality, and admonished the new students to live by these principles. Everything was well executed and with great anticipation they anxiously awaited the review from the professor of Liturgy and Worship. Yes, they all remembered and, as if reliving the very moment of the review, simultaneously they mimicked the professor: 'Gentlemen, your conduct is speaking so loudly that I cannot hear what you are saying.'

[F]athers, ... bring them up in the discipline and instruction of the Lord.'

(part of verse 4)

We are challenged to practise what we preach and to remember that example is the best teacher. It is not enough to extol virtues and admonish others to live by them; if our teaching is to have any impact, others must see us living out these teachings.

† Lord, mould us so that our lives may be good examples for those whom we seek to nurture, and may we first learn so that we can teach others. Amen

Every 'can' is not an 'ought'

My father was a schoolmaster of the 'old school' and during my secondary education we both travelled a daily round trip to school of approximately eighteen miles by public transport. One day I said to him, 'Daddy, why don't you buy a car? I am sure you can afford one!' He looked at me and with his typical schoolmaster smile he slowly nodded his head and asked, 'You want a car? Christian, I will not buy you a car now.' 'Why not?' I asked. His response was 'When you start to work you can buy yourself a car; if I buy you a car now, you will never appreciate and value it as much as you will if you purchase it with your hard-earned cash.'

> *'If you then . . . know how to give good gifts to your children, how much more will your Father in heaven.'*

(part of verse 11)

Prayer in this passage is more than a shopping list. It highlights the nature of love and love's response in the father–child relationship, as petitions are fulfilled with gracious and wise gifts. We can confidently trust God our father always to answer our prayers with what is good for us.

† Lord, give us wisdom and insight in responding daily to requests made of us.

For group discussion and personal thought
- How difficult is it to emulate the care and counsel exhibited in the readings?
- Is your care and counsel based on ulterior motives or genuine compassion?

Care and counsel   Christian Glasgow

Order now for 2013!

It may seem early, but the copies of *Words for Today 2013* and *Light for our Path 2013* are now available to order.

Order now:

- with your local IBRA Rep*
- in all good bookshops
- direct from IBRA

online: http://shop.christianeducation.org.uk/

email: sales@christianeducation.org.uk

phone: 0121 472 4242

post: using the order form at the back of this book

If ordering direct, postage is free of charge.

*If you purchase 6 copies or more, and you live in the UK, you can sign up as an IBRA Rep and claim the 10% IBRA Rep discount on all IBRA products. You will also receive a free poster and samples to help you share IBRA more easily with family, friends and others in your church. Contact staff at IBRA to sign up now!

A whole year's Bible reading notes for only *17p* a week!

Consider a legacy

Help us to continue our work of providing Bible study notes for use by Christians in the UK and throughout the world. The need is as great as it was when IBRA was founded in 1882 by Charles Waters as part of the work of the Sunday School Union.

Please leave a legacy to the International Bible Reading Association.

An easy-to-use leaflet has been prepared to help you provide a legacy. Please write or telephone (details below) and we will send you this leaflet – and answer any questions you might have about a legacy or other donations. Please help us to strengthen this and the next generation of Christians.

Thank you very much.

International Bible Reading Association
1020 Bristol Road
Selly Oak
Birmingham
B29 6LB
UK

Tel. 0121 472 4242
Fax 0121 472 7575

Readings in Mark

4 Who is this?

Notes based on the *New International Version* by

Elisa Gusmão

Elisa belonged to the Presbyterian and the Methodist Churches in Brazil, before moving to the UK with her Scottish husband in 1987. She then became a translator, while serving the URC as an Elder and lay preacher. Between them, Eric and Elisa have 11 grandchildren born in the UK, Switzerland, Canada, Mexico and Brazil.

Introduction

Unlike other New Testament books, aimed at a special audience, Mark presents the good news in a universal perspective. In stories taken from oral tradition, Jesus challenges established Jewish beliefs and practices, proclaiming his authority as the 'Son of Man', and shows his power by performing healing and nature miracles. The book ends with great evangelistic activity, hence encouraging the Christian to go and proclaim the gospel.

Sunday 8 July: *Mark 6:1-13*

Who acts with power and vision

Jesus is in his upland home town of Galilee, among people who have always known him and are amazed at his wisdom and power. Mary's son has grown into a prophet and miracle worker. Jesus is also amazed – at their lack of faith. After being rejected by the larger towns, he turns his attention to the villages. Today, companies employ expensive resources to advertise their goods. Through posters, radio, television, and the Internet, publicity reaches us inside our homes. Jesus employed a different approach.

> *These were his instructions: 'Take nothing for the journey except a staff – no bread, no bag, no money in your belts.'*

(verse 8)

Having good news to spread, Jesus too organised his intelligent evangelism campaign. Sent out two by two, his disciples received instructions on how to focus on their task, placing their trust in God alone. Their success was great then, and, as you are reading me now, it was also global and long lasting!

† Dear God, make me a helpful participant in the campaign Jesus started, by fully using the resources you give me, and always trusting you.

Monday 9 July

Mark 2:1-12

Who forgives sins

The truly amazing thing experienced by the crowd filling that house is not simply the cure of a paralytic, but the fact that one among them – 'that fellow Jesus' – has claimed to have the authority to forgive sins, something reserved to God alone according to the Law. I see this as the focus of today's story.

> But that you may know that the Son of Man has authority on earth to forgive sins . . . .' He said to the paralytic, 'I tell you, get up, take your mat and go home.' He got up, took his mat and walked out in full view of them all. This amazed everyone and they praised God, saying, 'We have never seen anything like this!'

(verses 10-12)

Jesus' authority emerges side by side with his redemptive mission. He came to bridge the gulf between God and humankind, the original sin behind our individual and collective battles, our illnesses, and death. For the Jews, sin could only be forgiven at the Temple, through offering sacrifices. Mark is showing us how Jesus changed this. By defeating sin, his own resurrected body becomes the temple in which sin is defeated. The human race is finally drawn near to God. Here is a Master for whom it is as ordinary to forgive our sins as to do inconceivable miracles.

† Jesus, my Lord and Saviour, thank you for the freedom you brought to my soul and my existence through your life, sacrifice, and resurrection. I accept your loving authority and power over all I am and possess. Forgive me for the times when I haven't been a faithful disciple to you, and give me the strength to be one.

Who is this?   Elisa Gusmão

Who is a friend of sinners

Today we have another picture of Jesus' ministry, this time at the house of a tax collector. In Jesus' times Palestine was occupied by the Romans, whose officials received all the taxation money, passed to them by agents of the imperial government. They were the tax collectors, who, together with Samaritans, prostitutes, and other outcasts, were despised and ostracised by the population.

> [T]he teachers of the law who were Pharisees . . . asked his disciples: 'Why does he eat with tax collectors and 'sinners'?' On hearing this, Jesus said to them, 'It is not the healthy who need a doctor, but the sick. I have not come to call the righteous, but sinners.'
>
> (part of verse 16, and verse 17)

Mark has helped everyone who sincerely wants to understand and see Jesus. His carefully collected stories bring us reassurance and hope, and show us a Master who behaves in an entirely different way from all the pious leaders of the time, perhaps even of today. Jesus makes no distinction between people, he even spends most of his time with the destitute, the outcast, and 'sinners' of all kinds. Reading these stories, we are encouraged to do the same.

† Jesus, my Master, I know that it is by using my feet, my hands, my voice, that you can act in the world today. Come, and use them in order to get close to those who are sick in their spirit or their body. Help me to be a good friend to them, as you were. Amen

Elisa Gusmão

Who is this?

Wednesday 11 July
Mark 3:20-30

Who is full of the Spirit

Then Jesus entered a house, and again a crowd gathered, so that he and his disciples were not even able to eat. When his family heard about this, they went to take charge of him, for they said, 'He is out of his mind.' And the teachers of the law who came down from Jerusalem said, 'He is possessed by Beelzebub! By the prince of demons he is driving out demons.'

(verses 20-22)

Jesus endured such accusations during his entire ministry, and even after his death. But this time, very important men had come from Jerusalem to verify the nature of his power. The extraordinary quality of Jesus' miracles made evident their supernatural origin. But as his teaching and attitude did not agree with those adopted by the teachers of the law, they concluded his power was satanic.

Using illustrations, Jesus gave them a threefold answer:

- It would be illogical if Satan were acting against himself, so their conclusion was wrong.

- He claimed to be stronger than Satan, because 'In fact, no one can enter a strong man's house and carry off his possessions unless he first ties up the strong man' (verse 27). He was also making clear that he had invaded an evil space to obtain a victory there.

- They were committing a grave irreverence by identifying the Holy Spirit in him as Beelzebub, or Satan. By doing this, they had simply placed themselves outside the kingdom.

---

† God's Spirit, conductor of nature's symphony, who teaches the nightingales to sing and filled Jesus Christ with power, and with faith the souls of those who accept him, guide and inspire my life too, I pray.

Who is this?   Elisa Gusmão

Thursday 12 July

Mark 4:35-41

Who calms the storm

This story is the first nature miracle told by Mark. In it, as in the Old Testament, the sea represents chaos and the storm demonic powers. Storms like this violent one pictured by Mark are common in the Sea of Galilee. Perhaps to imply that no human guidance is needed, Jesus sleeps peacefully on the cushion where usually the helmsman sits to drive the boat. The disciples are terrified and, at the same time, resent Jesus' apparent indifference to their anguish. Are they being punished, as happened to disobedient Jonah? But why, if the trip was taken under Jesus' orders?

> *The disciples woke him and said to him, 'Teacher, don't you care if we drown?'*
> *He got up, rebuked the wind and said to the waves, 'Quiet! Be still!'*
> *Then the wind died down and it was completely calm. He said to his disciples, 'Why are you so afraid? Do you still have no faith?' They were terrified and asked each other, 'Who is this? Even the wind and the waves obey him!'*

(part of verse 38, and verses 39-41)

Admitting that Jesus had calmed a storm with his voice, the disciples' question contains the answer in itself. As they knew well, only God has power over nature. Therefore Mark proceeds in his revelation to an even clearer image of Jesus: he is not only a man with power and vision, who forgives sinners and is their friend, and is full of the Spirit; Jesus is God.

† 'When you lie down, you will not be afraid; when you lie down, your sleep will be sweet. Have no fear of sudden disaster or of the ruin that overtakes the wicked, for the Lord will be your confidence and will keep your foot from being snared' (Proverbs 3:24-26).

Elisa Gusmão

Who is this?

Friday 13 July

Mark 6:44-52

Who is divine

Carrying on with nature miracles, today's story emphasises Jesus' divinity through several signs. After feeding five thousand men, much more than Elisha had done, he makes the tired disciples climb into the boat, staying alone to dismiss the crowd, then going to pray. The fact that he prays after one miracle, and before another, clearly points to the Father as the source of his power. In the dark night the boat is tossed by the waves and, visible against the moon's silvery reflection on the lake:

> *He saw the disciples straining at the oars, because the wind was against them . . . but when they saw him walking on the lake, they thought he was a ghost. They cried out, because they all saw him and were terrified. Immediately he spoke to them and said, 'Take courage! It is I. Don't be afraid.' Then he climbed into the boat with them, and the wind died down. They were completely amazed, for they had not understood about the loaves; their hearts were hardened.*

(part of verse 48, and verses 49-52)

Since he is divine, Jesus comes walking on water, like God in the book of Job, 'He alone stretches out the heavens and treads on the waves of the sea' (Job 9:8). To leave no doubt in their minds, Mark shows Jesus, their rescuer, identifying himself in the same way used by God when addressing Moses, 'I am who I am' (Exodus 3:14a), 'It is I' (verse 50).

† My Lord and Saviour, like the disciples' hearts, mine too is sometimes hardened, failing to acknowledge who you are. I know that, no matter how poor my cries of fear, you always come to my rescue. Son of God, give me the spiritual perception always to see and believe in you.

Who is this?   Elisa Gusmão

Saturday 14 July

Mark 11:27-33

Whom I accept by faith

This Galilean rabbi was definitely different from other teachers, for he taught with authority (Mark 1:22). We have also seen (last Thursday) how the disciples had admitted that his power came from God. But a group of the highest authorities in Judaism, already part of the plot against Jesus, refused to admit what was clear to anyone prepared to see.

'By what authority are you doing these things?' they asked. 'And who gave you authority to do this?' Jesus replied, 'I will ask you one question. Answer me, and I will tell you by what authority I am doing these things. John's baptism – was it from heaven, or from men? Tell me!'

(verses 28-30)

'These things' could have been his aggressive cleansing of the Temple, triumphal entry into Jerusalem, miracles, or teaching. It may seem as if Jesus is not answering them, but he is. By summoning up John the Baptist's name, he is saying that his authority comes from the same source as John's. These men knew well about the Baptist, and that he was considered a God-sent prophet by the people. With their 'we don't know', those authorities were unwilling to admit what Mark's story makes obvious: that Jesus' authority is divine. Instead of trapping Jesus, they were trapped in their refusal. Accepting Jesus as Christ was never a question of rational proof, but essentially a question of faith.

† Dear God, I pray for greater faith in Jesus, the Christ, who suffered to the end the consequences of sin, coming out victorious to redeem all your creation.

For group discussion and personal thought

- Comparing the three gospels, what, in your opinion, is Mark's greatest contribution in showing who Jesus is?
- Which other answers would you add to the question, 'Who is this...?'

Elisa Gusmão   Who is this?

Readings in Mark

5 He is . . .

Notes based on the *New International Version* by

Selina Samuel

Selina Samuel is from India. She is a housewife and a freelance editor.

Introduction

India is not just a country of many people, but of many gods too. And Jesus is accepted as one among 300,000 or more supernatural beings. God for many is a name you can cry out for help. In such a pluralistic society the question that Jesus once asked his disciples, 'Who do you say I am?' (Mark 8:29), is a central question of faith. This week our meditations are on this question. In the gospels people encountered him as a healer, provider, miracle worker, and teacher; but is that all he is?

Sunday 15 July: *Mark 6:14-29*
A ghost?

'John, the man I beheaded, has been raised from the dead!'

(part of verse 16)

Today's passage has Herod and some of the people identifying Jesus as John the Baptist. King Herod had put John to death. John was a fearless prophet, a man who spoke the truth, a holy and righteous person. Though Herod loved to hear John, he made a choice to ignore the demands this made on his character. He was more worried about his position and status. He feared people's opinion. So now when he heard of Jesus' miraculous actions he actually thought Jesus was John the Baptist come back to life, perhaps to haunt him for his evil deeds. What was true of Herod could be true of many others too. 'Everyone who does evil hates the light, and will not come into the light for fear that their deeds will be exposed' (John 3:20). People's conscious rejection of Jesus' message is a result of the lives that they live.

† Almighty God, please open my eyes, my ears and my heart to see Jesus, to acknowledge him as the Christ, the Messiah, the Son of God. Amen

Monday 16 July

Mark 8:27-33

The Christt?

Jesus and his disciples went on to the villages around Caesarea Philippi. On the way he asked them, 'Who do people say I am?'

(verse 27)

After much travelling, healing, feeding thousands, exorcism and teaching, Jesus and the disciples were now in the region of Caesarea Philippi. This was a place full of pagan religions and man-made gods, and it was known as a centre of Baal worship. Here also was the temple built by Herod the Great for Augustus Caesar. It is in this context that Jesus asked the disciples the question 'Who do you say I am?' That he asked this question in a city like Caesarea Philippi is important, because the context of a place is equally relevant for our times too. We are surrounded by man-made religions, self-appointed gurus and gods, church attendance as a traditional requirement, pursuit after wealth and lifestyles that have no place for anything else but self. It is in this context that we have to confess who we believe Jesus is. Peter very boldly answered 'You are the Christ, the Son of the living God' (verse 29). The most important question to them and to each of us is 'Who do you say I am?' Jesus' question is very personal and the answer to that determines our destiny, and the quality of life here on earth. No one else can believe on our behalf. And it is not enough to believe that Jesus is one of many gods. He is the only true God.

† Almighty God, thank you for opening my eyes to see, understand and confess today that Jesus is the Christ, the Son of the living God, and in him and only in him is there life everlasting. Amen

Selina Samuel

He is . . .

Mark 3:7-12

The Son of God?

Whenever the evil spirits saw him, they fell down before him and cried out, 'You are the Son of God.'

(verse 11)

The impact of Jesus' ministry was indeed spreading, and large crowds were coming to see him, to listen to him, to touch him, and to be healed by him (verse 10). People everywhere seemed to be talking about him. Jesus saw the large crowds but he did not get swayed by this kind of fame. He continued to heal, feed, drive out demons, and teach both the crowds and the disciples. He set his heart on obedience and never lost focus. All through his life Jesus was clear about his identity and his purpose, and about his relationship with God as his father. He did not even accept the acknowledgement of the evil spirits. He did not need them or their authentication of who he was. Instead, Jesus rebuked the demons and told them to keep quiet. Unlike the religious leaders of his day, who feared people's opinions and also loved their praise, Jesus did not need anyone's endorsement. He came to give life and he did it in his own way and on his terms and in total obedience to God the Father.

'Who is this Jesus?' He is the son of God, who came to reconcile us to God through his death. He is the one who, without wavering and 'for the joy that was set before Him endured the cross, despising the shame and is seated at the right hand of the throne of God' (Hebrews 12:2). He held onto his purpose, without yielding to the pressures of fame or shame.

† Help me, Lord, to know you and your purpose for my life. Help me to be focused. Amen

He is . . .

Selina Samuel

Mark 9:9-13

A prophet?

'Elijah does come first, and restores all things.'

(part of verse 12)

The disciples were asked not to talk about the transfiguration experience until after the resurrection, and they kept quiet. But imagine what the event must have done to them in terms of their faith in Jesus as the Messiah! It must have been very encouraging and the most assuring of revelations. This revelation provides an immediate answer to such questions as 'Who is this man that the wind and the waters obey him and the evil spirits shudder and run? Who is doing the healing, the miracles such as we have never seen before? Who is this?' The transfiguration is truly significant. It comes at a time when the disciples were beginning to realise that Jesus had to suffer and die, which was not the image of the Messiah they had expected. Who is this man? Is he greater than Elijah and Moses, the two leaders who stood for the law and the prophets? Jesus, they now realise, is the Son of God, greater than Elijah and Moses or the systems of law and prophecy that they had put in place. Is this Jesus only another prophet? The transfiguration gave a glimpse to them, and to us through them, of the truth of who Jesus is, a truth that is crucial to the way we live. If we accept him as the Son of God, we become the children of God (John 1:12).

† Heavenly Father, bring me to that moment in my life when I shall see Jesus for who he really is. Help me to understand how crucial that is for my faith. Amen

Mark 14:1-9

One to be worshipped?

'She has done a beautiful thing to me.'

(part of verse 6)

A disturbing sight in India is that of people with leprosy, begging on our streets. Leprosy is perceived as a dreaded disease and most people shun any contact with those affected. This was equally true in Jesus' time. But Jesus was different. He touched lepers and healed them. In today's passage we find Jesus in the home of Simon the Leper. Simon himself may have been healed of leprosy but the tag remained – the home of Simon the Leper. For Jesus, however, society's tags on people are irrelevant. He was God who came into the world to show us the love of God.

It was here in Simon's home that a woman broke a jar of pure nard and poured it over Jesus' head. The people in the room, including his disciples, were indignant and rebuked her for wasting money. They felt the money could have been used for charity, given to the poor. While acts of charity are important they cannot take the place of worship from a grateful heart. Jesus acknowledged the woman's act as a beautiful act of gratitude and worship. She understood correctly who Jesus was and it is this understanding that evoked in her heart this act of worship. He alone is worthy of our worship. Who is this Jesus? He is the one at whose name one day 'every knee will bow . . . and every tongue will confess that he is Lord' (Philippians 2:10-11). Worship is born out of gratitude.

In the mad rush of our everyday life, it is time we stop to do something that Jesus can describe as beautiful and is genuinely from a grateful heart. Let us do something beautiful for God today.

† Father in heaven, make me willing to will something beautiful for you today. Amen

He is . . .

Selina Samuel

Friday 20 July
Mark 6:30-44

The leader?

When Jesus landed and saw a large crowd, he had compassion on them, because they were like sheep without a shepherd. So he began teaching them many things.

(verse 34)

The biblical word 'compassion' in its original Greek means a movement of the heart from oneself to the other. Our heart takes upon itself the suffering of the other. The gospels record many instances of the compassion of Jesus. And his compassion in this passage is because he saw the people who came to him as sheep without a shepherd. God is often described in the Bible as the shepherd of his people. And God also expects the leaders to be the shepherds of the people. But as it is today, in Jesus' time too there was a crisis – a crisis of leadership.

In Jesus, however, we have the ideal leader: the one who cared. He cared enough for the disciples to take them away from the crowds for rest after busy days of ministry. He cared enough for the crowds who came seeking him, and taught them the truth of God. He cared enough for the hungry, and fed them until they were satisfied. He cared enough for the disciples, and taught them the importance of saving what was left over.

Who is this Jesus? He is the good shepherd who lays down his life for his sheep. Jesus was the leader who set aside his own interest for the interests of others. His miracles were signs that bore witness to the truth that he was sent by God. And that is how it is even today. He works in our lives: he answers prayers, heals, guides and comforts. And all these point to the truth of his identity. Who do you say he is?

† Lord, even as I enjoy the miracles and answered prayers, help me to acknowledge and worship you. Help me to be compassionate. Thank you. Amen

Selina Samuel

He is . . .

The risen one?

'You are looking for Jesus the Nazarene, who was crucified. He has risen! He is not here.'

(verse 16)

Who do you see in Jesus of Nazareth? The one who was crucified? A good man killed unjustly by the rulers of his time? Jesus the martyr who died for a good cause, or Jesus the revolutionary – the inspiration for activists through the centuries? That seems to be the way Jesus' followers saw him when they watched him die on the cross.

Resurrection, however, changed their perception. Even though Jesus had told his followers often about his resurrection, when it actually happened the women 'trembled', were 'bewildered', 'fled' and 'were afraid' (verse 8). Jesus' resurrection was the revelation that he was the Son of God (Romans 1:4). Soon his followers knew for sure that Jesus was not just a good man, another prophet or revolutionary. He was, is and will be the God who became man. What you believe about the resurrection of Jesus is what you actually believe about him.

† May the truth of Jesus' resurrection change our understanding of you, O God. Amen

For group discussion and personal thought

- If you were asked 'What is unique about Jesus?', what would be your response?
- If Jesus did not rise from the dead, what difference would it make to your understanding of him?
- What one change could you make in your life in order to make it a more consistent expression of your gratitude to God?

He is . . .

Selina Samuel

Not to the swift

1   Running with an attitude

Notes based on *Today's New International Version* by

Chris Duffett

Chris Duffett is President of The Baptist Union of Great Britain. He is an evangelist and founder of The Light Project, a charity that aims to actively demonstrate the Christian message in a relevant way and to train others in evangelism (www.lightproject.org.uk).

Introduction

I ran the London Marathon last year. It hurt. I absolutely hated it. I also loved it so much that I want to run another one! There was the pain of running 26.2 miles – but also the loud cheers of the huge crowds. As this week's readings show, there is great joy in being a Christian, yet running the race hurts badly. To 'keep on keeping on' we need encouragement and support from past heroes of the faith and fellow athletes.

Sunday 22 July: *Hebrews 12:1, 12-13*

A constant barrage of cheers

According to Hebrews, all those who have gone before us – from well-known heroes of the faith to unknown followers of Christ – are eavesdropping and looking on at everything we do!

> *Therefore, since we are surrounded by such a great cloud of witnesses, let us throw off everything that hinders and the sin that so easily entangles. And let us run with perseverance the race marked out for us.*
>
> (verse 1)

We are not alone in our struggles and joys as we run as Christ's followers. There are people who have 'gone before us', who have faced unimaginable trials and hardships for their faith. They paid for our freedom. I often read biographies of past heroes of faith, such as Richard Wurmbrand's *Tortured for Christ*; they had to endure so much more than I ever have, and as I read I feel strengthened, as if I am being cheered on.

† Father God, I commit myself to the race of being a Christ follower, to become more like him every day. Help me to follow the example of those who have gone before me, to dedicate my whole life to you. In Jesus' name, Amen

Monday 23 July

Hebrews 12:2-4

Run in his footsteps

Today's reading reminds us that Jesus has gone before us and the best way to run is in his slipstream. We need to look up and fix our eyes on Jesus, 'the pioneer and perfecter of our faith' (Hebrews 12.2). I love the way Hebrews reveals a secret that is especially for us when we are worn out and our hearts are tired:

> For the joy set before him he endured the cross, scorning its shame, and sat down at the right hand of the throne of God. Consider him who endured such opposition from sinners, so that you will not grow weary and lose heart.

(part of verse 2, and verse 3)

Are you tired of being a Christian, or having a hard time for your faith? Consider Jesus, the one who endured the cross. Easier to say than put into practice! Last week I was in the centre of Glasgow with a team of Christians, teaching them about evangelism. They watched me as I held up a sign saying 'Free Hug'. I frequently do this as an expression of the love of God. Often, as people receive a hug they ask why I'm giving them out, and I say things like 'God loves you so much' or 'God has embraced the world through giving Jesus and I want to show that.' However, after five minutes of offering lots of hugs in Glasgow, a young man came up and spat at me and then swore. Because the trainees were watching, I pretended everything was just fine, but afterwards the spitting young man and what he had said to me really shook me up. It was only through taking time to consider what Jesus went through for my sins and fixing my gaze on him that my 'suffering' was put into perspective and I was able to move on.

† Jesus, today may I walk in your slipstream.
  Jesus, today may I run in your presence.
  Jesus, today may I consider what you went through for me. Amen

---

Running with an attitude

Chris Duffett

Tuesday 24 July

1 Timothy 6:1-6

Don't get sidetracked

Paul wrote to Timothy in a very different context to ours: for example, he commended slaves to work harder for their believing 'masters'. Yet this passage includes a gem of teaching that I wish many of the churches I have worked with would heed. If they did they would be at a much happier place! The need in many gatherings of Christians is to pay attention to Jesus and not get diverted. Paul says of those who are unfocused:

> *They have an unhealthy interest in controversies and quarrels about words that result in envy, strife, malicious talk, evil suspicions and constant friction between people of corrupt mind, who have been robbed of the truth and who think that godliness is a means to financial gain.*

(part of verse 4, and verse 5)

July

Do you think this is a rather harsh critique of the church today? Have you ever observed Christians in friction, or been part of it yourself? It's not nice. I saw an example of this kind of ugly behaviour last month when I was asked to preach at a local Baptist church. When I arrived I found a hurting congregation. They had recently fallen out with their pastor, who then decided to fall out with his flock and left under a bit of a cloud. So the service I had been invited to was rather uncomfortable, until someone stood up and said 'We need to stop arguing about who is right and who is wrong. As we bicker amongst ourselves there is an unreached community out there!' I liked this sentiment, and while that church was an extreme example of the pickle we can get into with one another, we really need to keep our eyes focused on him who says, 'Go! And, by the way, I am with you as you go!'

† Jesus, I want to be a follower who brings 'good news', who focuses on you and your heart for a fallen world. Not fussed with arguments and quarrels, but concentrating on being your hands and feet in this broken world. Help me to get on with the job in hand and reach this world for you! Amen

Chris Duffett   Running with an attitude

Wednesday 25 July
Isaiah 40:20-31

Get up and soar!

Once upon a time a mischievous boy took an egg from a nest at the top of an old tree and placed it under a broody hen on his uncle's chicken farm! The egg hatched and the baby bird was accepted as part of the flock. One day the young bird noticed different kinds of birds flying very high in the sky, soaring on the thermals. She asked, 'Why don't we ever do that?' 'We're chickens, we weren't made for flying at such great heights, we scrabble and scratch down here, come on, let's look for worms!' Later that day a majestic bird landed near the chicken farm and was transfixed by the young bird scrabbling around in the mud. He asked her what she was doing living on a chicken farm. The young bird replied, 'Well, it's obvious, I'm a chicken!' The majestic bird told her 'You aren't a chicken, you're an eagle!' The young bird looked up and asked whether she too could fly. 'Yes indeed!' replied the majestic bird. The chickens gathered around as the young bird unfolded her wings and began to flap. As she took flight, the chickens shouted at her, 'Hey! What are you doing? Get down! Where do you think you're going?' The young bird answered, 'I'd rather soar with the eagles than flap around on the ground with you chickens!'

Even youths grow tired and weary,
and young men stumble and fall;
but those who hope in the LORD
will renew their strength.
They will soar on wings like eagles;
they will run and not grow weary,
they will walk and not be faint.

(verses 30-31)

† The old has gone and the new is here! You make me soar on wings like eagles. I am so grateful. Amen

Running with an attitude   Chris Duffett

Thursday 26 July
2 Timothy 1:1-7

Tools for training

As I write it is –7 degrees outside and thick snow covers much of the United Kingdom! Therefore I am sitting at the best place in the house – right next to a roaring fire. The fire is dancing around in the hearth doing a lovely job of keeping me very warm. Yet to get it to this roaring stage I actually got very 'light headed' as I blew and blew on it and coaxed the embers to light the wood and coal. Paul writes to Timothy that this is what we should do to the gifts God has placed in us:

> I remind you to fan into flame the gift of God, which is in you through the laying on of my hands. For the Spirit God gave us does not make us timid, but gives us power, love and self-discipline.
>
> (part of verse 6, and verse 7)

People often quote bits of this text – the bits they like! Many of us are happy to have the gift of power, but reluctant to receive love and self-discipline. Yet Paul isn't offering us a choice but listing three vital ingredients for living a close relationship with God. Please spend some time meditating on these wonderful gifts that we must fan into flame.

† Father, show me where I need more of your power in my life; show me where I lack love for my family and friends; and help me where I lack discipline. Then I shall become more like Jesus, your love will overflow to others, and I shall be able to accomplish the good intentions that I can't get done.

Chris Duffett

Running with an attitude

July

Friday 27 July

Ecclesiastes 9:11-18

Jesus' rules are very different

The race is not to the swift
or the battle to the strong,
nor does food come to the wise
or wealth to the brilliant
or favour to the learned;
but time and chance happen to them all.

(part of verse 11)

This wisdom from Solomon seems topsy-turvy. Whoever heard of a slow sprinter, a weak wrestler or a feeble boxer? Yet this out-of-the-ordinary order sits well amongst other upside-down biblical teaching such as who gets first place in the kingdom (Matthew 23:11-12), who is blessed (Matthew 5:1-12) and what it means to be made strong (2 Corinthians 12:9). My prayer today is for those of us who feel weak and unable. May we find strength to keep on going, knowing that it is 'not by might, nor by power, but by my Spirit says the Lord' (Zechariah 4:6). May we receive the truth that while we may not be swift, we can still win the race!

---

† Emmanuel, you came to this world and turned things upside down. You made foolish things wise and weak things strong. Emmanuel, you are God with me in my circumstances and you know the ebb and flow of my seasons. Emmanuel, you humbly journey with me, and scoop me up when I am unable to carry on. Emmanuel, let me know your beautiful presence. Amen

Running with an attitude   Chris Duffett

Saturday 28 July
Psalm 19

A prayer for the Olympics

I am so excited! Today is the start of the biggest ever sporting event! The world is watching as the United Kingdom hosts the Olympics and Para-Olympics this summer. Today we can use the reading as a prayer for the millions of people world-wide involved in the 2012 Olympics. In particular we will pray for the awesome opportunity the church has to herald the good news of Jesus! As you meditate on Psalm 19, pray for the Olympics this summer.

The fear of the LORD is pure,
enduring forever.
The ordinances of the LORD are sure,
and all of them are righteous.
They are more precious than gold,
than much pure gold;
they are sweeter than honey,
than honey from the honeycomb.

(part of verse 9, and verse 10)

† Pray for much-needed purity over the Olympic time, that the Lord will put a stop to any sexual exploitation, forced labour and other forms of abuse. Gold is the goal of the athletes: pray that they and their families may find something much more precious over this time. And pray for the church in the UK and the many initiatives of 'More Than Gold', the umbrella organisation in which many thousands of Christians are serving (www.morethangold.org.uk). Amen

For group discussion and personal thought
• Which sport do you think best describes your Christian walk?
• In what ways are Jesus' rules very different to those of the world?
• In what way can you let someone who isn't a follower of Jesus know something of the gospel this Olympic season?

Chris Duffett   Running with an attitude

Not to the swift

2   Live the ongoing race

Notes based on the *Contemporary English Version* by

Elizabeth Bruce Whitehorn

In her working life, Elizabeth Bruce Whitehorn was a school teacher, adult educator and editor. Now retired and living in Cambridge, UK, she is a voluntary tutor for the University of the Third Age, sings in a choir and is an active member of her local United Reformed Church.

Introduction

In this first full week of the Olympic Games, people all around the world will be following the performances of their sportsmen and women. Thanks to modern technology, it is possible to be 'armchair spectators', following developments from afar. According to this week's Bible passages, however, there is no room for 'armchair spectators' in the Christian life. Faith demands total involvement and commitment. We are called to 'live the ongoing race': to enter fully into what God calls us to do.

Sunday 29 July: *2 Timothy 2:1-5*
Be a good team member

> *You have often heard me teach. Now I want you to tell these same things to followers who can be trusted to tell others.*

(verse 2)

Paul's words make me think of Christians as runners in a relay race. Each runner is responsible for receiving and passing on the baton according to the rules. The smallest mistake can cause the whole team to lose the race or be disqualified. Paul reminds Timothy that he is responsible for passing on what he has learned. Since then, countless people have shared their faith and now the baton has been passed to us. The health and well-being of the church, both now and in the future, depend on each of us, whether we are 'ordinary' members or prominent leaders.

What does it mean for me to be part of such a team?

† God of the past, thank you for the people who helped me believe in you. God of the present and the future, help me to be a responsible member of your team today and every day.

Monday 30 July

Philippians 3:7, 10-12

Keep on running

I have not yet reached my goal, and I am not perfect. But Christ has taken hold of me. So I keep on running and struggling to take hold of the prize.

(verse 12)

These words make me think of a marathon runner struggling to keep going. Whatever natural advantages he began with, they count for nothing. He may have earned a wonderful reputation previously, but now it is a question of effort and endurance in this particular event. In ancient Greece, athletes literally stripped for action; they laid everything aside and performed naked so that nothing would prevent them doing their best. Similarly, Paul has realised that all his advantages of birth and upbringing (verses 5-6) are of no value to him in his relationship with Christ (verse 7). Sometimes God asks us to set aside things which are not wrong in themselves but are keeping us from fulfilling our calling. For example, we may be hampered by our attitude to material things, whether we have too much or too little.

In spite of Paul's many missionary achievements, he was very aware of his shortcomings and his need of Jesus' help to keep going to the end. His passionate desire to know Christ (verse 10) inspired him to keep on running even in the hardest times. How much more do we need to be 'taken hold of' by Christ so that we can keep going to the finishing line, however near or far it may be.

What might be preventing me from doing my best?

What changes might God be asking me to make in my life?

† All-knowing God, you know me better than I know myself. You know what holds me back. Please set me free and help me to keep on to the end of what you want me to do.

Elizabeth Whitehorn   Live the ongoing race

Tuesday 31 July

Acts 20:17-21

Stay focused

Some of the Jews plotted against me and caused me a lot of sorrow and trouble. But I served the Lord and was humble ... I told Jews and Gentiles to turn to God and have faith in our Lord Jesus.

(verses 19 and 21)

As Paul looked back on his time in Ephesus, he could claim that he had remained focused on serving the Lord regardless of obstacles and opposition. For athletes taking part in a hurdles race, the important thing is to keep going, even if they knock some hurdles over. Runners need to focus on the race; they won't win if they allow themselves to be distracted by what is going on around them. Major sporting events can be overshadowed by scandals relating to drugs, match-fixing or betting scams. Sometimes the pressure to win or the lure of money is such that people try to take shortcuts to fame and success.

Paul had such a strong desire to share his faith with the people of Ephesus, and many other places too, that he kept going in spite of problems and opposition. He continued to preach his simple but uncompromising message: 'turn to God and have faith in our Lord Jesus'. Our lives too can be full of obstacles, hurdles and temptations – or are they opportunities to allow God to work in us and through us? To use a different metaphor, with God's help stumbling blocks can become stepping stones.

How would I sum up my Christian service so far?

What do I particularly need God's help with at the moment?

† All-powerful God, I offer you the stumbling blocks in front of me just now. Please turn them into stepping stones and help me to stay focused on serving you humbly and with perseverance.

Live the ongoing race   Elizabeth Whitehorn

Acts 20:31-35

Remember your training

I now place you in God's care. Remember the message about his great kindness! This message can help you and give you what belongs to you as God's people.

(verse 32)

Even if people have many natural advantages (body shape, physical strength, mental attitude and so on), they need good training in order to make the most of their talent. In Britain, several years before these Olympic Games, young people were sought who could be trained to compete, even if they were currently involved in a different sport. For example, a young basketball player was selected to train as a rower because he had a suitable physique. It did not matter that he had never rowed before. Good sportsmen and women also need self-discipline to train regularly. Even the best coach can only take them so far.

In faith as well as in other areas of life, we can easily forget the basic training or teaching we received in the past. Rather than valuing and building on what we have been taught, we may think that it is no longer relevant. We may, for example, wonder whether the Bible has anything new to say to us after years of reading it and hearing sermons based on it – all the more reason to spend time reflecting on it, asking God to speak to us afresh. In verse 35 Paul seems to be suggesting that he taught by example, that he was a role model for the church leaders from Ephesus.

Who is your role model? Why?

How can you be a better example for others?

† Loving God, thank you for those who have been good teachers and trainers in my life. Please help me to build on their good work and also to be a good role model for others.

Thursday 2 August

2 Timothy 4:1-8

Run to win

[The Lord] judges fairly, and on the day of judgement he will give a crown to me and to everyone else who wants him to appear with power.

(part of verse 8)

Paul is in prison (2 Timothy 2:9) and knows he is nearing the end of his life. He does not fear the Lord's judgement but is looking forward to being rewarded for his faithfulness. The day of judgement has inspired artists and sculptors through the ages to produce grisly scenes of the wicked being punished while the good are welcomed into God's presence.

What sort of crown might Paul be thinking of? In the ancient Olympic Games, the winners were at first given valuable prizes. By Paul's time, however, the winner's prize ('crown') was a wreath of olive or laurel leaves to wear on his head. In Cambridge there are annual rowing races, known as 'the Bumps', in which the crew members of a boat which has caught up with ('bumped') the boat in front wear twigs of willow. On the other hand, a crown can be a sign of authority and responsibility for others, as when a monarch is crowned. Queen Elizabeth II is renowned for taking her responsibility seriously.

Paul instructs Timothy to work hard and well, as he himself has done, in spite of opposition and suffering. Nearly two thousand years on, would his message to us be any different?

How do I view the end of my life?

In what ways can I prepare to meet the Lord?

† God of love and of judgement, I confess that I deserve your judgement rather than your love. Please forgive me and help me to run the race that is my life in ways that express my love for you and bring you honour.

Live the ongoing race   Elizabeth Whitehorn

1 Corinthians 9:24-27

Finish well

I keep my body under control and make it my slave, so I won't lose out after telling the good news to others.

(verse 27)

The motto of the modern Olympic Games is 'Citius, Altius, Fortius' – 'Faster, Higher, Stronger'. It could be said that this is also the motto of humanity in general. Many amazing and invaluable discoveries and inventions have come about because of people's ongoing quest to go further and do better.

In Paul's time, Corinth was famous for its Isthmian Games, second only to the Olympic Games. It is quite possible that Paul attended the games when he was visiting the early church in Corinth. He may well have preached the gospel to the crowds of spectators and to the athletes. So it is appropriate that Paul used sporting metaphors when writing to the Corinthian Christians. Although he knew he had worked hard and served God well, he also knew he could not lessen his efforts; lack of self-control and self-discipline could still cause him to lose everything. Some parts of the news media love to point the finger at well-known figures (sportsmen, preachers and politicians, for example) who are discovered to be less than honest and upright. We all know it is easier to tell others how to live than to do it oneself; 'practise what you preach', we say. Self-discipline and personal integrity should both be key elements of our Christian life and character, as they were of Paul's.

Does my life match my words?

In which areas of my life do I need better self-discipline?

† Loving God, I need your help to . . . Please make me more Christ-like and help me to represent you better in the world.

Elizabeth Whitehorn   Live the ongoing race

Saturday 4 August

Acts 20:36-37

Hand on the baton

After Paul had finished speaking, he knelt down with all of them and prayed.

(verse 36)

I wonder what Paul prayed about. Did he ask for courage to face what lay ahead of him? Did he pray for the church elders who were there with him? If I had been in his position, I might well have been too upset to pray aloud at all. Luke makes it sound as though Paul was in full command of himself and of the situation. Nevertheless, Paul is effectively handing on the baton to these people; the church in Ephesus is now their responsibility.

In church life, it can be difficult to know when to stop doing a particular task and entrust it to other people. It can be hard to leave it to them, especially if they approach it differently. We need to trust that God knows and is guiding them.

Is there anything God is prompting me to hand on to others?

Is there anything I need to allow others to hand on to me?

† God of succeeding generations, help me to recognise when it is time for me to hand a task over to others, and enable me to do it graciously and lovingly.

For group discussion and personal thought
- Look back at each day's question(s) and consider them again carefully and prayerfully.
- What has comforted/encouraged/challenged you in this week's readings and notes and in your own reflections?
- What action(s) is God prompting you to take, individually and as a group?

Live the ongoing race   Elizabeth Whitehorn

Missing the mark

1 Prophets, kings and judges

Notes based on the *New International Version* by

John Birch

John Birch is a Methodist lay preacher and worship leader based in south-west Wales. With a keen interest in Celtic spirituality, in his spare time he writes prayers, articles and church resources and hosts www.faithandworship.com, a prayer resource.

Introduction

In his letter to the Roman church Paul reminds us that all have sinned and fallen short of God's glory. The word he uses for 'sin' has a meaning of missing the mark, as in the sport of archery. I find the word 'all' quite reassuring. It means that in the Christian journey there is a level playing field on which we're all equally capable of falling short, all subject to distractions that can mess up our aim. This week we're going to meet a few biblical characters who did just that!

Sunday 5 August: *Romans 3:21-26*

Messing up

The former Bishop of Durham, Dr Tom Wright, commenting on today's society said, 'We have grossly underestimated the way in which human beings can still mess things up.' Scripture reminds us that humankind has struggled with this problem since the dawn of time. The Old Testament is full of examples of people falling short, being tempted and turning their back on God. Did all this 'messing up' stop as the New Testament began? Of course not, because Paul reminds us that we are all capable of failing to be the people we could be. We all miss the mark now and then.

[F]or all have sinned and fall short of the glory of God.

(verse 23)

Paul's words may be uncomfortable ones for today. People don't like to admit their mistakes. Fortunately, Paul also reminds us that God's forgiving love is bigger than our faults, and his hand steadies our aim.

† Lord God, I come to you as I am: knowing that you love me; knowing that you want the best for me; knowing that you accept me as I am. Accept the confession of my heart and transform me daily, that I may be a blessing to you and others. Amen

Monday 6 August

Exodus 32:1-6, 18-24

Digging a hole

If you've ever made a mistake and tried to explain it away, or even blame someone else, then you are probably familiar with the concept of digging a hole. The harder you try and extricate yourself from the situation, the more complicated it gets and the deeper the hole you find yourself in! You're in good company because Aaron had that problem. This is Aaron the brother of Moses, called by God, founder of one of the priestly tribes, now digging a very big hole. His brother is away doing business with God on Mount Sinai, and the people are complaining day and night. They've had enough of their God, and want a different one who will go before them. They persuade Aaron to melt their jewellery down and create a golden image that they can worship. So what happens when Moses comes back and sees what has happened? Does Aaron apologise? No, he blames everyone but himself!

'You know how prone these people are to evil.

(part of verse 22)

Then he explains away his actions by telling Moses that all he did was throw the gold into the fire and a golden calf just happened to pop out! There really was no way out of that hole. But all it did was prove the truth of Paul's words that there really is a level playing field when it comes to falling short of God's standard.

Did Aaron agree with the people as they complained against God, or was he just trying to be popular? We're not told, but now and then life presents us with the temptation to do something which seems oddly out of character, and which we know deep within our heart is wrong. How we respond to that temptation says a lot about our relationship with God.

† Loving God, you have richly blessed our lives and yet so often we repay your love by messing up. Keep us close; enfold us in your arms and protect us from all that would separate us from your love. Amen

Prophets, kings and judges

John Birch

Tuesday 7 August

Numbers 20:1-13

A momentary lapse

Decisions made on the spur of the moment often have long-term implications, some bad, others good. In Alabama in 1955, on the spur of the moment, Rosa Parks, the African-American civil rights activist, refused to obey a bus driver and give up her seat for a white passenger in 1955. There was a cost – she lost her job – but this act of defiance became an important symbol for the modern Civil Rights movement and her name lives on in history books.

In today's reading the people of Israel are complaining bitterly because there is no water in the desert. Moses and Aaron bear the brunt of the people's anger. They turn to prayer and find that God is perfectly willing to supply his people's needs. God tells Moses to take his staff and simply speak to the rocks, from which water will pour out. What a demonstration of God's glory that would be! What does Moses do? He shouts at the people in anger and frustration, and slams the staff down onto the rock, twice. Water comes pouring out, but who do the people think did this, God or Moses? And because of Moses' momentary lack of composure, letting his anger and frustration boil over, God tells him and Aaron that they won't be allowed to bring the people into the Promised Land:

'Because you did not trust in me enough to honour me as holy in the sight of the Israelites.'

(part of verse 12)

God saw within that action of Moses a lack of faith. He had been given a simple task but by allowing his emotions to get the better of him, he let himself rather than God become the centre of attention. Can you remember occasions when you suffered the consequences of decisions made on the spur of the moment?

† Lord, give us wisdom and courage to make the right choices, particularly when decisions affect not only our own lives but those of others. Give us also the humility to admit our mistakes. Amen

John Birch   Prophets, kings and judges

Wednesday 8 August

Judges 16:4-22

A moment of weakness

I would imagine all children who go to Sunday school know something of the story of Samson, but probably just the exciting parts! Although chosen by God before his birth to deliver Israel from the Philistines, Samson's wasn't a perfect life by any means. Among his less desirable qualities Samson was demanding of his parents, left his first wife, went with prostitutes and seems to have had a poor choice in girlfriends.

When Delilah saw that he had told her everything, she sent word to the rulers of the Philistines.

(part of verse 18)

The Bible is full of real people with real faults. If it were populated by impossibly good characters with shiny halos then there would be something wrong. God deals with ordinary people like you and me, people with faults who experience real moments of weakness. But that doesn't mean that God cannot or will not use us. Far from it! What it means is that through using us, God starts to build us into the people he wants us to be. Samson tells us that God accepts us for who we are, and that is the way we should look at our own lives. When Sir Peter Lely was commissioned to paint a portrait of Oliver Cromwell, his instinct was to show off his subject as handsome and perfect in appearance, which was the custom of the day and I guess still is with magazine photo shoots. Cromwell is reported to have told him to paint 'The whole thing; not concealing the less attractive parts.' Samson knew what his strengths were, and where his vulnerability lay, but allowed his weakness for a pretty face to be his undoing. How many of us can honestly say that we have never succumbed to a moment of weakness?

† Lord, you accept us for who we are. Help us to do the same, accepting that we are not perfect and that we are prone to moments of weakness. But that does not mean that you love us any less. Take us, just as we are, and use us to the glory of your kingdom here on earth. Amen

Prophets, kings and judges

John Birch

Thursday 9 August

1 Kings 11:1-13

The slippery slope

Newspapers are full of politicians, TV and sports stars ruining their lives by deliberately breaking the law, or deceiving a partner, while on the surface apparently leading a normal life. They get away with it for a while, but then a reporter gets wind of a scandal and within hours the whole world seems to know. These are people who seem to have everything: big house, expensive car, beautiful wife, more money that they know what to do with. Yet they still seem to want more.

We read that Solomon was greater in riches and wealth than any other king on earth. He was also someone revered for his wisdom – 'the wisdom of Solomon' was and still is used to describe someone who has great discernment. So what made this rich, wise old man turn his back on God who had so richly blessed him? What made him take hundreds of wives from other nations and allow himself to be led astray and worship other gods, to step onto the slippery slope to his eventual downfall?

The Lord became angry with Solomon because his heart had turned away from the Lord, the God of Israel, who had appeared to him twice.

(verse 9)

Could it simply be that he had so much, but failed to appreciate its true value? Many will gamble hard-earned money this week on a lottery that might bring untold riches into their lives; and yet we keep hearing stories of how such riches have ruined lives and relationships. Could there be more to life than riches, fame and wisdom? I think there is! Real happiness comes in being content with what we have and in the strength of our relationships, both human and divine.

† Lord, I pray for those who seem to have so much, and yet in reality have so little. Help me appreciate the blessings of this life: friends, family, food to eat, and remember to thank you daily for all that you provide.

John Birch   Prophets, kings and judges

Friday 10 August

1 Kings 14:1-18

Responsibility

In the 2002 film *Spiderman* the main character, Peter Parker, reflecting on his other life as Spiderman, says 'Whatever life holds in store for me, I will never forget these words: "With great power comes great responsibility." This is my gift, my curse.' Jeroboam seemed to have had his eye on the top job for a while, but it was as a result of Solomon's sin and subsequent downfall that God eventually chose him to be king. It was God's will that Jeroboam should follow him faithfully and do what was right for the people under his care. In return he and his descendants would be blessed. But Jeroboam's enduring legacy was to be known as the man 'who made Israel to sin' and he eventually felt the wrath of God.

'You have done more evil than all who lived before you.'

(part of verse 9)

There is a great truth in those words of Spiderman. If we are given a position of authority, then we must accept that with power comes great responsibility. There is a duty of care to those who work for us or who are dependent upon us. We look up to those in authority and expect a high standard of behaviour and morals. How often do we hear a country's citizens complain there is corruption within their government, trust has been broken and respect for those in authority has evaporated? We might not be asked to lead our country, but the call may come to serve God in a particular place, as it did to Jeroboam. How we do that affects not only our own lives but those of others with whom we come into contact. It is a responsibility not to be taken lightly.

† Lord, may we follow you more closely every day, and as you lead us to new places and opportunities may we be a blessing both to you and to others, through our words and our actions. Amen

Prophets, kings and judges

John Birch

Saturday 11 August

Jonah 3:1-5, 10 – 4:11

Missing the point

Jonah was a most reluctant prophet. Told to go to Nineveh he catches a boat in the opposite direction. Thrown overboard in a storm to save the lives of the other sailors, he ends up where God wanted him in the first place. But even after delivering God's judgement to the population of Nineveh and seeing them repent and be forgiven, he is not a happy man. The people did exactly what God was hoping they would do, and he was happy to forgive and bless them. Jonah meanwhile had other plans for God.

> But the Lord replied, 'Have you any right to be angry?'

(verse 4)

One of my problems is short-sightedness. Without my glasses I cannot see very far. I have a similar problem with God. In my mind I have sketched out a future which I try and convince myself is God's plan. If tomorrow doesn't turn out as I feel it ought to, I feel justified in registering a complaint. But of course I've missed the point, just like Jonah. 'Your will be done' is what Jesus taught his disciples to pray, not 'My will be done!'

† Lord, may it be always your will that is done in my life and in the lives of those around me. Amen

For group discussion and personal thought

- How would you define 'sin' to a group of people both inside and outside the church in your neighbourhood? Is there one definition that would be readily understood by both?
- What can we do to avoid those moments of weakness when we let ourselves and God down?
- How important is it to share the difficulties that Christians often face in the daily journey of faith, when telling others of the joys of the gospel message?

August

John Birch

Prophets, kings and judges

Missing the mark

2 Disciples and congregations

Notes based on the *New International Version* by

Martin Hayward

Martin Hayward works within the Reconciliation Ministry Team at Coventry Cathedral. He also ministers to the parish of St Francis in the north of the city and has been a sitting as a magistrate for longer than he cares to remember.

Introduction

In his letter to the Roman church Paul reminds us that all have sinned and fallen short of God's glory. The word he uses for 'sin' has a meaning of missing the mark, as in the sport of archery. We are all subject to temptations and distractions which can mess up our aim; we all need God's help to keep us on target.

Sunday 12 August: *Matthew 26:47-56*
Jesus arrested

Then all the disciples deserted him and fled.

(part of verse 56)

August

Matthew's cameo of Jesus' arrest highlights at least three different sorts of sin. Judas is marked down in history because his sin was premeditated and deliberate, committed in collusion with others and for financial gain – all indicators that make a British court treat an offence as being of greater seriousness. For the man who chopped off the servant's ear, however, there is some mitigation: it was a reflex action made in defence of his friend and teacher. 'I tell you, whoever publicly acknowledges me before others, the Son of Man will also acknowledge before the angels of God. But whoever disowns me before others will be disowned before the angels of God' (Luke 12:8-9).

But what about the disciples running away? Was this, too, a reflex action? Being known as a follower of Jesus had suddenly become personally dangerous and so the disciples deserted him and fled. Any one of us might have done the same, but what mitigation can you find?

† Lord, thank you for your faithfulness to us in all circumstances. Please help us to remain faithful to you in our witness to the world.

Monday 13 August
Luke 22:54-62

Running before we can walk

As Jesus was being arrested he asked the soldiers to let the others go free (John 18:8-9), which was a clear signal to the disciples that they should not follow him. In spite of this, Peter followed the soldiers and their prisoner to the house of the high priest. No doubt his motivations were excellent: he wanted to support the Master whom he loved so much. His mistake was to allow his loyalty to cloud his judgement and lead him into more trouble than he could cope with. Peter's first sin was his disobedience which led him to the place of denial.

How often do we jump the gun and make false starts? We often struggle and wonder why God delays: he doesn't always answer prayer the moment we ask, he sometimes allows us to fail exams or interviews that we are so sure form part of his plan for our lives. With the wisdom of hindsight, however, we can often look back on events and understand why God's timing was so much better than ours would have been.

'God is faithful; he will not let you be tempted beyond what you can bear' (1 Corinthians 10:13). The disciples had been taught by Jesus to pray 'Lead us not into temptation'. Perhaps the cockerel's insistent crowing reminded Peter that not only had he sinned by denying his Lord three times, but that it would have been avoided had he listened and obeyed the Master earlier in the evening.

[H]e went outside and wept bitterly.

(verse 62)

---

† Heavenly Father, please help us to listen to your voice and to obey you in order that we may not be led into temptation.

Martin Hayward

Disciples and congregations

Tuesday 14 August

John 21:15-19

Allowing our emotions to show

Poor Peter! A few days earlier he had denied knowing Jesus. Not just once but three times. And now Jesus brings him back into his kingdom by asking him that probing question not just once but three times:

'Simon son of John, do you truly love me more than these?'

(part of verse 15)

Peter felt hurt that Jesus didn't take him at his word the first time, but this public questioning of his faith led to him being publicly restored by the risen Jesus into a vital leadership role in the church.

The other disciples had failed Jesus, too. They had fallen asleep in the Garden of Gethsemane during his hour of anguish, and many of them had even failed to support him with their presence at his crucifixion. Being human, they may have minimised the problems on their own consciences by pointing their fingers at Peter for his more public failure. But now they saw his repentance and they saw Jesus restoring him back to full apostleship and leadership – but only after they had seen Peter's pride being dented. We can only guess at the reactions provoked in the onlookers by this display of emotion. Was it an encouragement to them, or would it have made them reluctant to have their own encounters with the Master?

'In everything set an example by doing what is good. In your teaching show integrity, seriousness and soundness of speech that cannot be condemned' (Titus 2:7-8). When we have leadership roles in the church (parent, teacher, pastor or preacher) then we have the awesome responsibility to lead by example. When we fall by our actions and words we risk pulling others down with us; when we are forgiven it can be an encouragement. Even when we give voice to our emotions we are leading by example.

† Dear Father, please help me to lead my life today to your glory and as an encouragement to the faith of others.

Disciples and congregations   Martin Hayward

Wednesday 15 August

Acts 5:1-11

'To thine own self be true'

Followers of Jesus are called to a life where there is a harmony of words and actions – a lifestyle which witnesses in a selfless way to the faith that they profess. It's a lifelong challenge in which the vital ingredient is honesty. From earliest childhood we seem to be programmed to react 'It wasn't me' or 'I didn't do it', even when the evidence to the contrary is quite clear. As adults we sometimes continue to say what we think we ought to say rather than expressing our true inner selves.

In courts of law the accused are asked if they plead 'guilty' or 'not guilty' to the charges against them. Often their reply seems to reflect what they think they can get away with, or a wish to justify themselves, rather than truth. And we all do it to a greater or lesser degree! Maybe not in law courts but in our everyday living we hide behind the facades that our own egos have built. And the real, mortal danger is that we begin to believe our own lies. Ananias and Sapphira died not because of the money, nor even because they had lied to Peter about their greed, but because they had acted contrary to the leading of their consciences:

> You have not lied to men but to God.

(part of verse 4)

As Shakespeare says in Act I of *Hamlet*:

> This above all: to thine own self be true,
> And it must follow, as the night the day,
> Thou canst not then be false to any man.

God will forgive us our sins when we confess them with repentance; he cannot forgive those sins that we won't admit or recognise as sin even to ourselves.

† Dear Lord, please help me to live this day such that my conscience is guided by your Holy Spirit and my words and actions are in line with my conscience.

Martin Hayward

Disciples and congregations

Thursday 16 August

Acts 13:13, 15:36-40

Choosing to give encouragement

I wasn't much good at sports when I was at school and I well remember those anxious times as the leaders selected their teams. 'Please don't let me be the last, the one no one wants!' Unfortunately, the other boys remembered past games days and my missed goals or fumbled catches. I couldn't seem to escape from the past until that wonderful day when I was one of the first to be picked for the hockey team. I nearly burst with pride, played for all I was worth, and from then on became an increasingly useful player. All I had needed was the encouragement to unlock my talent.

In the adult world it can be like that getting a job: past failures or, worse, a criminal record mean that you will get passed over. It can be very discouraging. Paul and Barnabas each had very different recruitment policies. As the commentator Warren Weirsbe says in his book *'Be Daring': Acts 13-28* (David C. Cook, 1988): 'Paul looked at people and asked "What can they do for God's work?" while Barnabas looked at people and asked "What can God's work do for them?"' Both questions are important and have to be kept in balance, and both groups of people need encouragement.

'Brothers, if you have a message of encouragement for the people, please speak.'

(part of verse 15)

Thank God that he loves each one of us just as we are. He forgives and forgets our confessed and repented sins and wants to encourage us to do better in the future; He gives us the gifts we need to do his work. God's workforce is made up of people who are all the same: fallible human beings relying on the presence of the Holy Spirit in their lives to succeed in doing God's work through them and in spite of them.

† Lord, please help me to encourage others today so that your kingdom may grow.

Disciples and congregations   Martin Hayward

Friday 17 August
Galatians 2:11-21

The sin of disunity

Rather than facing up to doctrinal differences, Peter ignored the arguments between the Jewish Christians and the Gentile converts in Antioch. The differences resulted in separate tables for Jews and Gentiles – and broken fellowship within the church. When Paul found out about this he accused Peter and the others of hypocrisy – of living their lives contrary to their teaching:

> *'We who are Jews by birth and not 'Gentile sinners' know that a man is not justified by observing the law, but by faith in Jesus Christ. So we, too, have put our faith in Christ Jesus that we may be justified by faith in Christ and not by observing the law, because by observing the law no one will be justified.'*

(verses 15-16)

How easy it is for us to fall into that same trap of thinking that Christians from other churches are somehow less valuable in God's eyes than people from our own church. There is a temptation to think that only our way of observing the law, of 'being church', our worship style and our interpretation of scripture can be in line with God's ways. What is needed is not fighting with each other, but an honest assessment of our differences and a celebration of all that binds us together. An issue of the *National Geographic* magazine included a photograph of the fossil remains of two sabre-tooth cats locked in combat. To quote the accompanying article by Dr. Peter A. Alwinson of the Reformed Theological Seminary, Orlando : 'One had bitten deep into the leg bone of the other, a thrust that trapped both in a common fate. The cause of the death of the two cats is as clear as the causes of the extinction of their species are obvious.' While the church indulges in in-fighting the world looks on in disbelief.

† Dear Lord, help me to respect all those who worship and follow you; may your church witness your saving grace as one to the world.

Martin Hayward

Disciples and congregations

Saturday 18 August

Galatians 3:1-5

Competitors in training

Olympic competitors have to rely on past performance against progressively stiffer competition in order to be selected to represent their countries. In order to help them as they train, modern sports coaches use state-of-the-art video and computer technology to analyse performance so that they can help their trainees to see their bad habits and improve their techniques.

What a blessing that the Christian life isn't like that! Unlike the sports competitors, past failures are not held against us and we are not in a competition against each other. We are part of a team and can all attain the goal that Paul urges us to reach: eternal life in the presence of God. But we can't do it just by the Old Testament law, which, like the trainer's video, shows where we go wrong but doesn't help us to do better.

> *After beginning with the Spirit, are you now trying to attain your goal by human effort?*

(part of verse 3)

The only thing which can really help us is the indwelling of the Holy Spirit – God himself at work in our hearts – and the encouragement of others as we run the race.

† Dear Lord, thank you for encouragement and all the gifts we need to reach our final destiny: home with you so that we may praise you for ever.

For group discussion and personal thought

- If you were in a court of law accused of being a Christian, would there be sufficient evidence to convict you and would you have the courage to plead guilty?
- Is your church's relationship with other churches a positive witness to the gospel and to the unity we have in Christ?
- Do you ever race ahead with great enthusiasm without first seeking God's will?

Disciples and congregations   Martin Hayward

Genesis 37–50

1 'Listen to this dream that I dreamed'

Notes based on the *New International Version* by

Robert Kwasi Aboagye-Mensah

Robert Aboagye-Mensah is an ordained minister of the Methodist Church Ghana. From October 2003 to 2009 he served as the Presiding Bishop of the Methodist Church Ghana. He now works partly with the All Africa Conference of Churches (AACC) as the Vice-President for West Africa.

Introduction

This part of Genesis follows the fortunes of Jacob and his sons and later descendants. None of them is a saint, all of them fail, yet through it all runs the thread of God's plan for his people and his use of this family to fulfil that plan.

Sunday 19 August: *Genesis 37:1-11*

'I had another dream…'

None of us chooses our parents and the family we are born into. Our father and mother met somewhere when we were nowhere and later gave birth to us. We then became their children and they our parents. Within the family there are certain crucial things that happen to us in our relationships that greatly influence our future. God did not wait for the Jacob family to become perfect before graciously choosing a family member who was at the centre of a love–hate relationship as an instrument to fulfil his divine purpose. All Joseph had to do throughout the ensuing story was to wait patiently, trusting God to fulfil his divine purpose through him. Yet his words in these first few verses set off the events that follow:

> 'Listen,' he said, 'I had another dream, and this time the sun and moon and eleven stars were bowing down to me.'

(part of verse 9)

Like Joseph, finding ourselves in a similar situation we need the assurance that the sovereign God is with us, and must trust him completely to journey with us in fulfilling the dream he has for us.

† Gracious Lord, enable me to trust you totally as you journey with me in life.

Monday 20 August

Genesis 37:12-24

'We shall see what comes of his dreams'

The fulfilment of God's dreams for our lives usually starts with an ordinary, simple assignment. My call into the ministry as a pastor began when, as a young person, I was asked to read a lesson from the Bible during Sunday morning worship. That simple event kept me in the church. Similarly, the fulfilment of God's dreams for Joseph began when Jacob sent him off 'to see if all is well with your brothers and with the flocks, and bring word back to me' (verse 14). Joseph set off on what seemed a simple errand. But his brothers

saw him in the distance, and before he reached them, they plotted to kill him.

(verse 18)

The very people who sought to destroy the dreams were the ones used as important links in the process of fulfilling them. Neither Jacob nor his sons knew that Joseph's greatness would depend on this simple act of sending him to serve his brothers who hated him. A lesson for all of us is that the road to greatness lies in being sent to serve others in love and not in lording it over people. Our Lord Jesus Christ made this clear to us: 'Whoever wants to become great among you must be your servant, and whoever wants to be first must be slave of all. For even the Son of Man did not come to be served, but to serve, and to give his life as a ransom for many' (Mark 10:43-45).

August

† Lord, grant me the grace to seek daily to fulfil the dreams you have for my life by being a servant to all.

'Listen to this dream that I dreamed'   Robert Aboagye-Mensah

Tuesday 21 August

Genesis 39:1-10

How do you make God's dreams for your life secure?

When Joseph left Hebron he was wearing his precious ornamented robe. It was the pride of his father and the envy of his brothers. At Dothan his brothers stripped him of this robe. He lost everything. He became a slave in a foreign land.

However, there was something no one could take away from Joseph, even in a foreign land. It remained his most treasured possession: his faith in the living God. The Lord honoured him with great responsibility in the house of Potiphar as a result of his total dependence on God. He also became an instrument of blessing to Potiphar and his entire family:

> Potiphar put him in charge of his household, and he entrusted to his care everything he owned . . . the LORD blessed the household of the Egyptian because of Joseph.

(part of verses 4-5)

In Joseph's greatest hour of temptation from Potiphar's wife, it was his faith in this living God that saved him (verse 9). Even though Joseph would be imprisoned on false charges, he would remain faithful to God. The Lord also continued to be with him in all things and all places. Security and the fulfilment of the dreams given us by God depend on our maintaining absolute faith in him. By remaining faithful to God Joseph lost all the material possessions he had at Potiphar's house, but he maintained his integrity, moral authority and respect before God.

† In my daily walk with you, dear Lord, keep me closer to you so that I will remain faithful at all times.

Robert Aboagye-Mensah   'Listen to this dream that I dreamed'

Wednesday 22 August

Genesis 39:11-23

Imprisonment cannot imprison the dreams

The prophet Habakkuk asked God questions that are relevant for today's reading. Knowing that God's 'eyes are too pure to look on evil', and that God 'cannot tolerate evil', he asked God: 'Why then do you tolerate the treacherous? Why are you silent while the wicked swallow up those more righteous than themselves?' (Habakkuk 1:13).

There are people who are in prison for crimes they did not commit, perhaps through being blackmailed. Their personal dignity has been seriously distorted. Yet God who knows that they are innocent did not immediate intervene to vindicate them. Like Habakkuk we are too quick to ask God why he would permit the innocent to suffer in humiliation. Interestingly God did not answer Habakkuk's series of 'why' questions. Instead God asked him to get on with his job: 'Write down the revelation and make it plain on tablets so that a herald may run with it' (Habakkuk 2:2). In such a situation the only approach for the innocent is to hold on to faith in God. In faith Joseph got on with his job in prison as if nothing had happened to mar his reputation. He trusted in God who never left him.

[W]hile Joseph was there in the prison, the LORD was with him; he showed him kindness and granted him favour in the eyes of the prison warden.

(part of verse 20, and verse 21)

† Gracious God, when I am wrongly accused, grant me your wisdom to know what to do, so that you will be glorified and I will continue to be a blessing to others.

'Listen to this dream that I dreamed'   Robert Aboagye-Mensah

Genesis 40:1-15

Interpretation of dreams belongs to God

As human beings we shall from time to time go through periods of hardship and face injustice and pain. Our ability to go through such circumstances will be determined by the attitude that we adopt. If we become bitter, resentful and angry we are likely to be unfruitful. If, on the other hand, we develop a positive attitude towards negative things that happen to us, we are likely to see great good come out of the unfortunate situation.

As a result of Joseph's cheerful attitude towards his work, and his readiness to serve the people put under his care, the cupbearer and the baker were willing to open up to him with their problems. He was able to point them to God who alone has the wisdom and the power to assist them. Joseph helped the two prisoners to know that God is the genuine interpreter of dreams. He also used the opportunity to share his own needs with the cupbearer after God had used him to interpret his dream for him.

'But when all goes well with you, remember me and show me kindness; mention me to Pharaoh and get me out of this prison.'

(verse 14)

† Through the Holy Spirit, dear Lord, enable me always to serve with joy.

Robert Aboagye-Mensah

'Listen to this dream that I dreamed'

Genesis 40:16-23

'I too had a dream'

A few years ago a close family friend approached me with a request. Both his parents had been admitted to two different hospitals in Accra, the capital city of Ghana. I had been visiting both of them at separate times as their pastor. One day his mother died in one hospital, while the father was still in the other hospital. My friend came to me and asked me to break the news to his father. It was one of the challenging moments in my ministry. I had to pray for wisdom, guidance and the sensitivity to inform my friend's father. Eventually I did carry out the difficult assignment with fear and trembling.

It could not have been easy for Joseph to tell the baker the truth about the meaning of his dream. The bad news was that he would be hanged by Pharaoh and that there would be no decent burial for him. Joseph had to do it because it was part of his job to share both good and bad news. The apparent bad news for Joseph himself was that

The chief cupbearer, however, did not remember Joseph; he forgot him.

(verse 23)

We all face the challenge of sharing both good and bad news with people as we seek to fulfil our dreams. In all cases we need wisdom from above.

† Gracious God, let your peace rule in my heart today, and give me wisdom in all my dealings with other people.

August

'Listen to this dream that I dreamed'   Robert Aboagye-Mensah

Saturday 25 August

Genesis 41:1-13

Giving each man the interpretation of his dream

I have difficulty remembering the names of people I have met before. I have to apologise to them when they expect me to call them by their names. Perhaps you are like me and have difficulty in remembering people and their names. The chief cupbearer of Pharaoh had forgotten the name of Joseph. He only remembered him as 'a young Hebrew', 'a servant of the captain of the guard'. However, there was something else that he remembered so well, even two years after the event. It was the good work that the Hebrew young man did for him when they were in prison together:

We told him our dreams, and he interpreted them for us . . . And things turned out exactly as he interpreted them to us.

(part of verses 12-13)

We may not remember the names of all the people who come our way. But one thing is sure, people will always remember us for the way we treated them the first time we met.

† Help me, good Lord, to do good to all people, especially those who are poor and in need.

For group discussion and personal thought
- Reflect on the way God led and guided Joseph before his dreams finally became a reality. Have you had similar experiences in your own life?
- How do you deal with the problem of evil in your community and church?

Robert Aboagye-Mensah   'Listen to this dream that I dreamed'

Genesis 37–50

2 'One in whom is the spirit of God'

Notes based on the *New Revised Standard Version* by

Oral Thomas

Oral A.W. Thomas is a minister in the Methodist Church in the Caribbean and the Americas (MCCA) and lecturer at the United Theological College of the West Indies. He is an Antiguan by birth and a Jamaican by marriage.

Introduction

Last week's readings ended with Joseph in prison, a slave, falsely accused, and then belatedly remembered by the chief cupbearer. How was God going to fulfil Joseph's youthful dreams? Now Joseph's fortunes change as God sets his plans in motion. He seems to have been at the mercy of others, but it is God who is in control.

Sunday 26 August: *Genesis 41:14-16, 25-32*

Not I but God

In circumstances of established human control, God's will breaks through. For all his power, Pharaoh and his administrators cannot discern the signs of the time, that seasons of famine and plenty are about to come upon the land of Egypt. Pharaoh's power might be on display but it is God's will that is done. Pharaoh sends for Joseph, who knows that he has no power to help himself as a slave in a foreign country:

> *And Pharaoh said to Joseph, 'I have had a dream, and there is no one who can interpret it. I have heard it said of you that when you hear a dream you can interpret it.' Joseph answered Pharaoh, 'It is not I; God will give Pharaoh a favourable answer.'*

> (verses 15-16)

God rules the world, not Pharaoh. The working out and working through of God's will may be long delayed but it cannot stay unrealised.

† Creator God, we are assured through your love for the world expressed through the life, death and resurrection of Jesus Christ that you will never leave nor forsake your created order or abandon it to the devices of your creatures. Amen

One in whom is the spirit of God

It could not have been foreseen, either by the family of Joseph or by Pharaoh's court, that when Joseph was sold into slavery he would end up as overseer. But God's providence is mysterious; God is sovereign. Joseph gives Pharaoh the advice that God has put into his mouth, perhaps little dreaming that he would be chosen to put it into practice.

> *Pharaoh said to his servants, 'Can we find anyone else like this – one in whom is the spirit of God?' So Pharaoh said to Joseph, 'Since God has shown you all this, there is no one so discerning and wise as you. You shall be over my house, and all my people shall order themselves as you command.'*

> (verses 38-39 and part of verse 40)

The slave is made a member of the ruling class by the ruler, who renames Joseph and gives his hand in marriage to a daughter of the ruling class (verse 45). Joseph is given authority but not power, Pharaoh remains the supreme ruler (verse 44). But who is in control? For the narrator, God is. God still is, for us. Vast economic resources, military might and the power, and the means of cultural imperialism do not wrest control of the world out of the hands of God. God's hand may be difficult to discern, but God's purpose for good can always be trusted, however long it takes.

> God moves in a mysterious way
> His wonders to perform
> He plants his footsteps in the sea
> And rides upon the storm.

> (William Cowper, 1774)

---

† Sustaining and patient God, however long it may seem to us for your will to be on earth as it is in heaven, may we hold to faith in your will for good for us all. Amen

Oral Thomas   'One in whom is the spirit of God'

Genesis 41:46-57

Remembering

In the Caribbean we have a proverb that says 'When you are going up the ladder, treat those you meet coming down well because you may meet them going up when you are coming down.' It is disturbing when someone from humble beginnings or oppressive circumstances who has 'made it' seeks to erase their past. In Egypt, the slave is now a member of the ruling class, an overseer. As overseer, he ensures that the economy booms and the status quo remains intact. Joseph engineers a surplus economy. But what happens to him as a person? The naming of his children provides a clue:

> *Joseph named the firstborn Manasseh, 'For', he said, 'God has made me forget all my hardship and all my father's house.' The second he named Ephraim, 'For God has made me fruitful in the land of my misfortunes.'*

(verses 51-52)

As Joseph settled down in Egypt, was he forgetting his origins? Had his own family not also been successful? The once oppressed slave is now ruler; will the oppressed become the oppressor? Will he liberate, tolerate, and forget? We wait to see – and to see where God is leading Joseph. We can redeem our past by practising the biblical injunction to 'do to others as you would have them do to you', and by asking God to help us to remember where he has brought us from.

† Liberating God, when our hearts are full of joy help us to remember and give you all the praise and glory. Amen

August

'One in whom is the spirit of God'   Oral Thomas

Wednesday 29 August

Genesis 42:1-17

Joseph and his brothers

In today's reading a number of questions arise about Joseph's dealings with his brothers. Is Joseph getting his own back? Is this revenge? Or is Joseph showing how dishonest they are? Joseph is determined to judge the claim by his brothers to be 'honest men' (verse 11) and discover 'whether there is truth in you' (verse 16). Dreams do come true as the brothers literally bow down to Joseph:

> Joseph's brothers came and bowed themselves before him with their faces to the ground.

(part of verse 6)

Noticeably in this episode God drops out of the story; there is no reference to God or mention of the activity of God. Life goes on. The story seems to drift on. But is this all part of the mysterious ways of God's providence? Is there really drift? On closer examination, we see God working his purposes out in the fulfilment of dreams, in Joseph's rise to a position of authority, and later in Genesis in the painstaking revelation of the truth that Joseph is not dead. Slowly the tangle of the past is unravelled and becomes a blessing for the present. God may seem to be absent, but in fact 'he who keeps you will not slumber. He who keeps Israel will neither slumber nor sleep' (Psalm 121:3-4).

† Keeping God, we are comforted in the faith that you neither slumber nor sleep. Amen

Oral Thomas   'One in whom is the spirit of God'

What's going on?

Joseph's brothers are in the dark. What's going on? The question reflects ignorance, uncertainty, and the inability to draw conclusions on the information presently available. For Joseph's brothers, 'what's going on' is that, unknown to them, they are being punished for the crime of selling their brother Joseph into slavery. But in ignorance and confusion they are asking 'Why this probing and testing of our character? Why is it that our transaction is not according to the usual business practices? Why us? Is something afoot?' For Joseph, 'what's going on' is a process of bringing to the light of day the mysterious ways of God's providence, a process that must be quite painful for Joseph as his own flesh and blood are involved. Now it is the brothers who, in their confusion and uncertainty, bring God back into the story:

'What is this that God has done to us?'

(part of verse 28)

It is not clear whether their question indicates guilt, is blaming God, or trying to make sense of their confusion. On the other side, Joseph, in spite of his pain, is not simply keeping his head but also his faith in God.

† Faithful God, in our times of confusion, uncertainty and anxiety we thank you for keeping faith with and in us.

August

'One in whom is the spirit of God' Oral Thomas

A family up against it

When you are 'up against it' nothing seems to work or work out, better times seem a distant reality and you are too confused and de-energised to think and act clearly.

'What's going on' is still unclear to Joseph's brothers. Their confusion is turning to anger as they hold to their integrity and family honour, and the view that Joseph is dead. But was the placing of the money in their sacks a test of honesty or a clue? The plot thickens. Panic is setting in. For Jacob, the forces are against him. He, too, holds to the view that Joseph is dead and is finding it unbearable to grieve over the loss of two sons. Joseph is pushing the family to the limit.

> *'If harm should come to [Benjamin] on the journey that you are to make, you would bring down my gray hairs with sorrow to Sheol.'*

(part of verse 38)

When in life we find ourselves 'up against it', our thoughts and prayers turn to God as we attempt to find spiritual meaning in our experiences. Escape seems the easier option. It is more difficult and daunting to confront the opposing forces and work through the issues, although this may be the best and only way to well-being and liberation.

† God of our difficulties, grant that in our experiences of pain we may hold firmly to the faith that you will not break the bruised reed but will strengthen and sustain. Amen

Oral Thomas   'One in whom is the spirit of God'

Saturday 1 September

Genesis 43:1-10

Forced into action

In the Caribbean we have the saying 'Force makes water go uphill'. In other words, force of circumstances pushes you to act, fast, and achieve the seemingly impossible. Chapter 42 ended with Jacob's defiance and deep sorrow. Chapter 43 begins with Judah baldly confronting his father with the reality of the situation.

> 'Send the boy with me, and let us be on our way, so that we may live and not die – you and we and also our little ones . . . If we had not delayed, we would now have returned twice.'
>
> (part of verse 8, and verse 10)

As the famine worsens and with it the possible loss of lives and livelihoods, there is increasing pressure for the family to act, fast. Money is not the problem. Time is. The family's predicament is driving their actions. What remains a dilemma for them is but the ripening of God's purposes. While God is sovereign, he is not a bully. God's way is to stand at the door and knock. He may appear to be moving slowly, but his purpose is sure.

---

† God of solidarity, our faith and hope in you increase, knowing that with and in you we may be down but never out, perplexed but never driven to despair, and that we can triumph in defeat, and right will win the day.

For group discussion and personal thought

- Joseph starts as a slave in the Pharaoh's court and ends up as an overseer. As an overseer, do you think Joseph would have been an oppressor or a liberator?
- How is God portrayed in these chapters of Genesis? Is this the God you worship and serve?

September

'One in whom is the spirit of God'   Oral Thomas

Genesis 37–50

3 'It was not you who sent me here, but God'

Notes based on the *New Revised Standard Version* by

Jules Gomes

Jules Gomes is Dwelly Raven Canon at Liverpool Cathedral and Lecturer in Theology at Liverpool Hope University. Ordained in the Church of North India, Jules started work as a journalist. He has a Cambridge doctorate in Old Testament studies.

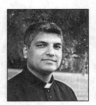

Introduction

What makes a great story? A great story resonates with readers in any culture and age because it is about archetypes, not stereotypes. We see ourselves in it. A great story is about great values – what's worth living and dying for. It takes us beyond the factual to the essential. It changes and transforms the lives of its characters completely and irreversibly, and forces them to make choices that reveal their essential nature. The Joseph story has all the above elements and more.

Sunday 2 September: *Genesis 43:11-15*

Tales of transformation

> *'May God Almighty grant you mercy before the man, so that he may send back your other brother and Benjamin.'*

(part of verse 14)

The pressure intensifies. The famine worsens. The characters are forced into making choices: Jacob sends his sons back to Egypt for food, and Benjamin with them. Joseph's brothers are being transformed. Judah once sold his brother Joseph. Now he pledges himself for Benjamin. Once Joseph's brothers received money from the Ishmaelites: now they are carrying double back to Egypt. Once the brothers united to get rid of Joseph. Now they unite to save Benjamin. Jacob, too, is being transformed. He is willing to let go of his son and return double the money to Joseph. There is a new streak of honesty to his old cunning as he sends gifts to Egypt – as a bribe? Above all, he entrusts the entire venture to El Shaddai – the God of his ancestors.

† Almighty God, help us to know when you are turning our world upside down. May we see your hand in the reversal of events and trust in your providence and your plans. Enable us to make the right choices when we are faced with pressures and let our character be transformed into the image of Christ. Amen

Monday 3 September

Genesis 43:16-30

It's God, stupid!

He replied, 'Rest assured, do not be afraid; your God and the God of your father must have put treasure in your sacks for you; I received your money.'

(verse 23)

A great story has a sense of the reader knowing what the characters often don't know. Here it is God's providence. Although God has not been mentioned often, although Jacob and his sons are skilled at calculation and manipulation, God is working even through their human devices. God will have the final word and the last laugh. The Egyptian steward seems to know this better than the 'sons of Israel'. He attributes the treasure in their sacks to the God of Israel. Of course, as readers we know that it was the steward who put the money in the brothers' sacks. But we know that God's plans are worked out through human agents. Joseph's brothers need to be reminded that God is in control. Their strategies of human calculation and manipulation need to be subverted. They need to be toppled and thrust into the 'logic-surpassing world of forgiveness'. God had revealed his plans to Joseph through dreams and one of those dreams is coming to pass. The brothers bow before him just as Joseph had dreamt. The word that is used for bowing down here is used elsewhere in the Pentateuch only for bowing to God. This is yet another hint that God is at work here even in the subtlest and most hidden of ways. The scene in Joseph's house begins and ends in washing. The brothers wash their feet and Joseph washes his weeping face. Despite his eventual vindication, the once pampered and patronising Joseph is undergoing a deeper transformation. Instead of crowing over their humiliation, he now shows that on his part, too, there is a giving and a cleansing.

† God of times and seasons, God of humiliation and vindication, we pray that you will topple our calculation and manipulation and dismantle our strategies and schemes. Open our eyes to see your hidden hand in the sweep of history and the detail of our own lives. Surprise, subvert and sustain us by the glorious outworking of your providence. Amen

September

'It was not you who sent me here, but God'   Jules Gomes

Tuesday 4 September

Genesis 43:31 – 44:17

Twenty pieces of silver

A meal is a symbol of communion. But full communion has not yet been restored. Joseph eats with his brothers but not at the same table. There is no dialogue at the meal between Joseph and his brothers. Achieving full reconciliation is often painfully slow. In its raw honesty, the story offers no quick solutions to complex issues. This is no photo opportunity – at least, not yet! But at the same time, there are positive moves being made towards reconciliation. Joseph pays attention to his brothers' table. He generously shares his portions with them. He graciously reverses the injustice meted out to him years ago when his brothers had callously sat down to eat while he languished in the pit. He hints at his knowledge of them by seating them according to age. He then lavishes five times their share of food on Benjamin, testing them to see if they will resent this favouritism. But there is one final test that the brothers have to pass. Joseph orders his steward to fill his brothers' bags with grain and silver and to deposit Joseph's own silver cup in Benjamin's bag. A great story is one where there is a sudden and surprising twist in the tale. Joseph was sold for twenty pieces of silver. Now silver is used to test his brothers. The silver of betrayal will become the silver of reconciliation. Joseph tests his brothers to see if they will let Benjamin go into slavery as they once did with him. Now, in a stunning admission that recalls their real crime, Judah says:

> *'God has found out the guilt of your servants: here we are then, my lord's slaves, both we and also the one in whose possession the cup has been found.'*

(chapter 44, verse 16)

Without repentance there can be no reconciliation.

† God of mercy and compassion, thank you for reconciling us to yourself through the blood of your Son. Send us out as ambassadors of your reconciling love, both for people who are divided and, above all, for the broken body of your church, that we may enjoy the full communion that your Son prayed for, for Jesus' sake. Amen

Jules Gomes   'It was not you who sent me here, but God'

Genesis 44:18-34

The transformation that took twenty-two years

A great story transforms its characters completely and irreversibly. Such a transformation is taking place within Judah – slowly but surely. He first acknowledges a collective guilt on the part of the brothers. But Joseph, demonstrating both wisdom and justice, rejects the idea of collective punishment. He singles out Benjamin, the perpetrator of the alleged theft, for punishment. The rest of the brothers may 'go in peace', but without the youngest brother. The story now exerts the maximum pressure on the characters. Judah has to make the most difficult choice of his life. He steps up to Joseph and delivers the longest and most passionate speech in Genesis. He pleads for both his father and his youngest brother. He mentions his father fourteen times in his speech, hoping that it will soften Joseph's heart and cause him to change his mind. Twenty-two years ago he couldn't care less if his father would be left brokenhearted by the loss of one of his sons. But now he is willing to do anything so that his father may not suffer that way again. Judah knows that Benjamin is his father's favourite son: 'his life is bound up in the boy's life'. But now there is no resentment as there was twenty-two years ago for another favourite son. Judah's conversion is complete. His transformation is total. Twenty-two years ago he engineered the selling of one brother into slavery; now he offers himself as a slave – a sacrificial substitute – so that the other brother can be set free.

'Now therefore, please let your servant remain as a slave to my lord in place of the boy; and let the boy go back with his brothers.'

(verse 33)

Judah becomes the model not just of transformation, but of redemption.

† Sovereign God, do not leave us as we are or where we are. Transform us and take us where you want us to be and make us the people you want us to be. Grant us wisdom when faced with tough choices; grant that we may also be changed into the likeness of Christ by the choices we make. Amen

'It was not you who sent me here, but God'   Jules Gomes

September

Thursday 6 September

Genesis 45:1-20

God's providence overturns human disobedience

'So it was not you who sent me here, but God.'

(part of verse 8)

Joseph's Egyptian steward had already hinted at the mysterious ways of divine providence when he told the brothers that God had put the silver in their sacks. Now Joseph proclaims this doctrine fully, robustly and joyfully to his stunned brothers. In revealing himself, he reveals God as well. Three times he reiterates this theology of divine providence. His forgiving attitude reaches the limits of generosity when he tells his brothers not to be distressed about how they behaved, because through it God was working out his purposes. Joseph explains why God allowed this to happen. First, 'God sent me before you to preserve life' (verse 5), showing his love for all humanity – including the Egyptians. Second, 'God sent me before you to preserve for you a remnant' (verse 7), showing his love for his chosen people Israel. Joseph has been a hidden saviour to Israel and his family by working behind the scenes. God has been a hidden saviour to Joseph and his family, and Pharaoh and his people, by working behind the scenes. Yet divine providence does not exclude human agency. The fact still remains that Joseph is the brother 'whom you sold into Egypt' (verse 4). But this wrongdoing is now forgiven and righted as Joseph, recognising the providential grace of God in his life, extends it to his brothers. Where there is recognition of God's providential grace, there can be reconciliation, restoration and celebration! Pharaoh now extends his welcome to Joseph's entire family – the future nation of Israel – and offers them the best of all the land of Egypt. God's promises to Abraham are coming to pass. Through him, all the families of the earth will be blessed.

† Hidden God, you work in strange and wonderful ways your wonders to perform. We commit the many plans in our hearts to you, praying that your plans will prevail. We pray that in your own time you will let us see your hidden hand in the joyful and tragic events of our own lives. Amen

Jules Gomes   'It was not you who sent me here, but God'

Amazing love! How can this be?

Grace is another word for extraordinary and extravagant generosity. Grace is generosity gone mad even when the recipients do not merit it. Indeed, it is generosity gone absolutely insane when the recipients deserve to be severely punished but are instead rewarded beyond measure. This is what we see unfolding before our eyes. Joseph's brothers were probably rubbing their eyes in sheer disbelief. Just as they could not comprehend seeing him alive, now they cannot possibly comprehend his incredible generosity. The story describes in detail the gifts Joseph lavishes upon his brothers: silver, food and clothes, and donkeys. Benjamin is given an extra three hundred pieces of silver and five sets of garments. The reversal of wrongdoing is complete. Twenty-two years ago Joseph was sold for twenty pieces of silver and because his brothers were envious of his multi-coloured garment. Now Joseph gives Benjamin silver in abundance and garments galore. Instead of his brothers making restitution, it is Joseph who makes it. Instead of receiving gifts, Joseph gives them; he reverses the pattern, even as the story is now reversed for his father Jacob. Earlier he had said, "Joseph has been torn to bits . . . I shall go down to Sheol in mourning' (Genesis 37:33, 35). Now he says,

> 'Enough! My son Joseph is still alive. I must go and see him before I die.'

> (part of verse 28)

September

Great stories are timeless. We too should be rubbing our eyes in sheer disbelief as we explore the height and depth and length and breadth of God's incredible generosity to us in sending his Son to die for us even while we were his enemies. We should be rubbing our eyes in sheer disbelief as we discover that once we thought we were dead, but now we have been made alive!

† Amazing God, we find grace astonishing beyond our wildest imagination. We cannot understand why you did not condemn us to death when we deserved it, but in generosity gone mad, you sent your only beloved Son to die for us. Help us never to lose our wonder and amazement at this greatest truth of all. Amen

'It was not you who sent me here, but God'   Jules Gomes

Saturday 8 September

Genesis 46:1-7

The providence of God's promises

'I am God, the God of your father; do not be afraid to go down to Egypt, for I will make of you a great nation there.'

(part of verse 3)

This is the culmination of the history of the patriarchs, the last time that God will speak to them. The next time God speaks, it will be to Moses. God's promises to the patriarchs will be fulfilled. God has acted in different ways in the life of each of the patriarchs in order that his purposes may prevail. Thus far God has revealed himself in the story of Joseph through human agency and events. Now God reveals himself directly to Jacob. It is a daunting task for the ageing Jacob to migrate to Egypt. But God asks Jacob to undertake this challenging journey just as he had asked Abraham to leave his country and go to an unknown land. God reiterates the promise to Abraham that he will make of them a great nation – even in the foreign land of Egypt. Even in this so-called land of exile, God will bless Israel and fulfil his purposes. Are we ready for a challenge no matter what our age or circumstance?

† Prayer-answering and promise-keeping God, we thank you for your Word in Holy Scripture and your works in human history. We thank you for speaking and acting. We thank you for creation and for the hope of new creation. We thank you for our fathers in faith, Abraham, Isaac and Jacob and for Israel through whom you worked your purposes for humankind. Amen

For group discussion and personal thought

• Spend some time looking back over your own life. When has God used what seemed bad at the time (failure, disappointment, illness, ill-treatment) to bring about good in your life?

September

Jules Gomes   'It was not you who sent me here, but God'

Genesis 37–50

4 'God intended it for good'

Notes based on the *New International Version* by

Daniel Gheorghe Oprean

Daniel Gheorghe Oprean is a Romanian theologian, living in Oravita, Romania. He is the Director of Educational Programs at the Areopagus Center for Christian Studies and Contemporary Culture, Timisoara, Romania. Daniel is married to Ana and they have two boys, Cristian and David.

Introduction

This week's readings conclude both the story of Joseph and the Book of Genesis. After Jacob and his family are reunited, the focus moves to Joseph in his role as an Egyptian official dealing with a famine, then back to Jacob and his dying address to his sons, his death and burial. After their father's death, the old tension between Joseph and his brothers resurfaces and is calmed by Joseph, and Genesis ends with the death of Joseph.

Sunday 9 September: *Genesis 46:28-31*
The will of God for his obedient people

Joseph's life as told in Genesis 37–50 is an example of how to answer the call of God (Genesis 37). It is also a model of how man's faithfulness answers God's faithfulness (Genesis 38–39). And it is a demonstration of what God can do with us and through us (Genesis 40–45). This is the larger framework of the meeting between Joseph and his father after a separation of 20 years. The meeting is based on the revelation of God's will to Jacob/Israel, Joseph's father, and the obedient answer of Israel to the will of God (Genesis 46:1-27).

> Joseph . . . went to Goshen to meet his father Israel. As soon as Joseph appeared before him, he threw his arms around his father and wept for a long time.

> (part of verse 29)

† Eternal God, thank you for your faithful care for your people, which brings restoration, reconciliation, and renewal.

Monday 10 September

Genesis 47:1-12

The providence of God for his chosen people

One of the greatest truths with regard to God's dealings with humanity is that in his sovereign will he uses even the crises in life 'for the good of those who love him, who have been called according to his purpose' (Romans 8:28). Today's reading shows the wonderful way in which God, in his providence, assists his people. Even though all the tribes around Egypt were suffering an increasingly severe famine, and were forced to buy grain for bread from Egypt (Genesis 41:57), through his faithful servant Joseph God provides bread for free for the tribe of Israel, a tribe chosen to become the seed for God's people.

> So Joseph settled his father and his brothers in Egypt . . . Joseph also provided his father and his brothers and all his father's household with food.

(part of verses 11-12)

This story is a great illustration of the psalm that says 'In vain you rise early and stay up late, toiling for food to eat, for he grants sleep to those he loves' (Psalm 127:2). And of the other biblical truth about the providence of God for his people: 'I was young and now I am old, yet I have never seen the righteous forsaken or their children begging bread' (Psalm 37:25). In today's world, with its financial crises, famines and despair, we should still look to our heavenly Father for our daily bread. It comes to us from his providence is the reason for what we have, not through our abilities or efforts. Moreover, the acknowledgement of God's providence should motivate us to live obedient and thankful lives.

† Faithful God, our Provider, we acknowledge the perfection of your providence for us, your people. And we want to live a life of thankfulness as an answer to your faithful provision for us.

Daniel Oprean

'God intended it for good'

The protection of God for his people

There was no food, however, in the whole region because the famine was severe; both Egypt and Canaan wasted away because of the famine . . . Now the Israelites settled in Egypt in the region of Goshen. They acquired property there and were fruitful and increased greatly in number.

(verses 13 and 27)

The contrast between these two verses provides the key to today's reflection. In a context in which all the tribes from Canaan and all the people of Egypt lost their money (verse 14), their animals (verse 16), their land and even their freedom (verses 18-20), becoming slaves of Pharaoh, the people of Israel were safe and protected in the land of Goshen, where the presence of God in their midst made the difference not only in the peaceful times of Joseph, but also in the times of trouble in the future history of God's people (Exodus 8:22; 34:8-10). There is a lesson here for our lives today. For God, times of crisis reveal his complete sovereignty, his righteous judgement, and his eternal faithfulness). Wholly embraced in this threefold reality, God's people in all generations lived in God's hand and in his freedom, making his presence the centre of their lives and practices.

† Sovereign God, our protector, we rest in your marvellous protection and freedom in the midst of all the losses and slaveries of the world today.

September

'God intended it for good'   Daniel Oprean

Wednesday 12 September

Genesis 48:1-12

The transforming grace of God

The wise man in Ecclesiastes 7:8 says: 'The end of a matter is better than its beginning, and patience is better than pride.' This is true in Jacob's life. He started as a deceiver (Genesis 27:36), but as today's reading shows, towards the end of his life became a trusty person to bless others (Genesis 48:1-12). What transformed Jacob and his life was meeting with God (Genesis 28:10-22; 32:24-32), an experience with direct consequences for his thought and life. Even though he experienced suffering because of all his bad decisions, he was still under God's eye and at the proper time God changed Jacob's way of walking through life (Genesis 32:31) so that he could open the future for generations after him.

> Jacob said to Joseph, 'God Almighty appeared to me at Luz in the land of Canaan, and there he blessed me.'

(verse 3)

Instead of being overwhelmed by the past mistakes in our lives, we can be transformed by the grace of God, a transformation that begins in a real encounter with God and continues with his real presence being made manifest in our lives. The ability to see and experience this transformative presence comes, as in Jacob's case, from the day-by-day decision to obey God. In such a way we will become role models and trusty people through whom God will bless those who come after us.

† Graceful God, as we acknowledge the transformative power of your presence, we ask you to work in us through your grace, to change our minds, actions and ways in life so we can become a blessing for others.

Daniel Oprean   'God intended it for good'

September

Genesis 48:13-21

The guidance of God for the whole of life

'May the God before whom my fathers
Abraham and Isaac walked,
the God who has been my Shepherd all my life to this day,
the Angel who has delivered me from all harm
– may he bless these boys.'

(part of verse 15, and verse 16)

A paramount truth is expressed in these verses, of a great importance for us today. God is the shepherd of our entire life, from its beginning to its end. All the generations of believers before us lived under his guidance, and it is a sign of spiritual discernment to see his hand at work and his guidance on the path of our lives. We should acknowledge, as Jacob did, the permanent guidance of God in our lives, as the wise man says: 'In all your ways acknowledge him, and he will make your paths straight' (Proverbs 3:6). Someone who really sees and believes that God is a shepherd can be confident for his successors as Jacob was: 'I am about to die, but God will be with you and take you back to the land of your fathers' (verse 21). For Jacob this confidence in God grew clearer and clearer in a lifelong experience, and it can be the same for us. Growing in understanding should therefore mean also growing in thankfulness.

† Merciful God, our shepherd, we thank you today for the guidance you have always provided for your people. In all the complexity of our lives, may we rest today in your generosity in action.

September

'God intended it for good' Daniel Oprean

Friday 14 September

Genesis 49:29-33; 50:1-14

Fellowship with God beyond death

When Jacob had finished giving instructions to his sons, he drew his feet up into the bed, breathed his last and was gathered to his people.

(verse 33)

In today's reading we see that the unpleasant reality of death can be an occasion for the believer to celebrate the fact that death is not only an end of the earthly life but also a beginning of another life, eternal life with the triumphant people of God in the presence of God. Even though death came as a curse because of sin (Genesis 3: 19-22 and Romans 5:12), for the people that live in fellowship with God death is only a door from a temporal existence in which we live by faith – 'being certain of what we do not see' (Hebrews 11:1) – into an eternal existence in which 'we shall see him as he is' (1 John 3:2).

The instructions Jacob gave to his sons concerning his death and burial, instructions followed faithfully by the entire family (Genesis 50:12), transformed the sadness of Jacob's death into a memorial of God's faithful fellowship with his people that began with Abraham (Genesis 12–24), continued with Isaac (Genesis 25–27), and now ends with Jacob (Genesis 28–49). For the entire history of his people Israel, God was to be the God of Abraham, Isaac and Jacob.

† Eternal God, through your Son, our Lord Jesus, you transformed the sadness of death into the joy of resurrection. We thank you today for the continuous work of your Spirit within us, transforming what is perishable and clothing the mortal with immortality (1 Corinthians 15:54).

Daniel Oprean

'God intended it for good'

The generous follower of a generous God

'You intended to harm me, but God intended it for good to accomplish what is now being done, the saving of many lives.'

(verse 20)

This is a great attitude of generosity from a man that experienced many losses in his life. Joseph lost his family by being sold as a slave through his brothers' jealousy (Genesis 37); he lost his reputation through resisting temptation (Genesis 39). The only thing Joseph did not lose was his essential character, expressed in a generosity that mirrors the generosity of God. In his generosity Joseph became the saviour not only of the whole of Egypt and his family, but also of many tribes from Canaan (Genesis 41–47). When we understand that God can use even the many losses in our lives to save the lives of other people, then we can leave his Spirit to heal our wounds and replace the spirit of bitterness with a spirit of generosity. The example of Joseph foreshadows that greater gift of God's generosity, the one who saves not only from physical famine but also from the spiritual famine of humanity, the one who not only gives daily bread (Mathew 6:11), but who is himself the true bread of life (John 6:32-35).

† Generous God, we thank you today for your incomparable generosity. Help us in turn to be generous to others.

For group discussion and personal thought

- In a world of troubles can you see God's sovereign will changing the evil into good?
- Does your obedience to God's will contribute to the salvation of many lives?

September

'God intended it for good' Daniel Oprean

Jewish festivals

1 The biblical pattern

Notes based on the *New International Version* by

John Oldershaw

John Oldershaw lives in Wallasey just across the River Mersey from Liverpool in England. He is a United Reformed Church minister with pastoral care of a rural church and responsibility for running retreats and vision days for churches. John enjoys going to the theatre, reading poetry and spending time with family and friends.

Introduction

Festivals and celebrations are an important part of life. Families enjoy parties to mark key moments in life, and churches have a pattern of festivals during the year. This week we look at the biblical pattern of festivals set out in Leviticus 23 to explore the original purpose of these celebrations and to discover how elements of them have been carried into church life.

Sunday 16 September: *Leviticus 23:1-3*
The Sabbath

Time for rest and relaxation is essential for good health of mind and spirit as well as body. There is a long biblical tradition of a weekly day of rest. The creation story in Genesis tells us that on the seventh day God rested and in today's reading it is a God-given command:

> *'There are six days when you may work, but the seventh day is a Sabbath of rest, a day of sacred assembly.'*

(verse 3)

Christian tradition has taken the Sabbath but moved it to the first day of the week, not the last. It was on the first day of the week that Jesus rose to life and so the first disciples met then to break bread and remember Jesus. The fact that they did so points us to an important aspect of this instruction given to Moses: Sabbath is a time for sacred assembly, gathering together to spend time with God so that we may rest in him.

† God of creation, there are always so many things to do, even on a Sunday. Help me today to spend time with you, not constantly rushing about doing work for you. Amen

Passover

Today's verses set out the calendar details for celebrations which are to take place in the first month of the year, but we are not told here why the festival should be held.

> *'The LORD's Passover begins at twilight on the fourteenth day of the first month.'*

(verse 5)

The celebration harks back to the time when God's people were slaves in Egypt and Moses pleaded with the Pharaoh to let them go free. All to no avail until, after a series of plagues, the firstborn child in each Egyptian household died, but the houses of the Hebrews were passed over in this tragedy. The Passover festival is a reminder of this deliverance and the Feast of Unleavened Bread is a reminder of the need to make bread quickly to provide food for a speedy escape from Egypt. There was no time to add yeast and wait for the dough to rise. These festivals have a very long tradition and were annual commemorations of this key moment in the people's history, bringing reassurance at times of great difficulty in the nation's life.

They figure in Christian tradition too. We remember that it was at the time of the Passover festival that Jesus met in an upstairs room in Jerusalem and broke unleavened bread to indicate that his body would be broken in death.

† You are the God of yesterday and tomorrow as well as of today. I thank you for those experiences in the past that have revealed to me your truth and made me the person that I am. Today I give praise that you are part of my life and I pray that I will always know your presence. Amen

September

The biblical pattern   John Oldershaw

Tuesday 18 September

Leviticus 23:9-14

First fruits

This festival sounds fun, with the priest waving sheaves of corn as they are brought for dedication. There is no precise date set on which this celebration should be held, it is solely dependent upon when the harvest is ready. Harvests are very busy times, and probably everyone from young to old would be enlisted to help, so it is very significant that amongst all this activity the first sheaf is brought to the priest to acknowledge that the harvest belongs to God as well as to people. There are echoes here of the ritual described in Deuteronomy 26:5-10 where, when the harvest is gathered in, the produce is brought to worship and the farmers remember all the events, including the wandering in the wilderness following the escape from slavery, that have led up to them being in that place and time. In all of these festivals there is no getting away from history.

> The LORD said to Moses, 'Speak to the Israelites and say to them: "When you enter the land I am going to give you and you reap its harvest, bring to the priest a sheaf of the first grain you harvest".'

(verses 9-10)

At the end of today's reading we are told that this ceremony is to be carried out by future generations wherever they live, emphasising that the whole of creation is God's and not just one particular promised land.

† O Lord, our food comes from a long way away, as well as being locally grown. Wherever the harvest comes from, help me to remember that the earth is yours, and all that grows in it. The food I eat today will not be 'first fruits', but I do say thank you for it. Amen

John Oldershaw   The biblical pattern

Wednesday 19 September

Leviticus 23:15-22

Feast of Weeks

Following the ritual for the bringing of first fruits, a period of seven weeks and a day is set aside for the harvest to be gathered in and for the agricultural year to be brought to a close. The other name for the festival, Pentecost, refers to the fifty days. We are given a lot of detail about the celebrations which take place at the end of this fifty days; it sounds quite a party if you like that sort of thing. Of course, we need to remember this is all from a different age and culture.

However, the verse which ends today's Bible passage is extremely significant and is a challenge to us in our different age and culture:

'When you reap the harvest of your land, do not reap to the very edges of your field or gather the gleanings of your harvest. Leave them for the poor and the alien.'

(verse 22)

The inclusion of this instruction in the liturgical description shows that having care for those who are disadvantaged is also part of the worship offered to God, not simply a good or kind thing to do. This verse is challenging to us because it is another recognition that the harvest belongs to God, who has the ultimate say over its distribution, and also because this generous expression of love was to extend to people of different tribes and races, the aliens who lived among them.

† Lord, I know that I am sometimes selfish. I know that I should consider the needs of those people who are poorer than I am. Help me to do this and, as I do so, may I hear your reassuring words spoken to me: 'I am the Lord your God'. Amen

September

The biblical pattern

John Oldershaw

Thursday 20 September
Leviticus 23:23-25

Feast of Trumpets

The significance of this festival altered during Jewish history when there was a change of the calendar. Today's reading says:

'On the first day of the seventh month you are to have a day of rest.'

(verse 24)

But the Feast of Trumpets originally marked the beginning of the year, and was a noisy New Year celebration. The playing of the trumpets by the priests was a call for people to gather for worship and dedicate themselves to God at the start of the year. No regular work was to be done on this day, ensuring maximum attendance so that it was not just a personal act of piety but the action of a nation, a people meeting in a holy place with their God. Although brief, these few verses remind us that worship is not purely about personal faith; they indicate the value of a nation dedicating itself to seek the common good by ways of justice and peace.

In a time when there were no clocks, a distinctive sound was needed to call people to worship. In many Christian traditions church bells have been rung to tell people that now is the time to worship. Trumpets and bells have a penetrating noise which enables them to carry over long distances. In our personal lives there can be other sounds which are promptings to pray. For example, when hearing the sound of an aircraft we can pray for those on a journey, or the sound of water can alert us to pray for people facing droughts or floods.

† Living God, today may I listen for promptings to praise you and then to renew my desire to live my life following the teachings of Jesus. Amen

John Oldershaw

The biblical pattern

Friday 21 September

Leviticus 23:26-32

Day of Atonement

This is the most solemn of all of the festivals listed, and it is certainly not a feast day.

> *'It is a Sabbath of rest for you, and you must deny yourselves. From the evening of the ninth day of the month until the following evening you are to observe your Sabbath.'*

(verse 32)

The people are to make this day a sacred fast, and to do absolutely no work so that there is a strict observance of the Sabbath. This is the day when the high priest wore simple clothes and entered the Holy of Holies, the innermost part of the Temple in Jerusalem, to make a sacrifice for his own sins and another for the sins of the nation. It was the annual occasion when the nation sought to put itself right with God again. In the blood of the sacrifice the past is written off. The fasting and self-denial are acts of penance by the people. In all of this there would be reminders of the relationship between God and his people, with the responsibility of the people to keep the laws. Because this was an act of the whole nation it was important that everyone took part, and those who refused to do so were thereafter not considered to be part of the people of God.

Today's Jews call this day 'Yom Kippur', and this year it takes place on 26 September. If you would like to know more about the rituals for this day, read Leviticus 16.

✝ Father God, I ask for your forgiveness for the wrong things that I have done, and for the good things that I have failed to do. Please free me from the guilt of the past so that I can look to the future in hope. Amen

The biblical pattern   John Oldershaw

Saturday 22 September
Leviticus 23:33-44

Feast of Tabernacles or Shelters

The harvest is complete, and so there is a wonderful week-long celebration. Again we are given precise timings for when this festival should be held, and as before in this week's readings, the purpose is twofold. There is a party atmosphere as the stages of the agricultural year are celebrated and enjoyed, but also these festivals recall crucial events in God's dealings with his people.

> *'Live in booths for seven days . . . so your descendants will know that I had the Israelites live in booths when I brought them out of Egypt. I am the LORD your God.'*

(part of verse 42, and verse 43)

We are here brought back to the events following the Passover, when God's people were on the long journey to the Promised Land. There were times when they were certain of God's presence, and there were times of uncertainty.

At this festival, by building temporary shelters (booths or tabernacles) from branches of trees each year, there was confirmation of God's continuing presence.

† Father God, as I come to the end of the week help me to celebrate all that I have achieved and to rest secure in the shelter of your care. Amen

For group discussion and personal thought

- In what ways has thinking about these ancient festivals helped you to realise that God is present in festival times that you enjoy today?

- What key moments in your life do you remember each year, and celebrate with a party of some kind? Do you always thank God for those times?

- Some anniversaries are remembrances of sad times; do you open yourself to God at these times too?

John Oldershaw   The biblical pattern

Jewish festivals

2 Jewish festivals today

Notes based on the *New Revised Standard Version* by

Kate Hughes

Kate worked for the church in Southern Africa for 14 years. Returning to England in 1990, she is now a freelance book editor, and is also active in her local church and community. She is currently editor of *Light for our Path*.

Introduction

In the first week of this theme we looked at the biblical basis of the major Jewish festivals. But this is still a living tradition, and this week the readings are texts used at the celebration of the festivals today, which will help us to understand their meaning for contemporary Judaism.

Sunday 23 September: *Genesis 21:1-14*
Rosh Hashanah (New Year)

> *God said to Abraham, 'Do not be distressed because of the boy and because of your slave woman . . . for it is through Isaac that offspring shall be named for you.'*

> (part of verse 12)

Rosh Hashanah is the Jewish New Year; the two-day festival began this year on 17 September. Like the non-religious Western New Year on 1 January, Rosh Hashanah is a time for looking back with thanksgiving and penitence and looking forward to the future. It is an opportunity to look seriously at your life, your past achievements, your values and what you would like to achieve in the coming year. Rosh Hashanah is celebrated in the context of being God's chosen people, and in the long history of God's dealings with the Jews. Today's reading from Genesis is used in the New Year services, and reminds the worshippers of God's choice of Abraham and his descendants. Being the chosen people brings responsibilities as well as privileges. The story of Ishmael is also a reminder that to choose one thing is to reject something else; but although Ishmael was sent away from Israel, God continued to care for him. Privilege should not override compassion.

† God of the past and of the future, forgive us our old sins and help us to live as your sons and daughters in the days to come.

Yom Kippur (Day of Atonement)

The Day of Atonement, which takes place ten days after Rosh Hashanah, continues the New Year theme of penitence for the past, but with a much greater and more solemn emphasis on the seriousness of sin. The ten days between the two festivals (the Days of Repentance or Days of Awe) are spent putting right what has been done wrong, in particular asking forgiveness from people and sorting out relationships. Yom Kippur is also a day for asking God's forgiveness for broken vows, promises made to him that could not be fulfilled.

> *[T]he men feared the LORD even more, and they offered a sacrifice to the LORD and made vows.*

(verse 16)

The first chapter of Jonah is chaotic. Jonah's call, his running away, the storm at sea, the desperation of the crew, Jonah's conviction that only his being thrown overboard will save the situation, and the eventual reluctant agreement of the sailors, come tumbling one after another, finally ending in the sea becoming calm and Jonah having three days of quiet inside the whale to think things over. The crew, too, have been through a traumatic experience; they have had to accept throwing a man overboard as the will of God, and have seen the hand of God in the ending of the storm. Their response is praise, sacrifice and vows. On Yom Kippur this passage reminds God's people that, like Jonah, they have been less loyal and less devoted than those sailors – who may not even have been Jews!

† Help us, O Lord, to seek your will and to do our best to follow it, and forgive us when we cannot live up to what we promise to you.

Kate Hughes

Jewish festivals today

Sukkot (Tabernacles)

Tabernacles was one of the three great pilgrimage feasts of the Jewish year, when Israelites were expected to live in booths made of boughs of trees and palm branches. This custom continues today, with booths being built either at home or at the synagogue. The booth is a place for meals, which the ancestors are invited to come and share. It is also a place to sit and think. Tabernacles commemorates the Israelites living in temporary shelters as they crossed the desert. So it is a time for looking back over both the past of the nation and one's own past; living in a fragile, temporary shelter helps to focus on the important things of life and get material things and possessions in perspective. This reading from Ecclesiastes helps to emphasise this: everything in this life is transitory or, as the Teacher would say, vanity. Ultimately the only thing that matters – and that endures – is God.

Fear God, and keep his commandments; for that is the whole duty of everyone.

(part of verse 13)

† O God, many people today measure success and happiness in terms of material possessions. Help us to focus on what is truly important – you.

September

Pesach (Passover)

For Christians Passover is irrevocably linked to the final days of Christ's life on earth. But for Jews, of course, it had and has a different significance. It is the example *par excellence* of God's choice of the people of Israel, and his care for them. This choice and care are not simply an event in the past; the annual celebration of Passover is a reminder that God's choice and care continue into the present. The Passover Haggadah that retells the story says: 'In every generation one is obligated to see oneself as one who personally went out of Egypt.' The core of Passover is freedom: retelling the story of God's mighty act of freeing the Israelites from slavery, thinking of those who are not free, celebrating one's freedom to discuss, question, make choices – and questioning what is done with that freedom.

> *[T]his is my God, and I will praise him,*
> *My father's God, and I will exalt him . . .*
> *In your steadfast love you led the people whom you redeemed;*
> *You guided them by your strength to your holy abode.*

(part of verse 2, and verse 13)

✝ O Lord, thank you for the freedoms we have, above all our liberation from the slavery of sin. Help us to use our freedom to your honour and glory.

Kate Hughes   Jewish festivals today

Exodus 19:9 – 20:2

Shavuot (Pentecost)

As last week's readings reminded us, Shavuot, the Feast of Weeks, was the festival of the first fruits, a pilgrimage festival to offer the first of the harvest at the Temple in Jerusalem. This agricultural element is remembered in the reading of the book of Ruth during the Shavuot services. But as today's reading tells us, Shavuot also celebrates the giving of the Torah, God's law. A custom associated with the festival is to spend a night studying Torah. The giving of the law also marked the beginning of the covenant between God and the Israelites, a covenant that gives Jews their special identity.

> Then the LORD said to Moses, 'I am going to come to you in a dense cloud, in order that the people may hear when I speak with you and so trust you ever after.'

(part of verse 9)

Although it is Moses who goes up into the mountain and meets with the Lord, all the people have to prepare themselves for the great event. This is a covenant for the whole community; everyone has to recognise its seriousness, the holiness of the God with whom they are dealing, and the depth of commitment the covenant demands. In return, they will be special to God: 'If you obey my voice and keep my covenant, you shall be my treasured possession out of all the peoples' (Exodus 19:5).

In the Christian calendar, the feast of Pentecost has a different emphasis. But it still reaches back to its Jewish original and the idea of a covenant with God; Christians, however, are the people of the new covenant.

† O Lord, help all of us, Christian people and Jewish people, who see ourselves as people of your covenant, to take our commitments seriously.

September

Jewish festivals today

Kate Hughes

Hannukah (Dedication)

The word Hannukah means dedication and the festival commemorates the re-dedication of the Temple in Jerusalem after it had been desecrated by the Syrian ruler Antiochus Epiphanes IV in 168BC. The Syrians occupied Palestine and attempted to stamp out Judaism. The Jews fought back, led by a man called Mattathias and his five sons (known as the Maccabees). After three years of costly guerrilla warfare, they managed to drive out the Syrians and one of their first acts was to purify and re-dedicate the Temple. This included lighting the gold hanukiah or nine-branched lamp. A later story, found in the Talmud, tells that there was not enough oil left in the Temple to light the hanukiah for more than one day, but that small amount of oil miraculously lasted for the whole eight days of the dedication festivities. In commemoration, at the modern festival of Hannukah a candle is lit each night in a nine-branched hanukiah. Today's reading describes such a hanukiah (verse 2), but it is a later verse that encapsulates the deeper significance of Hannukah:

> 'This is the word of the LORD to Zerubbabel: Not by might, nor by power, but by my spirit, says the LORD of hosts.'

(part of verse 6)

The provision of oil was a miracle, but the greater miracle was that with the help of God a few men could defeat the might of Assyria, the weak could overcome the strong. The story of Hannukah is a source of hope.

† O Lord, at times when we have neither might nor power, may your spirit strengthen and protect us and help us to overcome evil.

September

Kate Hughes   Jewish festivals today

Purim

The book of Esther is another (fictional?) account of Jews overcoming attempts to exterminate them. The feast takes its name from the lot or pur cast by the villain Hamon to decide on the day when he would destroy the Jews (Esther 3:7), and is also known as the Feast of Lots. For many centuries it has been one of the most joyous Jewish festivals, marked by a festive meal and the giving of small gifts of food to family and friends, and to the needy (verse 19). It is also an occasion for riotous celebration of the downfall of Hamon, with satirical and humorous acting out of the story that includes plenty of audience participation, dressing up, feasting and drinking. Not only were the Jews saved from the evil intentions of Hamon, they were also authorised to destroy those who opposed them:

> when the king's command and edict were about to be executed, on the very day when the enemies of the Jews hoped to gain power over them, but which had been changed to a day when the Jews would gain power over their foes, the Jews gathered in their cities . . . to lay hands on those who had sought their ruin.

(part of verses 1-2)

Once again, God had looked after his people.

† O Lord, help us to celebrate your goodness and to rejoice that you are our God.

For group discussion and personal thought
• What can you learn from the thinking and theology behind the Jewish festivals you have considered this week?

September

Jewish festivals today   Kate Hughes

Jewish festivals

3 The festivals in the ministry of Jesus

Notes based on the *New International Version* by

Michael N. Jagessar

Michael Jagessar, a minister of the United Reformed Church, serves the URC as Secretary for Racial Justice and Multicultural Ministry and is also moderator-elect (2012–14). Michael has lived, studied and ministered in Guyana, Jamaica, Grenada, Curacao, Switzerland and the Netherlands. For more on Michael's work and writings visit his webpage: www.caribleaper.co.uk

Introduction

The gospel accounts of Jesus reflect a life and culture that is thoroughly Jewish in context. Growing up in a Jewish home, Jesus would have attended synagogue services each Shabbat, observed all the Jewish holidays and festivals, and respected the Temple by making pilgrimage to Jerusalem. When he began his ministry, Jesus did not set out to break the Law of Moses. His arguments with the religious leaders of the day were often over the finer points of incidental issues. Jesus ultimately objects to the hypocrisy reflected in practice, not the traditions or festivals themselves.

Sunday 30 September: *Matthew 12:1-14*

Mercy, not sacrifice: Jesus and the sabbath

'Sabbath rest' is meant to be a time to remember and celebrate God's goodness in creation and redemption. Such 'rest' does not, however, exempt us from love for our neighbour. Jesus points out that human need takes precedence over our religious observances: mercy and kindness are to become lived worship. In these conversations he was not trying to eliminate the sabbath or challenge the Ten Commandments or Torah. He was reminding his questioners of the real intent of the sabbath requirements: God's mercy for the oppressed, the poor, the sick and the hungry. This is a timely reminder for all peoples of faith. Practising faithfulness is more urgent than our rules!

> *'If you had known what these words mean, "I desire mercy, not sacrifice", you would not have condemned the innocent.'*

(verse 7)

---

† Sabbath God, transform our hearts with your love, that we may freely serve our neighbours.

Monday 1 October

A Sabbath-rest for all

Rest plays an important part in the biblical stories of creation. Human beings are not meant to be workaholics. The Christian faith has a lot to do with rest. God not only rested, but promises to give God's people rest. Jesus not only sought rest for himself in quiet place, he also offered rest to the tired. In our turbo-driven culture and our 'mad rush to nowhere', we usually rest because we are tired, exhausted and stressed out. It is not God's purpose for us to be anxious and tired human beings. In Christ we are invited to come into the rest that God offers for our lives. This offer underscores that God has completed everything already and we can live in the enjoyment of God's blessings in ways that honour the principle of Sabbath. The strength to face each day comes from resting in what God freely provides through Jesus. It is from the perspective of living in the promised blessings of God that we are invited to face life, seeking first God's kingdom and righteousness and knowing that all these things have already been given to us!

There remains, then, a Sabbath-rest for the people of God; for anyone who enters God's rest also rests from his own work, just as God did from his.

(verses 9-10)

† Patient God, instil in us a sense of peace and joy and a persevering heart, as we walk a life of obedient trust in you. Amen

October

The festivals in the ministry of Jesus   Michael Jagessar

Keeping the festival

The layered and complex stories of the Corinthian church read very much like those of many contemporary and modern-day congregations. How we handle difficult situations in the congregation today may differ from the approach of Paul, yet there are connecting insights that remain as pertinent as ever. In these few verses, Paul presents us with an analogy around dough, yeast and unleavened bread. As a new creation, both individually and as a congregation, Christians should strive to be the new people they already are in Christ, and not fall back into restrictive ways, habits and patterns. At a time when immense pressure is placed on followers of the Jesus Way to rethink and reconfigure who they are in order to meet the demands of diverse and complex contexts, there is the ever-present danger of moving away from this Way and the liberating message of the gospel – a message of release, sincerity and truth. Keeping the festivals and rituals of our faith tradition needs a different kind of bread – the bread of sincerity and truth.

[L]et us keep the Festival, not with the old yeast, the yeast of malice and wickedness, but with bread without yeast, the bread of sincerity and truth.

(verse 8)

† Vulnerable God, may your Spirit take hold of our lives and raise us up to walk your way of truth and sincerity, so that our celebrating of festivals is brought alive to reflect your way. Amen

Michael Jagessar   The festivals in the ministry of Jesus

Colossians 2:16 – 3:4

Made for goodness: a wider perspective on festivals

Here Paul gets practical. Those who aspire to walk the Way of Jesus must live lives characterised by goodness. We are called to walk the talk of the Jesus Way and to do so by remembering our first steps. We began our Christian walk by putting our trust in God in Christ. And that is the way we should continue. For in Christ we are already given fullness, having clothed ourselves with a renewed identity. The reminder is timely: to walk the way of God in Christ is about entering a relationship with Jesus. A renewed identity is not about giving up who we are as human beings. It is about renouncing or turning away from ways that deny fullness of life, and embracing goodness and a generous lifestyle. The question we all need to ask is: in what ways have we turned Jesus' offer of new life into rigid piety, puritanical ethics, and restrictive and excluding regulations? In Christ we have been remade for goodness, hence the imperative to live it! Besides, there is still more growing to take place . . .

These are a shadow of the things that were to come; the reality, however, is found in Christ.

(verse 17)

† Life-giving Saviour, give us new hearts, minds and spirits to live lives of holiness that will bring honour to your name as we continue to grow in your image. Amen

October

The festivals in the ministry of Jesus — Michael Jagessar

Thursday 4 October

John 10:22-42

Dedication festival

Are you really the Christ? What a question within the precincts of the Temple of Solomon! What did John have in mind? Perhaps the references to the festival of the dedication of the Temple (Hanukkah) and the season of winter are intended to underscore hope for the holy flock of God. Perhaps Jesus is here engaging with the dissenters of his time and the story is being retold by John in his first-century Jewish Christian communities, rife with conflicts and the creating of fences. The challenges and oppositions represented in this text are between Jesus and his followers and those with authority and privileged status who seem more inclined to follow the laws to the letter. Evidently his challengers were looking for definitive answers. The message of Jesus could not be plainer, though perhaps confounding: no one and nothing will remove God's people from the caring, restoring, life-giving embrace of God. Now who will ever desire to stay away from the voice that invites us to consider such an offer? It may be that we need to rediscover the dedication festival with our tradition!

'My sheep listen to my voice; I know them, and they follow me.'

(verse 27)

---

† Persistent God, we thank you for calling us and for sticking with us, even though we often fail to heed your invitation to take up your offer of fullness of life. Amen

Michael Jagessar   The festivals in the ministry of Jesus

Tabernacles and transfiguring love

For Matthew, Jesus stands in continuity with Israel's tradition of the Law and the prophets. Hence we read of Moses and Elijah (rather than Elijah and Moses as in Mark's account). Mountains are metaphorically where earth touches heaven, and in many religious traditions, especially Judeo-Christian traditions, mountains have always been considered places where a special relationship with the Divine is developed. And so on a mountain top Jesus experiences the appearance of God's glory – an affirming sign of God's grace and compassion. We are told to listen to Jesus, who calls us beyond the boundaries of our safe comfort-zones. The story of the transfiguration of Jesus is a story about the Divine who cannot be neatly gift-wrapped and given out like a bundle of assured grace. It's a story about a God who is beyond our control, who challenges us to change the way we think and feel and act. Perhaps what we also have here is an invitation to listen in on Jesus' conversation with Moses and Elijah. At the same time, we cannot remain in the private tents we have created. A consequence of our transfiguring encounters is the call to nurture spaces where God's vision of a present and future of peace and justice will take root and grow, 'tabernacling' and transfiguring in the valleys and plains of our messy living.

'This is my Son, whom I love; with him I am well pleased. Listen to him!'

(part of verse 17)

---

† Transfiguring God, open our eyes to see your love transfigured through Christ, the light of the world – your light. May your light shine upon us and be reflected in all our thoughts, words and acts. Amen

October

The festivals in the ministry of Jesus   Michael Jagessar

Saturday 6 October

Acts 2:1-13

Pentecost

One of the three pilgrimage festivals, Pentecost celebrated both the gathering in of the harvest and the coming of the divine Law on Sinai, when, according to legend, a flame came down from heaven and divided into as many tongues of fire as there were nations of the world. All could understand, but only one nation promised to keep the Law – the biblical Israel. This is the background to Luke's scene of wind and fire. God is acting again. The promise of an abundant flow of God's Spirit is being fulfilled. God's Word is being declared. These people with tongues of flames around their heads are again the true Israel, committed to obey God's Word. History is repeating itself, but in a new way. The focus on the biblical Israel is reflected in Luke's reference to Jews from all parts of the empire. This is a celebration of God and God's people. Later in Acts 10 the same blessing becomes available to people of other nations. Human beings may create walls and barriers, but God will have the last word that will disrupt our order and transform all lives. Such is the unpredictable nature of God's Spirit!

All of them were filled with the Holy Spirit and began to speak in other tongues as the Spirit enabled them.

(verse 4)

† Holy Spirit, break into our midst and move through our lives empowering us to bear faithful witness to the life-giving work of Christ. Amen

For group discussion and personal thought

- In what ways do our festivals and rituals enable us to 'listen to' Christ, and in what ways might they undermine our hearing of Christ?
- In what sense have we 'died' and been 'raised' with Christ? How is this reflected in our practices?
- How do we communicate transfiguration or other mountain-top experiences that God gives us?

October

Michael Jagessar   The festivals in the ministry of Jesus

Readings in Mark

6 Following Jesus (1)

Notes based on the *New Living Translation* by

Joan Stott

Joan Stott is a Lay Preacher in the Uniting Church in Australia, and in her 'retirement' is writing a three year series of prayers and meditations based on the Revised Common Lectionary readings from the Psalms entitled *The Timeless Psalms*.

Introduction

It is astonishing that God chose sinful people as close partners in proclaiming the 'good news' of God's plan for the liberation, renewal and restoration of humanity to its original relationship with God. God's plan was for unity, balance, cohesion and order within creation, especially in human relationships between all age groups, genders, cultures and traditions.

Sunday 7 October: *Mark 10:2-12*

Partners in God's grace

Jesus was teaching his 'kingdom' values to his new disciples as they followed him, moving often between theory and practical issues to help their understanding. Jesus refused to be drawn into a trick question about Moses' Law and divorce.

> But Jesus responded, 'He wrote those instructions only as a concession to your hard-hearted wickedness. But God's plan was seen from the beginning of creation, for "He made them male and female." This explains why a man leaves his father and mother and is joined to his wife, and the two are united into one.'
>
> (verses 5-7, and part of verse 8)

In his ministry, Jesus sought to enable people to live with God in a personal partnership of love and acceptance, and to experience the fullness of God's grace. Jesus told his disciples that his ministry objective was 'to give life in all its fullness' (John 10:10). Anything that diminishes that, especially within the 'oneness' of physical marriage relationships, is contrary to God's plan.

† Lord Jesus, each day may I live within the fullness of your grace.

October

Monday 8 October
Mark 3:13-19

Partners in ministry

Years ago, I was selected in a 'school' of twelve people for a three-year trial of a hospital-based nursing apprenticeship. Our group had various levels of education and life experiences, yet we developed a close bond as we lived and learned together, and shared our apprenticeship's 'ups and downs'. We had practical and theory sessions, but most of our 'hands-on learning' was with senior ward nurses in 'live' situations. After three years, I passed my tests and became a 'real' nurse.

> *[Jesus] called the ones he wanted to go with him. And . . . he selected twelve of them to be his regular companions, calling them apostles.*

(part of verses 13-14)

Jesus spent a night alone praying on a mountain before selecting twelve men from a larger group of people to be his apprentice apostles. These men became Jesus' new family, sharing the 'ups and downs' of their daily life with him; and a very close bond developed over those three years. These twelve men had times of theory and practical work as they tried to understand what Jesus was teaching them. They had 'hands-on learning', and they then tested, assessed and analysed with their teachers and with the other apprentices all they had learned and experienced. They gradually learnt their new vocation in discipleship from Jesus, and eventually became 'real' apostles – 'people sent with a message'. Jesus authorised these apostles with power to carry on his work amongst the people of Israel, God's chosen people, who for generations had failed to live by God's Law for spiritual and community living. Now in Jesus, and through his apostles' ministry, the new people of Israel and the new kingdom began to develop.

† Lord Jesus, each day may I better learn to follow you.

Joan Stott   Following Jesus 1

Mark 3:31-35

Partners in dreaming:

I grew up in a small rural town with mainly industrial-type career opportunities, and although there were reasonable education facilities, it was difficult for women to develop a 'good' career. Perhaps because of this, my parents had only a 'small dream' for me.

Following Jesus' birth, Mary and Joseph were visited by excited shepherds, who said that God's angels had given them a message about a new baby. They had rushed into the village to see everything for themselves and to share their news. 'Mary quietly treasured these things in her heart and thought about them often' (Luke 2:19). Jesus grew up in Nazareth and as the eldest son in a large family, he worked in Joseph's carpentry business until he reached the age of thirty, when his life focus changed and he began to fulfil his destiny.

When Jesus was called 'Rabbi', did Mary's family think Jesus had reached the pinnacle of his career? Did they have 'small dreams' for their brother and were anxious that he was over-extending himself? Mary's family's insights were limited by the teachings of 'old order' from Moses' Law, and they did not take into account the emerging revelation of Jesus' 'new order' in God's plan of salvation. Jesus' response to his family's arrival stunned his audience.

'Who is my mother? Who are my brothers? . . . Anyone who does God's will is my brother and sister and mother.'

(part of verse 33, and verse 35)

Jesus received familial support from his disciples and followers, but his own family joined the growing number of people who 'did not understand' Jesus or his ministry; and potentially, they were a limiting element on his ministry.

† Lord Jesus, may my dreams be large enough for your kingdom.

October

Following Jesus 1   Joan Stott

Mark 8:1-10

Partners in generosity

Years ago, I was a guest in a small Pacific island community that was experiencing very hard times both socially and economically. The normal Pacific practice is to offer special guests a welcoming feast which usually included fish, lobster, chicken, pork and other local delicacies; but in this instance, the 'feast' comprised rice, seaweed, grated coconut and just a few small fish. However, while the food was scarce, their welcome was generous and loving. This was a feast for the soul rather than the body.

So Jesus . . . took the seven loaves, thanked God for them, broke them into pieces, and gave them to his disciples, who distributed the bread to the crowd.

(part of verse 6)

Unlike the previous miracle, where Jesus fed the '5000' Jewish people in lush green pastures, this 'feast' was for Gentile people who were far from home and in desert-type surroundings. Jesus compassionately offered these people a feast for the soul and the body, symbolising the openness of God's heart to all people, not just the descendants of Abraham. It also showed the breadth of God's love dwelling in Jesus, that he met both their physical and spiritual needs.

The similarities and contrasts of these two miracles cannot be ignored. Following Jesus means travelling in both pleasant and harsh situations and in congenial and hostile circumstances. It also means having one's soul filled with God's forgiveness and grace, with love and mercy.

Mark described Jesus' disciples as being slow, forgetful, and unable to understand new concepts or insights. I find this very encouraging because we all fail at times to 'read the signs' or understand what is right in front of us.

† Lord Jesus, may I continue to experience a feast of the soul with you.

October

Joan Stott

Following Jesus 1

Partners in struggle

The Pharisees came to Jesus demanding a 'sign' of his authority from God to demonstrate finally to everyone that Jesus was a fraud; and to prove that Jesus was not the leader of any potential new threat to their religious hierarchy.

As the apprentice apostles journeyed with Jesus, they continued to share their knowledge, their experiences, their misunderstandings and their confusion. They were all travelling by boat back to Jewish territory when Jesus asked them nine questions, one after the other. Does your mind freeze when you are asked several questions at once, and you are not even sure why you are being asked those questions? The disciples could only answer the last two questions because they had been involved in counting the left-over food; the other seven questions made them even more confused. Then Jesus asked them:

'Don't you understand even yet?'

(part of verse 21)

The 'not yet' must have given them all some hope that eventually all would be understood, and that the apostles would finally fulfil their appointed role. The disciples knew Jesus was exasperated with them, yet they seemed helpless in their struggle to resolve their lack of understanding. Jesus knew that faith in him and his message could not exist or grow when visual evidence was always demanded as a requirement of that faith. What was the 'faith in Jesus' that the disciples misunderstood, and the Pharisees forcefully refused to accept? The writer to the Hebrews answers the question about what is faith in Jesus: '[Faith] is the confident assurance that what we hope for is going to happen. It is the evidence of things we cannot yet see' (Hebrews 11:1).

† Lord Jesus, may my faith in you keep growing.

October

Partners in vulnerability

Wearing a cross as jewellery is common, and clergy members often wear a cross as a symbol of their privileged right for access to people and places. However, this is not what Jesus meant by 'taking up my cross'. Taking up the cross daily is a holy and deliberate act of submission and acceptance of Jesus' lordship, and not a whimsical choice of what jewellery to wear today.

Jesus was on his way to Jerusalem and towards all that would happen there. Jesus needed to make future challenges and situations clear to his disciples; but also to the crowds who followed him everywhere; and to everyone who would follow Jesus in every succeeding generation.

> *Then he called his disciples and the crowds to come over and listen. 'If any of you wants to be my follower,' he told them, 'you must put aside your selfish ambition, shoulder your cross, and follow me.'*

(part of verse 34)

Jesus was open and honest with all his would-be followers. He repeatedly told them that in following him they should not only selflessly love God, but equally love their neighbour. They should expect to be misunderstood and rejected; and there was no room in the coming kingdom for procrastination or second thoughts. Instead, they would experience risky times which would affect relationships, employment and lifestyle. Jesus did not want 'hangers on' in his kingdom! He wanted and still wants people who are prepared to be vulnerable, just as Jesus was – and indeed, just as God was vulnerable – by allowing God's own self to rely on flawed humanity to continue Jesus' work of bringing in the kingdom.

† Lord Jesus, may I take up my cross each day for the sake of your kingdom.

Joan Stott   Following Jesus 1

Saturday 13 October

Mark 10:13-16

Partners in the kingdom

Several years ago, it was my unforgettable privilege to visit the Kingdom of Tonga as a guest, to lunch with the Queen of Tonga, lead worship and address a meeting in the presence of Her Majesty, and ride in the royal limousine. However, for cultural and historical reasons there are restrictions on being a guest of Tongan royalty. God's kingdom has no such restrictions; this is how Jesus commenced his ministry: '[He] went to Galilee to preach God's Good News. "At last the time has come!" he announced. "The Kingdom of God is near! Turn from your sins and believe this Good News!"' (Mark 1:14-15). Jesus, as God's herald, pronounced the coming kingdom; as God's presence amongst humanity, he invited people to repent and become transformed members of the kingdom; as host to children who were not normally brought to worship, he challenged his disciples not be distracted by the artificial barriers of culture or class, gender or age; and he ignored existing protocols by blessing the children and placing them centrally within God's kingdom. He said to them,

> 'Let the children come to me. Don't stop them! For the Kingdom of God belongs to such as these.'

(part of verse 14)

Children cannot pay or earn their way into God's favour, so in their innocent simplicity they model for us the way to enter into the fullness of life in Christ and receive the gifts of God's kingdom.

† Lord Jesus, may I accept the gift of God's kingdom with childlike faith.

For group discussion and personal thought
• When do we graduate from being an apprentice disciple?
• Can faith in Jesus grow even while people are confused or doubting?
• How do you react to the concept that God is vulnerable?

October

Following Jesus 1

Joan Stott

Readings in Mark

7 Following Jesus (2)

Notes based on the *New International Version* by

Anne Roberts

Anne's working life was divided between school teaching (including two years in Uganda) and church administration and teaching. Now almost retired, she works for part of the year in college administration and is still actively involved in the church.

Introduction

Reading this week's passages at one sitting gives a strong sense of what a serious thing it was to follow Jesus – no flower-strewn path in pleasant sunshine. There was to be no compromise; the impossible was expected; earthly security must be abandoned; Jesus himself would die a terrible and apparently untimely death. There would be deception and persecution, leading to a deep sense of isolation, but faith and endurance would ultimately be rewarded.

Sunday 14 October: *Mark 10:17-22*
Hanging on

> *Jesus looked at him and loved him.*

(part of verse 21)

Here was a young man determined to live according to God's law as regards duty towards his neighbour. But Jesus saw in him only disappointment, duty and no love, discerning that when it came to parting with his wealth to help the poor there was a deep resistance. He was torn apart on the inside and Jesus saw this and loved him.

If our experience falls short of the abundant life Jesus promised, we must question the quality of our discipleship. There are times when the circumstances of life will deprive us of any sense of satisfaction, fulfilment or meaning, but generally speaking if that is how we are, we need to examine our hearts and question our priorities. We must be sure we are letting go of everything that hinders us in following Jesus and enjoying eternal life.

† Lord, help me to see myself clearly, and if I am hanging on to anything that hinders my following of you, give me the strength to let go of it.

Monday 15 October

Mark 10:23-27

Letting go

'It is easier for a camel to go through the eye of a needle than for a rich man to enter the kingdom of God . . . all things are possible with God.'

(verse 25 and part of verse 27)

Rich people may be tempted to suppose that their own abilities have secured their riches. To some extent this is true. However, it does not take much discernment to note that someone of equal ability may for any number of reasons end up poor, and a touch of humility and gratitude to God does not come amiss in the rich. If the rich then make the mistake of assuming that their supposed abilities will also equip them to gain admission to the Kingdom of God, they are doubly deceived. So it is not riches as such that hinder entrance to God's kingdom but the pride that so easily comes with them, because that entrance and inclusion are purely a matter of grace and gift. Anything that gives rise to self-sufficiency in spiritual matters is a serious hindrance, since by definition grace and gift cannot be earned.

Many of us are possessed of a determination to pull ourselves up by our own bootstraps, to earn our way into the kingdom. As with the young man in yesterday's reading, Jesus looks at us and loves us and longs for us to let his Spirit do the impossible. As we surrender our wills to his, the eye of the needle becomes the gateway to God's kingdom.

† Lord, thank you that you want to give me only the best. Help me to let go of all that is second best and enter into the glory and wonder of life in your kingdom.

October

Following Jesus 2

Anne Roberts

Tuesday 16 October

Mark 10:28-31

Leaving all

Peter is confident that he and the other disciples have let go of all that would hinder them in following Jesus, and he is not slow to assert this. Jesus assures him and others listening that the compensations will far outweigh the sacrifice. God's people will be our home and our family if we are called to separate ourselves from those places and people in which we used to find security. Throughout Christian history this has proved to be the case, especially in those situations where persecution forced the removal – and Jesus does not hide the fact that there will be persecution.

'But many who are first will be last, and the last first.'

(verse 31)

Having drawn his listeners' attention to the age to come, Jesus warns them that even then there will be surprises. We can bring false values into the kingdom with us and inflict our old sense of hierarchy on how we view people. The apostles, the leaders, those who have made the greatest sacrifice, even died for their faith, will surely come first in the age to come. Not so, says Jesus. He knows the hidden ones: the widow who gave everything she had, the centurion who stayed at his post. He understood the predicament of those who could not leave home and family. Today he sees those who are tied to disabled children or parents. He sees the children of HIV/Aids parents who stay put to look after those parents and their siblings. He knows that their sacrifice is in staying rather than leaving, and they will receive their reward.

† Lord, continue to challenge our worldly values. Help us to see things, and more especially people, the way you see them, through your redeeming love.

Anne Roberts

Following Jesus 2

Wednesday 17 October

Mark 10:32-34

All the way

'They will condemn him to death and will hand him over to the Gentiles, who will mock him and spit on him, flog him and kill him. Three days later he will rise.'

(part of verse 33, and verse 34)

Jesus seems determined to court trouble. Another way of looking at it is to say that he was willing to leave or risk everything for the gospel and did not expect of others anything he would not do himself. He was prepared to be stripped of all outward dignity and suffer painful torture and death. At every step of the way he turns human values upside down. He does not seek anyone's favour or try to avoid trouble – he walks straight into it. Amazingly, all this will not mean the failure of his mission but guarantee its success. On the third day he will rise! He will be the first of those who are last to become first. The epistles make many references to the self-abasement of Christ and they encourage us to follow him in this, through death to resurrection.

There is significance in the fact that both Jews and Gentiles would be implicated in his death. This is a world event, not a minor blip in the history of a minor enclave of the Roman Empire. There is cosmic significance in its outcome. He would rise, to become the firstborn from the dead, thus guaranteeing our salvation.

† Father, when we are discouraged in our walk with you, give us grace to persevere. Help us to keep on keeping on, through the many little deaths that will lead to our resurrection with your Son. Thank you, Jesus, for your willingness to go through all that would secure the world's salvation.

October

Following Jesus 2

Anne Roberts

Thursday 18 October

Mark 9:38-49

Drastic measures

In words recorded in chapter 9, before our readings so far, Jesus had already sought to undermine the apostles' concept of status. Yet they now demanded to know what right those not called to be apostles had to cast out demons in Jesus' name. Jesus accepted willingness to be associated with his name as sufficient qualification. Even the children who place faith in him and who must be welcomed (verse 37) are to be treasured and protected.

> *'If your hand causes you to sin, cut it off. It is better for you to enter life maimed than with two hands to go into hell.'*

(part of verse 43)

Having your values turned upside down, recognising who and what are important and being consistent in living out your new understanding, may hinder you in terms of worldly progress but what you achieve will be of eternal value and will lead to life. From a heavenly perspective, to hang on to whatever keeps you from living in this way is actually to end up on the scrapheap, however 'successful' you may seem. (Gehenna, the word here translated 'hell', was the place outside Jerusalem where offal and rubbish were permanently on fire.)

Church and social hierarchies today still leave plenty of potential for sin of the kind Jesus is highlighting. We can covet status or give undue importance to those who have it and regard as unimportant those who don't or are just not 'one of us'. Reputation and recognition are important in the way many people think, but we may have to do without them and must learn impartiality if we are to enter into life.

† Lord Jesus, you did not show or covet favour. Strengthen our resolve to do the same.

October

Anne Roberts

Following Jesus 2

Mark 10:35-45

Being like him

'Can you drink the cup I drink or be baptised with the baptism I am baptised with?'

(part of verse 38)

Even those closest to Jesus were slow to learn. James and John still wanted to be important, to be noticed, recognised, and not just now but in Jesus' glory. They hadn't yet seen the lengths to which Jesus would go in showing us that this is not the way to live, and that his glory would be in the prints of nails and wound of spear. Sharing his cup and his baptism meant for the time being inclusion in the entourage of a man who was being noticed. The nature of that cup and that baptism was about to change but despite all that Jesus had said, they didn't see this. They were expecting only good times. On hearing of this, the indignation of the other apostles was possibly because they wanted the places James and John were asking for. Jesus tenderly seeks once again to set them on a better course.

When Jesus calls us to follow him he is under no illusions. He is always encouraging us to be more like him, because in that way lies true freedom and full human-ness. But he has oceans of patience. He doesn't get annoyed or consider dropping us. He loves us with the everlasting love of the Father and we are promised that we are (however slowly) being transformed (2 Corinthians 3:18).

---

† Thank you, Father, for your patience and kindness. Thank you that you never give up on me but love me passionately and tenderly. Teach me to recognise your cup, your baptism, your cross in my life and to yield myself to them.

October

Following Jesus 2   Anne Roberts

Saturday 20 October

Mark 13:1-13

Only by grace

The disciples followed Jesus to Jerusalem and witnessed his triumphal entry, but he warns them that things will now get worse before they get better. They will follow him through suffering and death. However, they do not need to be passive sufferers. They must watch out, stay calm, be on their guard and not worry about what to say.

> *'All men will hate you because of me, but he who stands firm to the end will be saved.'*

(verse 13)

Minority groups are often blamed for calamity, but if this befalls Jesus' disciples the presence of God's Spirit is guaranteed and they will be enabled to endure.

The gospel promises only that we will be saved *in* suffering and not *from* it and we cannot avoid the difficult question of the fate of Christians who deny Christ at such times. Knowing our own weakness we may doubt our own performance. Does Jesus say that our salvation depends on the 'work' of endurance? Would apostasy prove that we never truly belonged in the first place? Think about Peter.

---

† Lord, it is only by grace that I can hope to be saved. I have no plea but the cross of Jesus and his lordship over evil, including that in me. Have mercy on me, a sinner.

For group discussion and personal thought

- What helps you to swallow your pride or deny yourself something in order to be true to your calling to follow Jesus?
- Think back over the 'little deaths' you have suffered and ask yourself what you learned from them and how they helped you to grow towards maturity.
- How do you build yourself up in preparation for those times when you might be tempted to deny Christ?

October

Anne Roberts

Following Jesus 2

Eyes of God

1   God sees us where we are

Notes based on the *New International Version* by
Jember Teferra
Jember Teferra and her team established the Integrated Holistic Approach Project and have worked with the poorest of the poor in the slums of Addis Ababa for the past 20 years, alleviating poverty and promoting social justice.

Introduction
This week's theme may confuse those who have not glimpsed something of God's entirety. Those who know and follow him know his omnipresence – he sees every step of our way; his omniscience – his justice. When things go right we human beings feel his goodness, kindness, depth, height and justice, but when things go wrong all our spiritual values are challenged. In the readings this week about Job, David and Hezekiah we see God's pleasures in creating human beings and then regretting it and questioning why. Those who know God know that he is the 'all seeing' and 'all knowing' God, even if our attitude changes according to our circumstances. Fortunately, he sees and knows and understands us well.

Sunday 21 October: *Job 34:12-15, 21*
All-knowing and all-seeing God

His eyes are on the ways of men,
he sees their every step.

(verse 21)

Job, like all human beings, is complaining about God's dealing with him. In his circumstance who wouldn't? In my own life when I suffered I have asked 'Why has God brought this upon us – upon me?' If we examine ourselves or our circumstances, God's purposefulness should convince us that he does not punish or allow suffering for nothing. Job doubted this because he suffered physically, mentally and psychologically. He felt let down by God, his friends sometimes condemned him, even his wife told him to disown God. We know what happened to Job at the end: double blessings and more.

† Heavenly Father, when things go wrong and we suffer as we sometimes do, help us to recognise that you are there – the omnipresent and omniscient God. Increase our faith.

Monday 22 October

Genesis 1:26-31

God's purpose fulfilled

So God created man in his own image, in the image of God he created him; male and female he created them.

(verse 27)

How many of us human beings treat any other human being like ourselves? The whole of this portion of the Bible clearly shows how much God loves human beings. 'In the image of God he created him.' The king of kings, the greatest, the mighty, the most high God took the trouble to create us like himself. Do we deserve that privilege? Unfortunately, the whole of the Bible shows that if he had not been a one-way loving father he would not have tolerated the sinfulness of human beings. I never get used to or take for granted how, with the best of intentions, God used his skill to create human beings and give them all the very best to own, command and enjoy. What a privilege! Are we even grateful for it? If we are, how do we show it in practice? Do we treat with respect our fellow human beings who have been created in the image of God? Well, if we did there would be no poverty, no inequality, no class system or, generally, no injustice on earth.

† Heavenly father, do not let me forget for one second that I am privileged to be made in your likeness. Thank you for all that it means to me, and may I give my fellow human beings similar respect.

Jember Teferra   God sees us where we are

Tuesday 23 October

Genesis 6:5-8

The divine purpose lost

The LORD was grieved that he had made man on the earth, and his heart was filled with pain . . . But Noah found favour in the eyes of the LORD.

(verses 6 and 8)

In this portion of the Bible we see that not only was God let down by Adam and Eve, having honoured them by creating them in his own image; but as human beings multiplied (as they should) God was deeply grieved by the increasing sin and total disobedience, not to mention Abel's murder by his own brother Cain because of jealousy. But one encouraging thing he found was Noah – I think God always looks out for something good. He is not a fault finder like us human beings. I remember seeing monks in the monasteries located near our city. When the Marxists took over and mass killing and imprisonment became the order of the day, people went looking for the monks to ask them to pray. It was comforting to know that they prayed all day and all night – that was their full-time occupation. To this day I feel that when God could have been angry and destroyed our land, he somehow saved us. I see those monks like Noah – God used them to help nations survive the reign of terror.

† Our Lord, king and father, forgive us when we constantly grieve and pain you. Even though you sent your Son to save us, we still grieve and pain you – give us your Holy Spirit to help us to stop offending you.

God sees us where we are   Jember Teferra

Wednesday 24 October

Psalm 33:13-22

God the superior ruler and judge

Those of us who have experienced the rule of dictators can testify to what it means to have the confidence that David expresses in this psalm:

> [T]he eyes of the LORD are on those who fear him,
> On those whose hope is in his unfailing love,
> To deliver them from death
> and keep them alive in famine.

(verses 18-19)

Those of us who survived that terrible period in my country, having been imprisoned and nearly executed, know how privileged we were to have that confidence. Many who love the Lord were also victims, but God must have a reason for that too. But those of us he has allowed to survive observe with surprise how the mighty were overthrown by another of their kind and today are still in prison or have been killed by those they never expected to take power. The lesson we learn is that ultimately God is the ruler and the judge of this earth. We learnt to hope in his unfailing love, and to know that his loving eyes are always on us to keep us safe.

† When things go wrong, and they frequently will, help us to remember that your eyes are upon those who fear you, so keep us hoping in your unfailing love and concern.

Jember Teferra   God sees us where we are

God: omnipotent and omniscient

David, who was given very special gifts to express what he felt about God, never ceases to surprise those who read the Psalms. In this portion David describes God in his totality: his sovereignty, his height and depth, his supremacy, his holiness, his presence, his complete knowledge of everything. In general terms, God's omnipresence – God's presence with us no matter where we are; and God's omniscience, his total knowledge of us. David confidently describes God, using his talent to try to give an accurate picture of him. No wonder God describes David as a man of his own heart. For any of us who think we are not understood or that God has forgotten us, especially when things go wrong, David has a message.

> *O Lord, you have searched me*
> *and you know me . . .*
> *For you created my inmost being;*
> *you knit me together in my mother's womb.*

(verses 1 and 13)

† How great you are, Lord; only in you can we be totally and completely confident. Help us to grow in faith, so that we can continue to look up to you, come what may.

October

God sees us where we are

Jember Teferra

Friday 26 October

Deuteronomy 26:15-19

Covenant relationship demands obligation

Look down from heaven, your holy dwelling place, and bless your people Israel and the land you have given us as you promised . . . The LORD your God commands you this day to follow these decrees and laws; carefully observe them with all your heart and with all your soul.

(part of verse 15, and verse 16)

Today's reading clearly shows a two-way relationship. If we wish to follow the Lord then there is both an obligation and a privilege in the covenant relationship. Sometimes we want to behave like a spoilt child – as the saying goes, we want 'to have our cake and eat it'. But we can't treat God that way; if we wish to follow him we have to go step by step all the way as he did. He loved us with his one-way love, persistently, while we sinners rejected him; and he loved us so much that he gave his only-begotten son. He has kept his side of the covenant. He looks out for us and blesses us, but we are inconsistent and do not obey him with heart and soul.

† Lord, who is a God and a father like you, who deserves obedience, loyalty and love? May your Holy Spirit enable us to honour our covenant relationship and obligation.

Jember Teferra   God sees us where we are

Saturday 27 October

Isaiah 38:1-8

Ask and you shall receive

Hezekiah prayed to the LORD . . . 'This is what the LORD, the God of your father David, says: I have heard your prayer and seen your tears.'

(part of verses 2 and 5)

We can learn something from Hezekiah's faith. Immediately he was told by the prophet Isaiah that he was going to die he turned his face to the wall to weep and pray. What a prompt response came from the Lord: he heard and saw, and increased Hezekiah's lifespan by 15 more years. However different the outward circumstances, I can still recall one sleepless night 20 years ago. I had four different, difficult problems to sort out just before starting my present urban ministry. I honestly did not know how they were going to be solved. It must have been the Holy Spirit who made me get up and go to our study at 4 o'clock in the morning. It was like standing before a king who was asking me what I wanted. To this day I vividly remember how I spoke to him, as if making an appeal and negotiating, using different approaches. I even asked him why he ws calling me to an impossible ministry and leaving me to get on with it! What a loving, caring and understanding father he is! Within that very day all four problems were solved in the most dramatic way and I began my new ministry.

† My Lord and king and yet my caring and loving Father, what a privilege to know you, to love you and for ever to follow you – you never let me down.

For group discussion and personal thought
• How do you understand God's omnipresence and omniscience?
• Can you recall any significant circumstances when you felt that God is 'all knowing' and 'all seeing'?

October

God sees us where we are   Jember Teferra

Eyes of God

2   God seeks us out

Notes based on the *New International Version* and *Today's English Version* (TEV) by

Aileen Khoo

After working in the Methodist Church in Malaysia for 33 years, Aileen Khoo is now retired but continues to spend her time leading Bible studies and training Bible study leaders, besides teaching music and playing in ensemble.

Introduction

We might sometimes feel, in our busy, hectic world, that it is difficult to see God and know God's presence with us. We think we have to seek God out before we can be in contact. As these readings show, however, the opposite is true – it is God who seeks for, and watches over, us. Many stories and encounters in the Bible illustrate the fact that God wants to be in contact, to establish a relationship. The same is true of God's Son, who showed an overarching understanding and concern for each and every person he met. And today, that same care and reassurance is ours.

Sunday 28 October: *Psalm 32:8-11*
God sees and teaches

> *I will counsel you and watch over you.*

> (part of verse 8)

The Psalmist reminds us that 'He who watches over you will not slumber' (Psalm 121:3). God's eyes sought out Adam and Eve and exposed their sins. He sought out Abraham and Sarah and promised to shield them from harm. He sought out Hagar and picked her up after she was rejected by the very people who were responsible for her safety and welfare. He sought out Jacob the scoundrel, to bring him back to a new life. He sought out the oppressed Israelites to free them from bondage. He sought out David, a shepherd boy, to lead a nation. His eyes continuously seek out the fallen, the vulnerable, the rejects, the oppressed and the lowly. He counsels and guides. Only when we look to God can we know the direction God wants us to take. God never takes his eyes off you. God is watching over you. God is watching you!

† Even if I go through the deepest darkness, I will not be afraid, Lord, for you are with me. (Psalm 23:4, TEV)

Monday 29 October

Genesis 3:8-13

God sees and seeks out: Adam and Eve

[T]he man and his wife . . . hid from the LORD God.

(part of verse 8)

God's design in creation was to establish a harmonious order in which people would live together in peace under God's rule and in relationship with him. Adam and Eve enjoyed an enviable relationship with God until the day they had to hide. At least, they thought they could hide from God. But God was not going to allow Adam and Eve's mistake to destroy his plan. We still play the childish game of hide and seek, but the eyes of God continue to seek us out, and we cannot hide. God had given Adam and Eve all they needed, but they went beyond that to decide for themselves to disobey, so they hid. Humankind's efforts to deal with guilt are never successful. But God did not abandon them. In the cool of the evening, God came looking for Adam and Eve.

Ever since that fateful day we have continued to think that we can hide our wrongs from God. In the days of Noah, too, 'The Lord saw that the wickedness of humankind was great in the earth, and that every inclination of the thoughts of their hearts was only evil continually' (Genesis 6:5). We purposely take ourselves from the presence of God but God seeks us out. We all try to hide our sinfulness. Adam and Eve hid after disobeying and God had to call out 'Where are you?' The whole biblical account is about us hiding and God seeking, seeking to reconcile us to him. God continues to gather the sinful, broken, lonely, guilty people into a fellowship of love and trust.

† My sins, O God, are not hidden from you; you know how foolish I have been.
  Don't let me bring shame on those who trust in you, Sovereign Lord Almighty!
  Don't let me bring disgrace to those who worship you. (Psalm 69:5-6, TEV)

God seeks us out

Aileen Khoo

Genesis 15:1-6

God sees and protects: Abram and Sarai

'Do not be afraid, Abram. I am your shield.

(part of verse 1)

Into a world of paganism and idolatry God called Abram and Sarai in order to make them a blessing to all families of the earth. Abram was 75 years old when he left the comforts of Mesopotamia, the region watered by the two great rivers, the Tigris and Euphrates. The people of Mesopotamia had built cities and invented writing. They were one of the earliest civilisations. The elderly couple left their familiar and comfortable surroundings based on the confidence that God would be their shield. Their names were later changed to Abraham and Sarah. They were called to be nomads in the rough and rugged terrain of Canaan, leaving behind the lush green and fertile land of Mesopotamia. Abraham was a homeless Aramean and he confessed to the Hittites, 'I am an alien and a settler among you' (Genesis 23:3). Abraham lived in tents, pitching them here today and there tomorrow, but it was never as though he had left God behind. Abraham and Sarah had their fair share of troubles with his nephew's servants, with their neighbouring tribes, within his own household. But he journeyed on trusting in the protection of God's watchful eye shielding him from all troubles and calamities. God's call to Abram and Sarai and the birth of the people of Israel and their settlement in the Holy Land was to be a blessing to all people. God's people today have a similar role. They experience God acting in grace and power and are called to be witnesses of that to the world. Now as then, they fail, now as then, God patiently calls. The covenant community is called, shaped, tested, watched over by God every step of the way.

† All who find safety in you will rejoice. They can always sing for joy. Protect those who love you; because of you they are truly happy. You bless those who obey you, Lord; your love protects them like a shield. (Psalm 5:11-12, TEV)

October

Aileen Khoo

God seeks us out

Wednesday 31 October

Genesis 16:1-13

God sees and provides: Hagar

'I have now seen the One who sees me.'

(part of verse 13)

The Old Testament records the history of women who have been more often than not victims of oppression. Sarah ill-treated her Egyptian slave-girl Hagar and ultimately, with the connivance of her husband, drove her out into the desert with her infant son Ishmael. One would have thought that being aliens themselves would have taught Abraham and Sarah to be kind to Hagar, an alien among them.

Jesus said, 'Are not five sparrows sold for two pennies? Yet not one of them is forgotten by God' (Luke 12:6). There is a large tree outside my house that bears cherries once every month. So many sparrows come to feast on these cherries that they cover the whole tree. This is one of the times when you see sparrows fall. They fall, they die. The rest of the flock does not know about it or even if they do, they continue to fly on, leaving the dead or dying bird behind. Hagar is like the fallen sparrow in Jesus' story. She is dispensable, used by her mistress Sarah and then rejected. Somehow the realities of our lives do not seem to square with the assurance of Jesus that no sparrow is forgotten by God. God seems to be careless over the million-odd sparrows that fall. He seems to be careless of the thousands and millions hit by typhoons, earthquakes or wars. What has become of the sparrows that fall? They fall into the hands of God. Consider carefully how God deals with injustice.

God found Hagar. God is the God of those deserted, of those who are left out. One of my favourite hymns is by Civilla D. Martin (1869–1948): 'His eye is on the sparrow, and I know He watches me.'

---

† As I lie in bed, I remember you; all night long I think of you, because you have always been my help. In the shadow of your wings I sing for joy. I cling to you, and your hand keeps me safe. (Psalm 63:6-8, TEV)

October

God seeks us out   Aileen Khoo

Thursday 1 November

Genesis 28:10-17

God sees and directs: Jacob

Jacob, having cheated his brother and deceived his father, was running away. When Jacob was running for his life, God came to him in a dream. The fugitive hears holy words,

> 'I am with you and will watch over you wherever you go, and I will bring you back to this land. I will not leave you until I have done what I have promised you.'

(verse 15)

We often, like him, feel ourselves in spiritual exile, lonely travellers through what often seems an empty land. We long for the mystical feeling of God. We long for Jacob's ladder to bridge the gap between God and us. In any event, the wilderness seems to be an unlikely place in which to find comfort. Jacob does not deserve this vision, but he needed it. And all his life, in his groping and unworthy ways, he had desired it. Even on the rocky slopes where Jacob was alone there arose the shining stairway that brought the heavenly glory, with angels going up like the prayers of people to God and angels coming down like the grace of God to men and women. Therefore God comes to us not when we deserve him, but when we need him. People's contact with God can begin wherever they are and whenever their need reaches up to find the heavenly answers. Watch God carefully guard Jacob's step to maintain the covenant even amid deception. In verses 20-22 we read Jacob's conditional promise: 'If…'. Compare this with God's unconditional promise in verses 13-15. In return Jacob promised to give God one tenth, God gave his all.

† How wonderful are the good things you keep for those who honour you! Everyone knows how good you are, how securely you protect those who trust you. (Psalm 31:19, TEV)

Aileen Khoo

God seeks us out

God sees and rescues: Moses

The LORD said, 'I have indeed seen the misery of my people in Egypt, I have heard them crying out because of their slave drivers, and I am concerned about their suffering. So I have come down to rescue them from the hands of the Egyptians.'

(verse 7 and part of verse 8)

I have seen, I have heard, I am concerned, I have come down to rescue them. In Chinese folk religion there is worship of a high god who created the world. After that he disappeared and never came down again. He is not worshipped as much as the other gods because this high god does not meddle with people's daily affairs as much as they do. But the God we worship is continuously interested in human affairs. Not only has God 'seen their misery' and 'heard their cry'. Not only does God 'know their sufferings', God empathises and shares their pain. God gets involved in history. He takes sides. Everywhere that people are being oppressed and enslaved, God is aware of their struggle. God sees them and knows their conditions. The message of Exodus is that God hears, God sees, God knows, God remembers, God acts. God's covenant with Abraham and his descendants is still valid. God is faithful to his part of the agreement. In the Exodus God fulfils the promise of deliverance. That promise is to everyone who is 'in Egypt', to everyone who is in bondage.

When God said to Moses, 'What is that in your hand?' Moses saw only a stick that stood as a symbol of himself – a Hebrew slave raised as an Egyptian, a runaway murderer, a stutterer living in the desert as a shepherd. But God saw a different man – a compassionate man that God could use.

† But you do see; you take notice of trouble and suffering and are always ready to help. The helpless man commits himself to you; you have always helped the needy. (Psalm 10:14, TEV)

God seeks us out

Aileen Khoo

1 Samuel 16:1-12

God sees what we do not see: David

'The LORD does not look at the things man looks at. Man looks at the outward appearance, but the LORD looks at the heart.'

(part of verse 7)

We go by first impressions and looks. We choose our parliamentary candidates by their oratory and promises. We choose our friends by what we have in common and similar interests. But the character of a person is more important, for this shows the real person. Looks are often deceptive.

God commanded Samuel to anoint David, one of the sons of Jesse, to succeed Saul as king. He thought Eliab would be a suitable candidate. But God said 'No'. According to our standards, God chose unlikely standard bearers: Abraham and Sarah, an old couple, to birth a nation; Jacob the scoundrel to carry on the Covenant; Moses, a stutterer, to speak the law; and David the shepherd boy to be king. The Bible says God purposely chooses 'what the world considers nonsense in order to shame the wise' (1 Corinthians 1:27). God looks beyond the external. These people whom God chose have one thing in common: obedience and faithfulness. The heart of the matter is really the heart.

† Examine me and test me, Lord; judge my desires and thoughts. Your constant love is my guide; your faithfulness always leads me. (Psalm 26:2-3, TEV)

For group discussion and personal thought

- What evidence do you see of God looking for you?
- Consider some surprising (by worldly standards), even limited, people that God has used in a mighty way. What weaknesses do you have that God might see as a potential that he can use?
- Recall the times when God guided you: how did he do it? Who were the people God used?

Aileen Khoo

God seeks us out

Eyes of God

3   The watchful God

Notes based on the *New Revised Standard Version* by

Kate Hughes

For Kate's biography see p.271.

Introduction

'Watchful' can sound suspicious, always looking for mistakes
or wrong-doing, like a divine security guard. That is not
God's watchfulness – he is looking out for us, taking care of us. He is also
watching for us in the sense of looking to see if we are coming – like the
father of the prodigal son, God keeps an eye on the road so that he will
catch the first glimpse of us far away and can run to welcome us.

Sunday 4 November: *Psalm 53:1-3*
God looks for those who seek him

> *God looks down from heaven on humankind*
> *to see if there are any who are wise,*
> *who seek after God.*

(verse 2)

St Augustine of Hippo wrote, 'You have made us for yourself, and our hearts
are restless until they find their rest in you.' Or in more modern idiom, human
beings have a God-shaped hole within them. So it is not odd for people to
want to find God, to move towards him. On the contrary, it is wise. The
writer of this psalm takes a gloomy view: 'There is no one who does good,
no, not one' (verse 3), but God is actively on the look out for those who are
different. The slightest move in his direction and he will be there, helping
and supporting the seeker, even though it may be a long road home.

† Thank you, Father, for the restlessness that drives us home to you, and for your loving
support on the journey. Help us to give that support to others on the road.

Monday 5 November

Psalm 121

God watches over us constantly

Some parts of England are very flat – often because the land has been reclaimed from the sea through drainage schemes. Such countryside has its own attractions, but I personally would not like to live there. I need something on the horizon; not necessarily mountains but at least a hill, a rise in the ground. Hills can be a barrier, shutting people in, making it difficult for them to leave; they can be dangerous terrain; they can collapse and bury whole villages. But for many people, hills are comforting. They are a clear landmark, a sign from afar that you are almost home; they provide shelter from the weather, and in countries with more warmth and sunshine than England, they can be a life-saving source of shade. And hills are always there, they don't move like sand dunes; they symbolise a stability that few people experience in their lives. So they are a good image for God. In Old Testament times, hills or mountains were also favoured places for encountering God, as Moses and Elijah found.

He who keeps Israel
will neither slumber nor sleep.

(verse 4)

Like the hills, God never sleeps or disappears. He constantly watches over us, providing for all our needs, accompanying us on all our journeyings in life, delivering us from evil.

† Father, I know that however busy I may be today and in the days to come – so busy that I may not be very conscious of your presence – you will not forget me. Help me to remember that you are always with me, guiding me and protecting me, and help me to remember to thank you.

Kate Hughes

The watchful God

Tuesday 6 November

Jeremiah 24:4-7

God's eyes are on his people

When I was growing up in the 1940s and 50s, there were still older people who had framed embroidered biblical texts hung on their walls. One of them, I remember, was 'God sees you'. It was obviously intended as a dire warning and threat: don't step out of line, because God will see what you do and punish you for it. But in today's reading, God seeing the exiled Jews in Babylon is a great encouragement.

I will set my eyes upon them for good.

(part of verse 6)

One of the problems for the exiles was whether God could be with them in a foreign land. Their worship had been very centred on the Temple in Jerusalem. That was where God revealed himself, in the Holy of Holies. Would he be able to do the same in heathen Babylon, which had no temple for him? So God reassured his exiled people that he could keep an eye on them wherever they were. He would still be looking after them, supporting them in their exile and planning to bring them back to their own country. 'If I ascend to heaven, you are there; if I make my bed in Sheol you are there' (Psalm 139:8). To wrongdoers, the thought that there is nowhere they can go to escape the eyes of God may be terrifying. But to those who are searching for God or have been found by him, there is immense comfort and support in knowing that God is constantly working for our good, wherever we may be.

† Thank you, Lord, that your eyes see me wherever I am, and that you are always working for my good, even though I may not always find your activity comfortable.

November

The watchful God

Kate Hughes

Lamentations 3:49-59

God sees his people's distress

My eyes will flow without ceasing,
Without respite,
*Until the L*ORD *from heaven*
looks down and sees . . .
*You have seen the wrong done to me, O L*ORD*;*
judge my cause.

(verses 49-50 and 59)

God's watchfulness over his people and his working for their good is not confined to the personal and domestic, He is equally concerned for justice and for intervening on behalf of his people in political situations. There are echoes in today's reading of the Lord's reply to Moses in Exodus 3:7-8: 'I have observed the misery . . . I have heard . . . I have come down . . . and [will] bring up.' With God, to see is to act, and especially it is to intervene in situations of injustice. This works both ways: God saw the disobedience of his people and acted by sending them into exile in Babylon. Here he needs to see and act against the sufferings of his people in the besieged and desolate city of Jerusalem. But it all starts with God seeing.

† Thank you, Lord, that your eyes are always open to the needs of your people, and that when we cry to you in our troubles you will deliver us.

Kate Hughes   The watchful God

Thursday 8 November

Matthew 6:1-18

God sees when we pray or do good

It may have seemed from the readings so far this week that God's watchfulness is only concerned with sorting out problems and difficulties – coming to the rescue, defending from harm. But today's reading reminds us that God sees other things as well. He doesn't just see our disobedience, he also sees our obedience. He sees our suffering, but he also sees and shares our joys and achievements. No one else may ever discover what we have done, but God sees our private actions, the secrets of our hearts, and the slightest effort we make to please him and show our love.

> [W]henever you pray, go into your room and shut the door and pray to your Father who is in secret; and your Father who sees in secret will reward you.

> (verse 4)

Our fasting should be done in the same way: secretly, so that only our Father can see us (verse 18). It is not important – in fact it is not at all helpful – that others should see our good deeds: 'Beware of practising your piety before others in order to be seen by them' (verse 1). The only seeing that matters, the only seeing that will encourage us and reward us, is God's seeing. Developing a relationship with God goes on in the privacy of our own heart, mind and soul. You cannot look at strangers in the street and know what is going on between them and God. And the relationship will not grow if, like a child who has planted bulbs, you constantly dig it up to see what is happening. But God can see what is happening in secret, and he can provide all the nourishment, support and pruning that we need.

† Thank you, Lord, for the seeds of faith and love that you have planted in me. Thank you that you can see what will help them to grow and blossom, and what weeds threaten them, and will provide all they need.

The watchful God   Kate Hughes

God sees the righteous

Jane was at the school that her son attended. Instead of the usual parents evening, all the mothers and fathers had been invited for a social get-together, with snacks and drinks. Jane's son Jonathan and other boys from his class were helping to look after the visitors. Jane was chatting to the teachers and the other parents but all the time her eyes were following her son, shining with love and pride at his good manners and self-confidence as he handed round plates of food and made sure everyone had something to drink. This was a good pride: pleasure that her son had grown into such a fine young man, not pride in her own parenting.

> *For the eyes of the Lord are on the righteous,*
> *and his ears are open to their prayer.*

> (part of verse 12)

Just as Jane delighted in her son Jonathan, so God delights in us when we co-operate with him and show evidence that we are becoming the people he created us to be, when we behave in the ways described in today's passage. Then he watches us with pleasure and approval, and because we are beginning to learn the right things to pray for, when he hears what we are asking he is able to fulfil our requests more often. Being watchful can sound like hard work, but it can also be a pleasure. Our growth and development is God's work, he has made it happen, so it is only right that he should enjoy watching his handiwork.

† Creator God, thank you for the times when we are able to please you, when you can delight in your creation and be pleased with your work in us.

Kate Hughes

The watchful God

Revelation 22:1-5

The face of God is the light of heaven

They need no light of lamp or sun, for the Lᴏʀᴅ God will be their light.

(part of verse 5)

St Augustine again, describing heaven: 'We shall rest and we shall see; we shall see and we shall know; we shall know and we shall love.' The same could be said of God: in heaven: he will see us, he will know us through and through, and he will love us. I live in Coventry, and in our cathedral there is a huge tapestry, covering the east wall behind the high altar, of Christ in Majesty by Graham Sutherland. Whenever I go to the cathedral, I gaze at the face of Christ, because the eyes are wonderful. At first sight they appear almost cold, but go on looking. This is a Christ who sees you. He looks deep into your heart, sees all the nastiness, failure and self-love – but sees too the good, the efforts to love God, the acts of unselfishness. His gaze is one of complete understanding and complete love, and it dominates the cathedral. In the same way, the face of God, with eyes full of knowledge and understanding and love, will dominate heaven and be its light. 'Now we see in a mirror, dimly, but then we shall see face to face' (1 Corinthians 13:12).

† Grant, O Lord, that we may come at the end to the glory of your gaze in heaven. Amen

For group discussion and personal thought
- Do you find the watchful gaze of God a disturbing or a comforting idea?
- Have you experienced God's pleasure when you have done well?

The watchful God

Kate Hughes

Eyes of God

4   Face to face with Jesus

Notes based on the *New International Version* by

Marti Pieper

Marti Pieper, M.Div. graduate of Southwestern Baptist Theological Seminary, writes and edits from her Florida home, where she also serves Awe Star Ministries, a student mission organisation, as Director of Prayer and Publication. She is married to Tom, a worship pastor, and has five amazing children and two wonderful sons-in-love. Find Marti at www.martipieper.com/ and www.awestar.org.

Introduction

Our world grows smaller every day. Social networking sites ensure our ability to stay in touch with hundreds or thousands. But can Facebook and MySpace substitute for face to face? God designed us for relationship. As he told Adam, 'It is not good for the man to be alone' (Genesis 2:18). Our identity means we need real – not virtual – contact. Upon Christ's Bethlehem birth, humankind met God in infant form. This week, we'll explore ways to encounter the eternal – face to face.

Sunday 11 November: *John 1:16-18*
Making him known

> *No one has ever seen God, but God the One and Only, who is at the Father's side, has made him known.*
>
> (verse 18)

The setting: a beautiful South Asian nation. The climate: sunny, warm, and 99.9 per cent Muslim. The danger: anyone suspected of sharing the Christian faith would face immediate deportation. The challenge for a student mission team: make kingdom impact in one brief month. Team leaders planned to host a children's club in a local park. But God's great plans took priority over the leaders' good ones. He cancelled the park opportunity and opened one in a local school. Before long, the teenagers were building relationships with teachers and students alike. One night, a student awakened after a dream of a man in white. 'Who was he? I need to know.' This young woman had never seen God. But Jesus, the one and only, was working to make him known.

† O God, the world needs to know you; make yourself known in your Son Jesus.

November

Recognising Jesus

The next day John was there again with two of his disciples. When he saw Jesus passing by, he said, 'Look, the Lamb of God!' When the two disciples heard him say this, they followed Jesus.

(verses 35-37)

'Who's that, Daddy?' My twelve-year-old son Andrew heard the question as he waited in the hallway, costumed and ready for his role as the boy Jesus in our church's annual Christmas musical. Perhaps he felt just a hint of self-importance as he watched the much younger child tug at his father's sleeve and point in his direction. The father, however, continued down the hall without answering his son. Turning back, the preschooler asked Andrew directly, 'Who are you?' Andrew smiled and gave what seemed an obvious answer: 'I'm what Christmas is all about!' 'Oh!' the little boy replied. 'I'm sorry, Santa!'

The child did what we often do: he came face to face with Jesus, yet failed to recognise him. In today's reading, John the Baptist does the opposite. When he came face to face with Jesus, he recognised him because he had known him from eternity past. John's faithful witness and example caused his disciples to follow Jesus right away. One of them, Andrew, was so moved that he immediately brought his brother, Peter, to do the same. Does your life point others to Jesus? Will you recognise him when you meet him face to face?

---

† Lord Jesus, I know you provide many opportunities for me to see you. Help me to know you so well that I recognise you right away. Make me a person whose life points others to you. May they want to follow Jesus because of my example. In your holy name I pray, Amen

Face to face with Jesus

Marti Pieper

Tuesday 13 November

John 3:1-15

Eyes to see

In reply Jesus declared, 'I tell you the truth, no one can see the kingdom of God unless he is born again.'

(verse 3)

Michael had a genius-level IQ. He amazed his secondary school teachers with his grasp of higher mathematical concepts and ability to debate complex issues. He led the school's academic quiz team to multiple victories. But Michael didn't understand common social graces. He often wandered down the hall with his shirt unbuttoned, his hair unkempt. Michael's learning didn't extend to practical matters, either. One day, he inadvertently set off the chemistry room's fire alarm. Gallons of water dumped from the ceiling as he searched, wild-eyed, for the 'Off' switch. His academic abilities didn't translate to real life. Perhaps Nicodemus could identify with Michael. Jesus referred to him as 'Israel's teacher' (verse 10), but the Master's simple words confused and confounded him. Nicodemus had all kinds of knowledge – but it hadn't translated into wisdom. Spiritual truth must be spiritually discerned. The Master's words seemed like foolishness because, although Nicodemus stood in front of Jesus, he had not yet met him face to face. Nicodemus had religion. He needed a relationship that would open his eyes and invade his spirit. That's why Jesus told him, 'You must be born again' (verse 7). Only real relationship with Jesus gives us the perspective we need. Only real relationship allows us to encounter him face to face.

† Father, I want to know you more. Help me receive from you the things I need that will help me know you most fully and meet you face to face. All relationships require time and attention. Please give me the discipline I need to keep meeting you face to face. Amen

November

Up a tree

He wanted to see who Jesus was, but being a short man he could not, because of the crowd. So he ran ahead and climbed a sycamore fig-tree to see him, since Jesus was coming that way.

(verses 3-4)

'Boys! Boys! Where are you?' My friend bellowed, anxious about his two small sons. He'd grown up on the family farm but had become a bit too accustomed to city life. Besides, the farm offered so many ways to get hurt. Where were those boys, anyway? Suddenly, he spied the sneaker-clad feet – about twenty feet up in a tree. 'Boys! Get down right now!' A little voice floated down through the leaves and branches. 'But, Dad—' 'Did you hear me? Get down from that tree right now!' 'But Dad – what do we do about Grandma? She's up here, too!' My friend's mother didn't make a habit of tree-climbing, but she did want to spend time with her grandsons. She didn't care how ridiculous it made her look. She didn't care what her citified son thought. Instead, she cared about spending time with his children – branch to branch, face to face.

Zacchaeus understood this perspective. He didn't climb the tree to build his reputation. His ascent represented his only hope of seeing the one everyone was talking about. He was willing to appear foolish because it gave him the opportunity to see Jesus face to face.

† Father, may I not put my own appearance, pride, or reputation above my desire to see and know you. Help me willingly to accept opportunities that make me look foolish but put me in a better position to experience your truth. Thank you for the example of Zacchaeus. Amen

Divine delays

When Mary reached the place where Jesus was and saw him, she fell at his feet and said, 'LORD, if you had been here, my brother would not have died.'

(verse 32)

The honk of car horns collided with the shouts of vendors and the excited chatter of schoolchildren. Bright colours swirled around the student mission team as they presented their evangelistic drama again and again. The pedestrian mall of Cinco de Mayo in Panama City, Panama, makes a perfect place to share the gospel. This day, however, it didn't seem so perfect. The day's schedule also included a park. But the team encountered one delay after another. What about the park? Didn't those people need to hear about Jesus, too? Hours later, the bus rolled into the park at last. Team leaders hurried off to secure an area for ministry. But wait – was that a band tuning up? Another delay? As the leadership spoke with the uniformed musicians, they learned something unusual. The band members all belonged to Panama's secret police. Would they watch the drama and share their opinion? Of course! Every step, every movement flowed with Holy Spirit power. After the gospel presentation, team members looked out onto a sea of hands. These professional soldiers wept at the recognition of their separation from God. The divine delay meant the right connection at the right time.

When Jesus failed to arrive in time to heal Lazarus, Mary felt confused. Faith, not anger, led to her sorrowful statement. What seemed like unnecessary tardiness resulted in a miraculous healing – and more glory to God.

† Lord, help me recognise delays as your handiwork. Please use them to bring yourself greater glory and to allow me to meet Jesus – face to face. Amen

Marti Pieper

Face to face with Jesus

Friday 16 November

John 9:24-39

Blind spot

Jesus said, 'For judgement I have come into this world, so that the blind will see and those who see will become blind.'

(verse 39)

'Set the stage!' The team leaders gave the command and the student missionaries began the familiar line-up. Excitement hung in the air as they waited to perform their drama at a new site: a homeless shelter in Foz de Iguaçu, Brazil. As the team knelt on the dusty cement floor, they passed out props for the pantomime drama. Masks: check. Extra costume pieces: check. Streamers: check. But wait! These streamers had bells on each end! I wonder how those bells got there after all this time, thought Lynne, one of the student missionaries. Anna must have decided to sew them on. Tiny jingle bells – what difference could they make? Lynda knew. Her team wanted the gospel to reach as many people as possible. The brightly-coloured streamers would communicate to most spectators. But for any blind audience members, the bells made a huge difference. We haven't seen any blind people yet. But it could happen. As they began their drama, the young missionaries looked out on rows of benches lined up for their performance. At the back of the shelter, four people waited in special chairs – four blind people. As Lynne skipped through her part, waving her jingling streamer, she realised again that everybody matters to God. He came to make the blind see – even through something as simple as a jingle bell.

† Dear Father, open our eyes to see and know you today. Thank you for the many things you use to help us encounter you. Whether we can see spiritually or not, please open our eyes to see you face to face. In Jesus' name I pray, Amen

Face to face with Jesus

Marti Pieper

Saturday 17 November

John 19:25b-30

The face of love

When Jesus saw his mother there, and the disciple whom he loved standing nearby, he said to his mother, 'Dear woman, here is your son,' and to the disciple, 'Here is your mother.'

(verse 26)

A glance explained this Mexican neighbourhood's nickname: Casa de Muerto (House of the Dead). Fear and prayers escalated as the student missionaries invited people to their drama. Shoes hung from criss-crossed power lines, gang language for murder. Blood spattered the doors and boarded-up windows. During their presentation, thirteen-year-old Ruth noticed a woman watching intently. Afterwards, she and her ministry group shared with Maria, who immediately received Christ. 'I want to go home to my small family of ten and tell them about Jesus,' Maria said.

When you care about people, you want to introduce them. That's why Andrew brought Simon to Jesus in Monday's reading. That's why Jesus introduced his mother to his beloved disciple. Does someone you love need to meet Jesus face to face?

† Lord Jesus, thank you for your redemptive work on the cross. Thank you for drawing people to yourself. Help us be faithful to introduce others to you. Amen

For group discussion and personal thought

This week, we've considered various aspects of meeting Jesus face to face. Scripture reveals this as both a one-time event and a continuing process.

- How does scripture say we come to know Jesus? Have you been aware of such a time in your own life?

- Once we've met him, how can we continue to advance our relationship with Christ?

- What do you believe is our responsibility in introducing others to Jesus? Can you share an example of a time you helped someone meet him face to face?

November

Marti Pieper

Face to face with Jesus

1 and 2 Thessalonians

1 Keep awake and sober

Notes based on the *New International Version* by

Corneliu Constantineanu

Corneliu Constantineanu is a Romanian Christian educator and pastor. He is Associate Professor of New Testament Studies and President of Institutul Teologic Penticostal in Bucharest, Romania.

Introduction

This week gives us a great opportunity to reflect on a rather neglected topic in our Christian life: watchfulness, vigilance, being alert. This was indeed one of the central admonitions that Jesus gave to his disciples. The readings this week help us to explore the call to keep awake and sober; the Apostle Paul gives warmhearted encouragement as he writes to the church in Thessalonica and speaks to us today. Since 1 Thessalonians is rather short, you may like to read the whole letter through at the beginning of the week before you reflect on the daily readings.

Sunday 18 November: *1 Thessalonians 1*
Faith, hope, love: the power of the gospel

Today's reading focuses on the three essential Christian virtues: faith, hope and love. These are both the evidence and the result of the transforming power of the gospel. Before Paul develops his argument for the need to be awake and sober, he reminds the believers of the reality of the gospel in their lives, the undeniable evidence of faith, love and hope working in them through the Spirit. Indeed, the Thessalonians' new life became a model for believers in the entire region as they

> turned to God from idols to serve the living and true God, and to wait for his Son from heaven, whom he raised from the dead.

(part of verses 9-10)

In order for Christians to 'keep awake' they must first be sure of their new identity in Christ, and always recall the reality and the transforming power of the gospel in their lives.

† Dear Father, we thank you for the wonderful work of the gospel in our lives, and we pray that you will enable us, through our faith, love and hope, to live in eager expectation and anticipation of your coming.

Monday 19 November

1 Thessalonians 2:2-12

Integrity, love and encouragement: the power of example

It is evident that in order for Christians to be awake and sober, they should not think and live in a 'worldly' manner. They have to live by a different moral standard to that of the surrounding culture in terms of motivation, attitude and behaviour. This is exactly what Paul tells the Thessalonians in today's reading. What is most impressive is the fact that Paul appeals to his own life, to his own example while he lived among them. He never had 'impure motives' (verse 3) or a hidden agenda, he 'never used flattery' or 'put on a mask to cover greed' (verse 5), he never played to the audience (verse 6). In everything he did, he worked with integrity and love as they could themselves testify:

You are witnesses, and so is God, of how holy, righteous and blameless we were among you who believed. For you know that we dealt with each of you as a father deals with his own children, encouraging, comforting and urging you to live lives worthy of God, who calls you into his kingdom and glory.

(verses 10-12)

We ourselves are reminded that we live in a world of exclusion and conflict, confusion and fears, a world of suffering and hopelessness. In such a context, for Christians to have any impact or to make any difference, we have to offer something radically new and refreshing; alongside our Christian message we must offer a new way of living. The message of the gospel has to be embodied in concrete manifestations of forgiveness and reconciliation, welcome, hope and love.

---

† Our heavenly Father, we praise you for all the wonderful examples of faith that we have encountered; help us to be good examples of integrity, justice, forgiveness and love to all those who come our way every day.

Corneliu Constantineanu   Keep awake and sober

1 Thessalonians 2:13-20

The word of God is at work

There are many situations in life which tempt us to believe that God is not present, that he has forsaken us, or that he is not interested in our lives. One such situation is when we experience opposition or suffering. Then it feels as if the promises of God lose their force. It is to such a situation that Paul is trying to respond in today's reading. He is reassuring the Thessalonian believers that their suffering and opposition do not mean that God is distant and uninterested. On the contrary, their suffering and opposition are a sign of their faithfulness to the gospel of Jesus Christ, a sign that the word of God is at work among them. And Paul is thankful for that:

And we also thank God continually because, when you received the word of God, which you heard from us, you accepted it not as the word of men, but as it actually is, the word of God, which is at work in you who believe. For you, brothers, became imitators of God's churches in Judea, which are in Christ Jesus: You suffered from your own countrymen the same things those churches suffered.

(verses 13-14)

It is an encouragement for us to know that suffering and opposition are an integral part of our Christian life. But what a wonderful promise we have, that God is present with us through these situations.

† Lord, we pray for all our brothers and sisters who experience trials, opposition or persecution. Give them a strong sense of your presence with them and may they experience today your comfort, peace and encouragement.

November

Keep awake and sober   Corneliu Constantineanu

Wednesday 21 November

1 Thessalonians 3

The encouragement of faith

It is no surprise to anyone that the Christian life of faith needs constant strengthening and encouragement. In a sense, this is not difficult to understand, since faith is a 'trust in things that are not seen' (Hebrews 11:1). The object of faith is always something that is not at our disposal. That is why faith needs encouragement – so that in moments of trial faith can resist and the believers stand firm in their commitment to the Lord. Knowing these things very well, Paul sends Timothy to Thessalonica

> to strengthen and encourage you in your faith, so that no-one would be unsettled by these trials.

(part of verses 2-3)

Faith is constantly being tested by the trials or persecutions that come in different forms in our life of faith. To resist them, to be awake and sober, faith needs strength and encouragement. And, indeed, the Thessalonians were very much encouraged and lifted up by the coming of Timothy, which, in turn, produced much joy for Paul: 'in all our distress and persecution we were encouraged about you because of your faith. For now we really live, since you are standing firm in the Lord' (verses 7-8). In order for us to continue to live an alert life in anticipation and hope of the coming of our Lord, we need to persevere in love, purity and holiness. And this is what Paul prays for the Thessalonians and this is also our prayer today:

---

† May the Lord make your love increase and overflow for each other and for everyone else, just as ours does for you. May he strengthen your hearts so that you will be blameless and holy in the presence of our God and Father when our Lord Jesus comes with all his holy ones. (verses 12-13)

November

Corneliu Constantineanu   Keep awake and sober

A life pleasing to God

Today's text is a wonderful reminder of the truth that we should live our Christian life in a manner that pleases God. And the text also offers 'instructions' for how we can pursue a life worthy of God. First, 'it is God's will that you should be sanctified' (verse 3). We can only please God through a personal life of self-control, purity and holiness. There is no place for sexual immorality, lust or any kind of sin that dishonours the physical body or wrongs another person: 'for God did not call us to be impure, but to live a holy life' (verse 7). Secondly, there is the community dimension of our Christian life. To please God is to live in harmony with other believers and to love them: 'you have been taught by God to love each other' (verse 9). This is significant: true spirituality and love for God is validated by love towards others both within the community of faith and, as we shall see, outside it. Thirdly, a life pleasing to God is lived with great care and responsibility towards those outside of the community of faith; it is an industrious and diligent life that gets respect from unbelievers:

Make it your ambition to lead a quiet life, to mind your own business and to work with your hands, just as we told you, so that your daily life may win the respect of outsiders and so that you will not be dependent on anybody.

(verses 11-12)

This is how we can keep awake and sober and please God: by a personal, bodily life of holiness, self-control, purity, and love towards believers, and a diligent and responsible life in the midst of the world.

† Lord, we love you and we want to live a life that pleases you. Help us to live a personal life of purity, self-control and holiness, and enable us to express our love for you by loving those around us; and help us to live as responsible citizens in the world.

November

Keep awake and sober

Corneliu Constantineanu

1 Thessalonians 4:13-18

The resurrection hope

There cannot be a more miserable life than one without any direction or hope for the future. There is thus great truth in Jürgen Moltmann's affirmation that hopelessness is among the greatest sins! To be without hope is to give up on God – it is not to believe any longer that he is able to fulfil his own word and promises. This sense of hopelessness is what Paul is trying to address in today's reading. The believers were very confused about what would happen to their relatives and fellow-believers who died. It is important that we know what the future brings after a believer's death and that we do not lose hope in the one who raised Jesus from the dead and will also raise us up with him. Paul is resolute:

Brothers, we do not want you to be ignorant about those who fall asleep, or to grieve like the rest of men, who have no hope. We believe that Jesus died and rose again and so we believe that God will bring with Jesus those who have fallen asleep in him.

(verses 13-14)

The hope of resurrection is vital for the Christian life. This not only gives us hope and therefore peace about loved ones who died in Christ. It gives us a great assurance that our Christian life of vigilance and expectation will be vindicated and that 'we will be with the Lord for ever' (verse 17). There is indeed great comfort and encouragement in these words (verse 18).

† Dear Lord, give us always the assurance and hope of your final vindication and redemption.

Corneliu Constantineanu   Keep awake and sober

Saturday 24 November

1 Thessalonians 5:1-11

Be alert and self-controlled

'The day of the Lord' is a very significant reality for all Christians, meriting considerable attention. But not in terms of the exact time or date when Jesus will come again – no one actually knows that except the Father. However, Paul points clearly to at least two crucial and significant aspects of the day of the Lord. First, it will certainly come. It will be a day of judgement for all those who have done evil and rejected Christ (verse 3). But for all those who are in Christ, this will be a day of salvation, rewards and redemption (verse 9). And secondly, since the day of the Lord is coming with certainty we have to live responsibly in the world:

> But you, brothers, are not in darkness so that this day should surprise you like a thief . . . So then, let us not be like others, who are asleep, but let us be alert and self-controlled.

(verses 4 and 6)

To be alert and self-controlled is to live with faith, love and hope. Christ's death and resurrection and our incorporation 'in him' are the guarantee that on the day of the Lord 'we will receive salvation through our Lord Jesus Christ' (verse 9). That is why we want to stay alert and self-controlled!

† Thank you, Father, for the certainty that your day of justice and redemption will come. Enable us to live with faith, hope and love in eager anticipation of the day of the Lord.

For group discussion and personal thought

- What are some practical implications of 'the day of the Lord' for our everyday life?
- Are there concrete issues in your personal life about which you are not necessarily alert and self-controlled? How could you address these issues?
- What about your relationship with outsiders? Do they regard you with respect and commendation? Or do you need to change anything?

Keep awake and sober   Corneliu Constantineanu

November

1 and 2 Thessalonians

2   Never tire of doing right

Notes based on the *New International Version* by

Gillian Kingston

Gillian Kingston lives in Ireland with her husband, Tom, a retired Methodist minister. An active ecumenist – locally, nationally and further afield – Gillian is the first Lay Leader of the Conference of the Methodist Church in Ireland and a part-time university chaplain.

Introduction

Paul is writing to a young church. Its members, mainly of Gentile background, are struggling with a variety of issues and, in particular, with misconceptions concerning the Second Coming: would their departed loved ones be excluded from the coming kingdom? They have been further confused by someone trying to persuade them that the Second Coming had already happened! Paul comforts them, and he gives practical advice on how to live in the interim. These letters are a model of pastoral concern for those bewildered by theological issues and worried about how to be faithful disciples.

Sunday 25 November: *1 Thessalonians 5:12-28*

Pass it on!

The new President was elected to thunderous applause. He quietly asked if he might have permission to ring his wife 'before this gets out on Twitter'! Such is the speed of twenty-first century communication – somewhat different in the first century!

I charge you before the Lord to have this letter read to all.

(part of verse 27)

Paul has a great deal of practical advice for his beloved friends in Thessalonica, but he can't write to individuals – the letter must be read publicly. Can you imagine the impact of this? This is not just for the few, it is for everyone and they hear it and absorb it together. Imagine the ensuing discussion and debate – the community is further strengthened as people absorb Paul's wisdom together, apply its detail, reflect on how it will affect their lives. It's a great model!

† Lord, may our congregations listen to each other, share with each other, and challenge each other as we learn together about you.

2 Thessalonians 1:1-4

I thank God for you!

Friends are one of the most precious gifts of a loving and generous God. And how wonderful it is when friendship is mutual and shared in community. Don't forget to thank God for your friends – and tell them so! All too often we leave saying good things about people until it is too late, at funerals perhaps. Paul reminds us to say such things now – when it will be appreciated and modestly enjoyed.

> *We ought always to thank God for you . . . and rightly so, because your faith is growing more and more and the love every one of you has for each other is increasing.*

(part of verse 3)

Paul, together with Silas and Timothy, opens this letter with blessing and affirmation. The community in Thessalonica is encountering persecution and Paul wants to commend their faithfulness. How enormously encouraging this must have been – the great apostle himself is boasting about them to fellow Christians! It is not easy to proclaim the faith in the face of persecution, but even so, the faith of these young Christians is growing and so is their sense of community, their love for each other. Some of us face active persecution, others face deadening indifference, still others strive to follow Jesus Christ in an environment of competing ideologies. In whatever circumstances, we should be able to find in each other a source of strength and encouragement. As John Wesley, the founder of the Methodist movement, urged, 'Let us endeavour to strengthen each other's hand in God!'

† Loving Lord Jesus, you told your disciples that they were not your servants but your friends. Help us to show love and encouragement to our friends as you do to us. Give us the grace to be good friends and supporters. Amen

November

Never tire of doing right

Gillian Kingston

Tuesday 27 November

2 Thessalonians 1: 5-12

Praying for you!

Sometimes, when we're under pressure, it is good to know that someone out there is praying. I am on the chaplaincy team of University College, Dublin. None of us knows what any day may bring – students with study issues, family problems, those who feel that life is no longer worth the effort. We may be stretched to the utmost, but we are there for each other. 'Say one for me!' I might text to my mate – and I know he will.

> [W]e constantly pray for you, that our God may count you worthy of his calling, and that by his power he may fulfil every good purpose of yours and every act prompted by your faith.

(part of verse 11)

Paul assures the Christians in Thessalonica that God will repay them for all the trouble through which they have been going. Some of the language he uses may seem strange and foreign to our understanding of a God of love and forgiveness (verses 6-9): we may need to recognise anew the evil of persecution and to appreciate Paul's anger on behalf of his friends. Be that as it may, he commits himself to praying constantly for them, and how strengthening that must have been. We are challenged to make a similar commitment on behalf of those we know – and those we don't know – who are facing difficulties. It is deeply comforting to be aware that someone is praying for us, especially if we are finding prayer difficult for ourselves.

† Loving Lord Jesus, you have taught us how to pray. Give us the grace constantly to hold those we know and love in prayer before you. And give the added grace to pray for those we will never know but who are also your beloved children.

Gillian Kingston

Never tire of doing right

2 Thessalonians 2:1-12

Don't believe everything you hear!

Some years ago, an American minister and his wife stayed with us. They were accompanying their youth choir on a tour of Ireland. A delightful man and built on the grand scale, he was open and frank about where he saw his particular church going – and he wasn't entirely happy about it. 'If you fall for everything, you stand for nothing!' he declared robustly. We have often had cause to remember his words!

We ask you . . . not to become easily unsettled or alarmed . . . Don't let anyone deceive you in any way.

(part of verses 1-3)

Like many teachers and leaders, Paul has his detractors. The Thessalonians have been confused by 'prophecy, report or letter' from an unnamed person – a man – who is undermining Paul's teaching on the Second Coming. Though not able to be with them in person, Paul writes to reassure and to warn. False teaching has serious consequences and the Thessalonians need to be alert.

Nothing changes much, does it? Even among those who name the name of Christ, there can be such a wide range of teaching on issues, particularly on ethical and moral issues, that we wonder if we are reflecting on the same matter. And, as in the first century, the consequences of erroneous teaching can be grave. Family and social relationships may be at stake. How we view the created world and our neighbours in that world may be jeopardised. Our prayers must be for discernment and for sound teaching. And we are in this together!

† Loving Lord Jesus, you told your disciples that the truth would make them free. Open our ears and our eyes, our hearts and our minds, to receive and live by that truth and to convey it with integrity to others. Amen

November

Never tire of doing right   Gillian Kingston

Thursday 29 November

2 Thessalonians 2:13-17

Hold on to the good!

The other day, we cleared out an old shed – there was so much accumulated rubbish in there that the temptation was to put the whole lot into bags and take it to the local dump! But if we'd done that, we would have thrown out some very useful, perhaps irreplaceable, things. It was worth taking the time to sift through the old boxes to find them.

> *[S]tand firm and hold to the teachings we passed on to you, whether by word of mouth or by letter.*

(part of verse 15)

In his first letter to the Christians in Thessalonica, Paul has urged that they 'test everything and hold fast to the good'. Here he reiterates that advice and we need to heed it too. It is too easy to take the line that anything old has had its day and anything new is automatically better – 'out' with the old hymns, 'in' with the new songs; 'out' with carefully worded translations, 'in' with trendy paraphrases! We need to be more discriminating than that.

The truths of the faith are eternal; the circumstances in which they are lived out change constantly. This doesn't mean, however, that we discard 'traditional' teaching, but rather that we carefully and prayerfully evolve new ways of living and proclaiming it. We must focus on the truth of the gospel message and on expressing it in a God-centred way.

† Loving Lord Jesus, thank you for all that has been passed on to us from our fathers and mothers in the faith. Give us wisdom and insight as we apply these great truths to the times and circumstances in which we live. Strengthen us to hold fast to what is good and to pass it on to others. Amen

Gillian Kingston

Never tire of doing right

Friday 30 November

2 Thessalonians 3:1-5

'Say one for me!'

Recently, a colleague on the chaplaincy team and I both had a 'big' day. 'Pray for me,' we asked each other – and we did. There is strength in knowing that someone is holding you in prayer – praying for you when perhaps you don't have the time or opportunity to pray for yourself, when the pressure is on. Never, ever, be afraid to ask!

> [P]ray for us that the message of the Lord may spread rapidly and be honoured . . . And pray that we may be delivered from wicked and evil [men], for not everyone has faith.
>
> (part of verse 1, and verse 2)

Paul is absolutely clear about the things for which he would like the Christians at Thessalonica to pray on his behalf: for the spread of the gospel and for his own safety. There is a sense of urgency that the gospel may be spread rapidly; times are uncertain, who knows what may happen next? The word of God must be honoured – there are less than honourable messages out there too. Paul is aware that personal attack can come in different ways; he needs protection, physical, spiritual and intellectual. 'What's new?' we ask in our own time!

With this personal request, he includes more prayer for his friends that they too may be protected from the forces of evil. We need to pray for each other faithfully and in an informed way. This is why prayer handbooks and prayer letters are so useful – they alert us to on-the-ground needs and concerns. Paul's letters are amazingly contemporary!

† Loving Lord Jesus, give us the grace to pray constantly for each other. We particularly hold before you those for whom it is difficult and dangerous to proclaim your Word. May they be kept safe in body, mind and spirit. Amen

Never tire of doing right   Gillian Kingston

Saturday 1 December

2 Thessalonians 3:6-18

Keep at it!

When I was teaching, I always found the last class of the day the longest and most tedious. After a day's work, the temptation was to do as little as possible and wait for the bell to go. But that wouldn't have been fair to anyone – and it certainly wouldn't have got the syllabus covered!

As for you . . . never tire of doing what is right.

(part of verse 13)

People are waiting for the Second Coming, not 'busy', but 'busybodies', living off the work and industry of others; Paul is not amused. Note that he is being critical of those who have chosen not to work; he is not talking about those who, for whatever reason, are unable to work. We need to be aware of this distinction so as not to cause hurt to vulnerable people. Asked what he would do if he knew the world would end tomorrow, Martin Luther replied that he would plant a tree. This is the spirit in which the followers of Jesus live and work.

† Loving Lord Jesus, keep me faithful to the tasks you have given me to do – right to the end of my time! Amen

For group discussion and personal thought

• In five minutes' time, someone is going to ask why you are a Christian, does it really make sense these days? What are you going to say?

• Some of us are in situations of real antagonism and persecution; others face apathy and indifference on a daily basis. Reflect on any difficulties you encounter because of your faith and how you handle them.

• Sometimes being mutually supportive in community can be really difficult – we know each other's weaknesses too well to be sympathetic! What is the best way to overcome this?

Gillian Kingston

Never tire of doing right

Wisdom

1 The identity and character of wisdom

Notes based on the *New Revised Standard Version* by

Nathan Eddy

Nathan Eddy is Free Church Chaplain to the University of Manchester and Manchester Metropolitan University. He was ordained in the United Church of Christ, USA. He has written on Paul for the preaching commentary *Feasting on the Word*.

Introduction

Advent is a time of urgent waiting and expectation of God's reign that runs counter to the consumer-driven rush to Christmas in Western society. As our time becomes crowded with work and family obligations in the run-up to the holidays, Advent is a refuge; a time to think about God's time – its beginning and its end when Christ comes in glory and judgment. The theme of wisdom this week calls us to question the hectic rush and attend deeply and simply to ways of peace, nature, true wealth, and daily decisions.

Sunday 2 December (Advent Sunday): *Proverbs 3:13-18*
Affluenza and its cure

> *[A] tree of life to all who lay hold of her.*

(part of verse 18)

Many of us in the West are gripped by what has been called 'affluenza.' We want more of everything, now, and with free delivery. In the UK, Christmas advertising campaigns begin in October, with shops claiming to be the 'centre' of Christmas. We are sick literally unto death with desire for what we lack. The wisdom coming into our world in Christ, and present in the words of the prophets and writings of the Hebrew Bible, promises a different kind of wealth. The wealth of wisdom is even more valuable than the silver, gold, and jewels that glitter in shop windows at this time of year. The ways of this wisdom are peace, satisfaction, and long life, not anxiety over what we don't have. And this wisdom promises to take root deep in our lives, if we open our hands to receive it, and hold on.

† Lord, as we start out on our Advent journey, help us to open our hands and hearts to all that you want to give us. Amen

Monday 3 December

Proverbs 8:12-21

You are invited. . .

'[T]hose who seek me diligently find me.'

(part of verse 17)

I serve as chaplain to one of the UK's largest universities, the University of Manchester. I love my work. On the faculty of the university are 25 Nobel laureates. The brightest students from around the world come here to study. There are brand-new glittering buildings all around my office window, filled with instruments I'll never understand. The New Testament students in the highly-rated Theology Faculty put my knowledge of scripture to shame.

What does it mean to be wise? Does it mean having a Nobel prize in physics? Being the cleverest person in the room? For the writer of Proverbs, wisdom is an invitation, not an achievement – an invitation to live attentively, seeking the fruit that is better than gold. Joan Chittester, the Benedictine nun and prolific writer, speaks of losing her father at the age of three and discovering that wisdom is the commitment to go on. In time, she found that places in her life that were inscrutable were actually calling her to live differently.

Recently I talked to a campus cleaner whose elderly mother had died. I don't remember his words, but I remember his conviction that life was worthwhile, even when difficult. His grief was real but, standing there in the basement storage room, he didn't have a shadow of the doubt that life would go on. 'I love those who love me, and those who seek me diligently find me.' Wisdom indeed, no Nobel prize required.

† Loving God, teach us acceptance. Teach us wisdom. Show us true wealth. Amen

Nathan Eddy   The identity and character of wisdom

Tuesday 4 December
Proverbs 30:24-28

Small and exceedingly wise

[The] lizard can be grasped in the hand,
yet it is found in the kings' palaces.

(verse 28)

One of the memorable scenes from the 2009 film *Creation*, about the life of the pioneering scientist Charles Darwin, shows a young Darwin examining beetles by lamplight deep in the hull of the ship HMS *Beagle* off the coast of the Galapagos Islands. For all his scientific breakthroughs, for his entire life Darwin was a keen and tireless observer of nature.

We have seen this week that wisdom is about shrewdness and skill that often runs counter to the ways of the world. In this reading, we see that wisdom also comes from closely observing nature. In recent times, wisdom, or reason, has often been pitted against nature – to the detriment of our world's complex and fragile ecosystem. In fact true wisdom takes us more deeply into nature. Nature, as Darwin observed, can be merciless, but nature can also illuminate human society in positive ways.

What can we learn from observing ants, badgers, locusts or lizards? Human society often privileges being born into the right family, or physical strength, or the winner taking all. But wisdom doesn't depend on physical size; a group can work together without coercive leadership and be stronger than an individual; and you can live in a palace without being the strongest, or from the right family. Just ask the ants, the badgers, the locusts and the lizards.

† God of small creatures, teach us to see the world as you do. Reveal to us true power. And keep us walking in it. Amen

The identity and character of wisdom   Nathan Eddy

Wednesday 5 December

Ecclesiastes 9:13-18

Wisdom under siege

Wisdom is better than weapons of war.

(part of verse 18)

Advent is a time when we confess belief in a peace coming to our world in unlikely ways, at unlikely times. A poor old man? A defenceless infant? Hardly obvious leaders capable of withstanding armies. Yet our parable-like story from Ecclesiastes, and the story of Jesus, challenge us to think again about the ways of God.

Our world pulses with coercive violence, but force will not have the last word. Can we be people who not only believe in peace-loving wisdom, but make ourselves channels of it? The wise man does not sit cross-legged on a cliff top far above society. He lives in a besieged city where the innocent suffer. He takes bold action in the midst of the turmoil of conflict. Wisdom is threatening and dangerous to the powerful in a violent world. Wisdom moves to the beat of a different drummer. The wise are rarely heeded initially; they are ignored at best, targeted at worst. The wise old man, the prophet Jeremiah, Jesus of Nazareth, and saints and peace activists down to our day all knew the wisdom and necessity of their action, and its cost.

† God of peace, we desire wisdom, yet we shrink from its cost. Show us that we are not alone, in whatever situations we face. Give us courage to act boldly, for the sake of peace. Amen

Nathan Eddy   The identity and character of wisdom

1 Kings 4:29-34

Consider the lilies

He would speak of animals, and birds, and reptiles, and fish.

(part of verse 33)

My 18-month-old daughter is fascinated with animals. She gets more excited over dogs in a park than over the ice-cream truck. She spots them from across a field, in photographs, on TV, in paintings. She never tires of our house cat. Through her the banalities of urban life come alive for me and my wife.

King Solomon was someone who spoke of trees, animals, birds, fish. People came from all over to hear him. Scripture tells us he was a powerful and respected ruler, a temple builder; yet he attended to the variety of trees, including the 'hyssop that grows in the wall' (verse 33). Perhaps today Solomon would be on BBC Radio 4's programme *Gardeners' Question Time*; he teaches us to be alive with practical wonder. He shows us that we are not the only creatures of God, not the only recipients of God's providential care.

Rational, intelligent faith does not remove us from our so-called 'animal' nature, nor does visionary leadership mean we must always look to the horizon. True wisdom shows us that we are a part of creation. It makes us attentive to what is growing around us, and opens us in wonder, even when it is our own house cat or garden tree.

† Creator God, give us delight in the things you have made. Show us that you, too, take delight in your creation, and in each of us. Amen

The identity and character of wisdom   Nathan Eddy

Friday 7 December

James 3:13-18

Actions speak louder. . .

Show by your good life that your works are done with gentleness born out of wisdom.

(part of verse 13)

Wisdom does not mean simply uttering wise aphorisms – wisdom is about action. Theologian Stephen Fowl has even compared James' words on wisdom here to Paul's words on love in 1 Corinthians. We could almost say, with Paul, that wisdom builds up, it doesn't puff up. Wisdom is more about our relationships with others – our generosity, our gentleness, our 'willingness to yield' – than it is about knowing complicated theorems. That is, the wisdom that comes from above looks a lot like foolishness: gentleness and mercy in the face of opposition; seeking peace when everyone else is waging war.

Was Jesus wise? Not obviously. He hung out with the wrong crowd, angered those in power, and taught that in order to be first we must be last and that he had to die in order to bring about God's reign. Yet in the folly of the cross is true wisdom: a gentleness that reconciles, a harvest of righteousness that sows peace because it both exposes sin for what it is and shows that it can be forgiven and even forgotten. Can we be open to the wisdom that comes as a gift 'from above'? Can we put actions behind our wise ambition – actions that reconcile, forgive, and seek peace? A child will be born – poor, defenceless, gentle, willing to yield, without a trace of partiality or hypocrisy. Will you make room for him? And will you follow him?

---

† God of the cross, your folly is wiser than our wisdom. Help us receive rather than achieve. Turn us into the darkness of your way. Open us in gentle trust. Amen

Nathan Eddy   The identity and character of wisdom

Saturday 8 December
Daniel 2:20-23

Sing out my soul!

'[God] changes time and seasons,
deposes kings and sets up kings.'

(part of verse 21)

Will Willimon, Dean of Duke University Chapel, tells a story about a student coming to him after an Advent service, confessing doubts about Mary's virgin birth of Jesus. Willimon responded, 'You think that's tough to believe? Come back next week – try believing that God, not the nations, rules the world.' Daniel, like Mary, received a vision of God overturning earthly rulers. For them, and for their Jewish people, this was good news indeed. For Nebuchadnezzar and Herod, it was profoundly threatening. Daniel and Mary were nobodies – Daniel and his friends were prisoners of a powerful foreign ruler, certain to be executed unless they could guess and interpret the ruler's dream. Daniel's God, and Mary's God, is a God who reveals and acts. Brute power seems unassailable, but God will overturn the mighty, as Nebuchadnezzar and Herod discovered. Will we take the side of the Herods of the world, relying on force, reacting defensively? Or will we be open to God's rule, which overturns rulers, sees in the darkness, and reveals and interprets the inscrutable and the impossible? Will we accept God's invitation to venture into the unknown? With Daniel and Mary this Advent we are challenged to believe, to be open, to say yes.

† God of justice, throughout the ages men and women have said yes to you. Give us the spirit to say this word. Be born in us. Free us. Amen

For group discussion and personal thought
- Why might Nebuchadnezzar have felt threatened by his prisoner, Daniel? Whom would Daniel's song threaten today? Whom would it encourage?
- What saints come to mind who have sung Daniel's and Mary's song in their own time?
- Is the wisdom God gives safe or dangerous? How do you feel about receiving it?

The identity and character of wisdom   Nathan Eddy

Wisdom

2   The acts of wisdom in creation and history

Notes based on *The Message* and the *New International Version* by

Chris Duffett

For Chris's biography see p.208.

Introduction

In two week's time we celebrate Jesus' birthday! As we consider the approaching nativity season the passages this week remind us of the mystery that Jesus has always existed. The incarnation is God becoming flesh through Jesus to reunite all things to himself. Paul writes, 'For God was pleased to have all his fullness dwell in him, and through him to reconcile to himself all things, whether things on earth or things in heaven, by making peace through his blood, shed on the cross' (Colossians 1:19-20, NIV). Throughout the Hebrew scriptures we see powerful cameo appearances of Jesus, spoken of through the prophets or seen in the creation story. Most strikingly, Jesus is glimpsed through the Wisdom literature, as the one who made all things and is to be pursued.

Sunday 9 December: *Proverbs 3:19-20*

God as a woman?

Describing attributes of the Trinity as female can upset us if we are familiar with God as 'Father' and 'Son'. As we get ready to celebrate the birth of the baby boy Jesus, it may surprise you that wisdom is described as a woman. The Hebrew word *Chakmah* and Greek *sophia* are both feminine nouns. Furthermore, wisdom is presented as a person rather than an abstract concept. This should help rather than hinder us in our growing faith. The very Christ who saves us is the same person who has always lived, who wove us all together and gives all things life:

> *With Lady Wisdom, God formed Earth;*
> *With Madame Insight, he raised Heaven.*

(verse 19, *The Message*)

---

† May I receive from you a renewed love for Jesus and enjoy how huge he is! May I worship you in Spirit and in truth. Amen

Proverbs 8:22-26a

Wonderful Jesus!

How big is your 'Jesus'? The Bible declares that he was with God the Father creating all things: 'things in heaven and on earth, visible and invisible, whether thrones or powers or rulers or authorities; all things were created by him and for him' (Colossians 1:16, NIV). John also declares, 'through him all things were made' (John 1:3, NIV). The writer of the letter to Hebrews declares that God has spoken to us by his Son, 'whom he appointed heir of all things, and through whom he made the universe' (Hebrews 1:2, NIV). Proverbs reminds us of our wonderful, ever-living, transcendent Jesus:

> 'God sovereignly made me – the first, the basic –
> before he did anything else.
> I was brought into being a long time ago,
> well before Earth got its start.
> I arrived on the scene before Ocean,
> yes, even before Springs and Rivers and Lakes.
> Before Mountains were sculpted and Hills took shape,
> I was already there, newborn.'

(verses 22-25, *The Message*)

Please take time to think about Jesus, the Son of God. He has the same nature as the Father. He is eternally God and therefore, while there was never a time when he was literally begotten, rejoice that our wonderful Jesus, maker of all things, is right with us now.

† Father, thank you that you had a rescue plan for this world. Thank you that you sent Jesus, your beloved Son, for me. Thank you that I belong to him and he belongs to me. Amen

Wisdom in creation and history   Chris Duffett

Tuesday 11 December

Proverbs 8:26b-31

Delight in creation

Yesterday a good friend came round for supper. She is an avid butterfly spotter and had just come back from a museum where she had taken hundreds of pictures of the collections of butterflies. My wife and I looked at the photos and marvelled at how striking the vibrant colours and shapes were. We were quite in awe of how clever God is and how he created such amazing things for our enjoyment. Our friend observed our fascination and in contrast commented on how spectacular it was that evolution had formed these insects by chance over millions of years. After our friend had gone we reflected on our evening before going to bed. We wondered how anyone could see such detailed beauty and not see the creator behind the created.

Day after day I was there, with my joyful applause,
always enjoying his company,
Delighted with the world of things and creatures,
happily celebrating the human family.

(part of verse 30, and verse 31, *The Message*)

We too can join in the delight of the Trinity in how things have been so wonderfully made. The *Westminster Catechism*, part of a document of the English Reformation presented to Parliament in 1648, includes these famous words: 'The chief end of man is to glorify God and enjoy him for ever.' Do you enjoy God? Do you take time to enjoy what he has created? Glorify him by delighting in the wonders of his creation! Take time today to thank him for all that is around you that has been so skilfully made.

† Lord God, you created all things.
   Lord Jesus, you delighted in how this world was put together.
   Lord Holy Spirit, you are a genius in the detail and beauty of creation.
   Help me to appreciate all you have done around me. Amen

Chris Duffett   Wisdom in creation and history

Wednesday 12 December

Job 12:7-13

Big hands

Hands are among the first things that we register as human beings. A baby feels secure held firmly by loving hands. Although hands can be used to harm and hurt, for many people they signify security, protection, loving care, connection. Job's poem reveals that our God's hands are huge!

> *'But ask the animals what they think – let them teach you;*
> *let the birds tell you what's going on . . .*
> *Isn't it clear that they all know and agree*
> *that God is sovereign, that he holds all things in his hand –*
> *Every living soul, yes,*
> *every breathing creature?*
> *Isn't this all just common sense,*
> *as common as the sense of taste?*
> *Do you think the elderly have a corner on wisdom,*
> *that you have to grow old before you understand life?'*

(verses 7 and 9-12, *The Message*)

Surrendering to God's control can be a humbling thing to do. It means recognising that we are not in charge of our diaries, families or circumstances. All living things (including you and me!) are held in his hand. In Job's extreme suffering and trials he refused to curse God, but rather held tight to the truth that it is God who is sovereign and holds all things. This understanding brings wisdom.

---

† Sovereign God, I need to trust in you. Sometimes I panic and wonder whether you are in control. Sometimes I am overwhelmed with all that I have done and need to do. At times I worry, lack peace, and hurriedly try to keep my life in control. Please come to me now, scoop me up into your hands, and embrace me. Amen

Wisdom in creation and history   Chris Duffett

The fear of the Lord

True wisdom comes through having a right perspective of who God is. The 'fear of the Lord' (verse 28) doesn't mean that we should hide away from him and worry that he will punish us. As people hidden in Christ (Colossians 3.3) and seated in heavenly places (Ephesians 2.6) we are able to trust and know that we enter into his presence with boldness (Hebrews 4.16.) Yet Job challenges us about how we view God. Is he your 'All-matey' God or your 'Almighty' God? Over-familiarity with God as our Father can bring a slapdash approach to our relationship with him, one where we demand and order him to do things for us. He calls us to seek him and to seek his wisdom:

> 'God alone knows the way to Wisdom,
> he knows the exact place to find it . . .
> After he commanded the winds to blow
> and measured out the waters . . .
> He focused on Wisdom,
> made sure it was all set and tested and ready.
> Then he addressed the human race: "Here it is!
> Fear-of-the-Lord – that's Wisdom,
> and Insight means shunning evil."'
>
> (verses 23, 25, and 27-28, *The Message*)

✝ I want to be wise and fear you, worship you, love you and give my all for you,
I want to be wise and allow you to lead me, rather than me commanding you to come,
I want to be wise and turn my back on all that is evil, and follow close after you. Amen

Our true God

Today we meditate together on this passage from Jeremiah and ask God to speak to us through his word. You may need to find a quiet spot in your home away from any distractions for the next ten minutes or so!

By his power he made earth.
His wisdom gave shape to the world.
He crafted the cosmos.

In the stillness, thank God for his creation and how he made it. Bring to mind images of your favourite walks or scenes from nature programmes that you have watched on TV. Thank him for all he has made.

He thunders and rain pours down.
He sends the clouds soaring.
He embellishes the storm with lightnings,
launches the wind from his warehouse.

Reflect on God's might. Ask him to reveal more of his handiwork to you.

Stick-god worshippers look mighty foolish!
God-makers embarrassed by their handmade gods!
Their gods are frauds, dead sticks—
deadwood gods, tasteless jokes.
They're nothing but stale smoke.

Give thanks for our true God, the one who is permanent and ever present. Ask him to increase your awareness of his presence.

But the Portion-of-Jacob is the real thing;
he put the whole universe together,
With special attention to Israel.
His name? God-of-the-Angel-Armies!

(verses 15-19, *The Message*)

† Thank you God that you are mighty, Lord of all.

Wisdom in creation and history   Chris Duffett

Saturday 15 December

Psalm 104:24-30

Redemption of the world

God is renewing all creation, which groans (Romans 8:22) until the full time when there will be a new heaven and a new earth (Revelation 21:1). Today's reading has two verses which remind me of this rescue plan that God has for you and me and the world:

> *What a wildly wonderful world, God!*
> *You made it all, with Wisdom at your side,*
> *made earth overflow with your wonderful creations . . .*
> *Send out your Spirit and they spring to life –*
> *the whole countryside in bloom and blossom.*

> (part of verses 24 and 30, *The Message*)

God – with his wisdom – has made our breathtaking world and despite how humankind has ruined it and shattered the intimate relationship we had with God, he himself has made a way: God is redeeming back the mess and making all things new. The literal meaning of redemption is to purchase back something that had been lost, by the payment of a ransom. Jesus' death on the cross as the compensation for sin means we are reconciled to God. He now sends his Spirit to bring life all over this world, wooing the lost children back to the Father, making hope blossom.

† Jesus, thank you that you alone are the saviour of the world. You are amazing in how you redeem us and rescue us. I love you. Amen

For group discussion and personal thought

- In what way is it helpful for you that the Bible describes wisdom as a woman?
- How did you feel about reading that God has big hands? When have you been aware of him carrying you?
- The way God sends his Spirit to make the countryside blossom reminds us of the Spirit bringing new life. In what way could you take time to pray for your community this week?

Chris Duffett   Wisdom in creation and history

Wisdom

3   The call of Wisdom

Notes based on the *New International Version* by

Anthony Loke

Revd Anthony Loke is an ordained minister with the TRAC Methodist Church in Malaysia and a lecturer in the Old Testament in Seminari Theoloji Malaysia, the largest ecumenical seminary in the country.

Introduction

Wisdom is often pictured searching out human beings who will listen to her, accept her teachings, and follow her ways. In the New Testament, particularly in Matthew, Jesus is presented as one who calls people to follow him and accept his teaching as the new realisation of wisdom. This week's readings explore different aspects of this invitation and teaching.

Sunday 16 December: *Proverbs 1:20-33*
Who will listen?

'But whoever listens to me will live in safety.'

(part of verse 33)

To get young people, especially young men, to listen to the voice of wisdom, it was personified as a woman. This helped to dramatise and make vivid what was otherwise an abstract concept. To represent wisdom as a fine lady made it more understandable to the target group of young men who would one day become leaders in society. In these verses, wisdom is also portrayed as a street evangelist who actively calls out to everyone. Some people will reject her, others will listen to her. Those who reject her are called the 'simple ones', the naive and easily deceived, the 'mockers' and 'fools'. Because they reject wisdom, they will bring trouble upon themselves and eat the fruit of their foolish ways. Wisdom does not need to condemn them because they have already condemned themselves by their waywardness and complacency (see also John 3:18). Listening to wisdom brings safety and ease; to those who do so, she will pour out her heart and make known her thoughts. Therefore one of the important decisions in life is to make the right choice: to listen to wisdom's voice and not reject her.

† Lord, help me to heed wisdom's voice when she calls, lest I reject her and eat the fruit of my own foolishness and waywardness. Amen

Monday 17 December

Proverbs 8:1-11

Wisdom calls

'I raise my voice to all [hu]mankind.'

(part of verse 4)

Proverbs 8 is generally considered to be a wisdom poem extolling the virtues of seeking and following after Lady Wisdom. The praise of wisdom, which was only touched on briefly in the earlier chapters of the book, now breaks forth in full flow. Wisdom is described by several metaphors in these verses. She is portrayed in verses 2-3 as a street evangelist standing at the city gates and crying out to the city folk. She has a message not only for all humankind, but especially for the 'simple' and 'foolish'. Those who are 'simple' can gain prudence from her; those who are 'foolish' can gain understanding. This group of people are called to leave behind their old ways and find life.

In verse 5 wisdom is portrayed as a guide with precious words for everyone. She has 'worthy things' to say and speaks of 'what is right'. In her, there is no deceit or perversion, only what is right and just. Blessed are those who are able to discern this truth and follow her. In verse 11, wisdom is as valuable as precious rubies and nothing can be compared with the joy of finding her. Those who choose to follow her will find her instruction and knowledge more precious than silver and gold. What wisdom has to offer goes beyond material benefits, for she will bestow prosperity and wealth upon those who seek her (verse 21). With such a clear invitation, why do people not heed her call?

---

† Lord, take my eyes off earthly things, even if they are precious jewels and metals, and set my eyes on wisdom, which surpasses all.

Anthony Loke   The call of wisdom

Proverbs 8:32-36

Find wisdom, find life!

'For whoever find me finds life
and receives favour from the Lord.'

(verse 35)

At the end of the poem on wisdom, in a final metaphor she makes a last call to her 'sons', like a mother to her children. Mother Wisdom entreats her children to listen to her motherly advice. Twice in these verses those who listen to her are described as 'blessed', a word which can also be translated as 'happy' (compare Psalm 1:1 and Matthew 5:3). Wisdom's children are 'happy sons' when they listen attentively to their mother's advice, her proven and tested home-grown truths. It is the 'happy man' who daily waits attentively at wisdom's door, knowing that he will receive good advice to help him walk on the right path. Those who listen to her instructions are also called 'wise' (verse 33). There is a deliberate wordplay or pun on this relationship in the Hebrew language: those who listen to *hokmah* (wisdom) are indeed the *hakam* (wise)!

There are two opposing responses to Mother Wisdom: listen to her or ignore her. Those who listen and find her will indeed find life and receive divine favour from the Lord (verse 35). Those who choose to ignore her, or literally 'hate' her, will find the opposite: they will harm themselves through their own foolishness and stupidity and inevitably choose the path that leads to death, which is separation from the Lord (verse 36).

---

† Lord, help me as her child to heed Mother Wisdom's advice and find life. Let me not be an unruly child and end up loving death instead!

The call of wisdom

Anthony Loke

Wednesday 19 December

Proverbs 9:1-6

Lady Wisdom's banquet

*'Come, eat my food
and drink the wine I have mixed.'*

(verse 5)

Chapter 9 is the last chapter of Proverbs before the short proverbial sayings begin in chapter 10. Here, wisdom and foolishness are both personified and compared as two great rivals: Lady Wisdom (verses 1-6) and Lady Folly (verses 13-18). Both are described as offering a banquet in contrasting styles and wooing the same target group of people, called 'the simple' (verses 4 and 16).

In today's passage, Lady Wisdom speaks. Her residence with seven pillars conveys the idea of a grand house. Her menu is meat with wine mixed with spices and a fine table setting. Invitations are sent out through her maids and she calls from the vantage point of the city. Her banquet is open to the simple and to those who lack judgement, naive, foolish and ignorant people who are easily swayed by others and deceived. Yet she invites them to come in and feast at her banquet. There are no dress codes, no prerequisites, no entrance fees, and no RSVPs. All who seriously desire wisdom are invited to come and feast with her. In doing so, they are invited to leave their simple ways and walk in the way of understanding. The consequence of people finding Lady Wisdom is that they will find life abundant, purposeful and meaningful. To follow Lady Wisdom is another way of saying that we are following God. When we find wisdom, we find life. It is the same when we find God.

---

† Lord, always remind me that following Lady Folly is like infatuation or puppy love. It is only by following Lady Wisdom that we find our true love that grows deeper and truer with time.

Thursday 20 December

Matthew 5:1-12

A new wisdom?

And he began to teach them, saying, 'Blessed are the poor in spirit.'

(verse 2, and part of verse 3)

Jesus is portrayed in Matthew's Gospel as a wisdom teacher who called people to follow him and accept his teaching as a new realisation of the wisdom of the Old Testament. The Jews of Jesus' time were familiar with the wisdom books of Proverbs, Job, and Ecclesiastes and probably also Ben Sirach (Ecclesiasticus) and The Wisdom of Solomon. Added to this list were the numerous rabbinic sayings and traditions. But here was someone who came teaching in a new way and was going against the traditions of the forefathers: 'You have heard that it was said to the people long ago . . . but I tell you…' (Matthew 5:21, 27, 31, 33, 38, 43). No wonder the crowds were amazed at Jesus' teaching 'because he taught as one who had authority, and not as their teachers of the law' (Matthew 7:29).

In the Old Testament, wisdom is described as calling people to listen to her instruction and teaching. Jesus is wisdom personified in the New Testament and he calls people in a similar fashion. He offers them not something 'new' but wisdom 'dressed for the occasion and time'. Wisdom principles remain the same throughout the ages but need to be contextualised in order to be relevant and appropriate. Jesus is the wisdom teacher par excellence! Listen to his words: 'See how the lilies of the field grow... But seek first his kingdom and his righteousness... Do not judge, or you will be judged... Ask and it will be given you... Enter through the narrow gate... Therefore everyone who hears these words of mine and puts them into practice is like a wise man who built his house on the rock.'

† Lord, am I that 'wise man'? Is my house built on the rock that is Christ?

The call of wisdom

Anthony Loke

Friday 21 December

Matthew 10:16-20, 24-26, 40-42

Call and challenge

'He who receives you receives me, and he who receives me receives the one who sent me.'

(verse 40)

Jesus calls people to follow him and be his witnesses. These followers are to go on his behalf to spread the good news of the kingdom of God. The call will not be easy for some, as Jesus reminds us that his followers are sent out like sheep among wolves (verse 16). Because his followers go in his name, the enemy will not be happy and will seek to devour some of them. Hence, in answering Jesus' call we are reminded to be wise and shrewd in our dealings with an often hostile world. But there will be times when the hostilities will be strong and overpowering and we shall find ourselves suffering for the faith. Jesus promised us that he will give us the appropriate words to say when the time comes (verse 20). We should not be surprised to find the world being hostile to us because if the world was first hostile to Jesus, so it will be for his followers (verses 24-25).

But there will be some people who will gladly receive us for the message we bring. In receiving us, they are actually receiving Jesus (verse 40). Jesus also promised a great reward to those who will show mercy to others (verse 42). Sometimes we think that the little deeds we do out of love for others are not appreciated or remembered. Jesus promises us that even the little deeds that we do will not be easily forgotten.

† Lord, when you call me, you also issue a challenge. Am I willing to take up the challenge as I obey your call?

Anthony Loke

The call of wisdom

Saturday 22 December

Matthew 11:25-30

Invitation for the weary

'Come to me, all you who are weary and burdened, and I will give you rest.'

(verse 28)

Verses 28-20 are the favourite verses of many Christians. The offer by Jesus to come to him and find rest is indeed reassuring. There are many people who, like an animal labouring under a heavy load, struggle to make ends meet, to pay their mortgages and bills, or to find meaning and purpose in life. The constant effort wearies them and they go through life carrying huge burdens on their backs. Jesus' invitation is to come to him and unload our burdens onto him so that we can find rest in him. The picture of a yoke in verse 29 also conveys a picture of animals trudging along carrying a heavy yoke on their shoulders. If two unequal animals are yoked together, the stronger one will shoulder more of the weight than the weaker one. Jesus tells us that we do not need to pull the yoke all by ourselves, for we can take his yoke upon us and he will yoke himself with us. Then we will find that our side of the yoke is manageable and the burden lighter. Jesus gives us wisdom for life.

† Lord, exchange my yoke for yours and help me to realise that you are carrying it with me.

For group discussion and personal thought

- Why do people find it hard to listen to wisdom's call?
- The ancient Jews spoke of Lady Wisdom in order to get their young men to be serious in pursuing wisdom. In our modern age, how can we speak of wisdom to get young people to pursue it?
- Are you willing to take up Jesus' call and challenge people to follow him?

The call of wisdom

Anthony Loke

Wisdom

4   Jesus Christ, the wisdom of God

Notes based on the *New Revised Standard Version* by

Helen Van Koevering

Helen has lived in northern Mozambique for fifteen years. She has worked as an ordained priest in training community priests and lay women and men for ministry with her church, the Anglican Church of the Diocese of Niassa.

Introduction

In the Old Testament wisdom is prized as a way of life grounded in and leading to God. During Advent, wisdom provides a different lens through which to reflect on the presence and purposes of God at work in the world with the coming of Jesus. Wisdom is a rich and powerful way to speak of Christ who was present in the beginning with God, the source of life and true understanding, and acting in our world today to reveal God's purposes.

Sunday 23 December: *Matthew 13:53-58*
Surprising wisdom

> *[T]he people . . . were astounded and said, 'Where did this man get this wisdom and these deeds of power?'*
>
> (verse 54)

Aren't we always 'astounded' when someone we know as 'one of us' comes to be somehow 'other than us'? Like the woman who sang in church becoming the celebrated winner of a national television competition; or the abandoned child who became a president. Jesus was known in his hometown, 'one of us'. Something special had been noted: 'as Jesus grew he advanced in wisdom and in favour with God and men' (Luke 2:51). But now, as Jesus' public ministry begins, something more is seen in this 'one of us' – a wisdom from somewhere else, unusual power, unexpected authority. God was being revealed through Jesus – the divine life and presence, meaning and power making sense in the incarnation of wisdom, in the very Son and Word of God. A surprising wisdom as 'one of us', with us and for us all.

† Lord Jesus, you came as one of us, to be known and to know us. Yet you are God's wisdom with us and for us, God's incarnate Word. Remind me who you are today, and teach me to seek and recognise wisdom with me always. Amen

Monday 24 December

Ephesians 3:1-11

Grace-filled wisdom

[T]his grace was given to me to bring to the Gentiles the news of the boundless riches of Christ, and to make everyone see what is the plan of the mystery hidden for ages in God who created all things; so that through the church the wisdom of God in its rich variety might now be made known to the rulers and authorities in the heavenly places.

(part of verse 8, and verses 9-10)

One of the most popular hymns, even amongst non-churchgoers, and sung at weddings as well as funerals, is 'Amazing Grace'. But what is grace? The essence is captured in part by taking the first letters of the phrase 'God's Riches At Christ's Expense', and more fully with the words Generosity, Reconciliation, Acceptance, Compassion and Encouragement. But it is within the life of the church that grace comes alive, revealed as a rich and varied wisdom powerfully different yet mysteriously related to the power of heavenly rulers and authorities. Where generosity towards ourselves and others is active; reconciliation between enemies, conflicting interests and hardened viewpoints are pursued; acceptance of all difference tangible; compassion marks our service to others; and encouragement is freely given to build up others – then the grace of God is seen and known in greater ways than with words. The church, in all its diversity, shared pain and joys, incompleteness and struggles in becoming what in God's grace it's meant to be, is God's dream. Today's reading holds God's promise to bring that dream to pass through God filling and enabling with saving grace. And the dream includes each of us living God's grace-filled life, each day, just where we are.

† Lord, God of all wisdom and grace, fill me today with your presence. Where I am tempted to be mean, make me generous; where I disagree, reconcile me; where I avoid any other, let me accept; where I dislike, open my heart to love; and instead of discouraging, may I bring encouragement. Amen

Jesus Christ, the wisdom of God   Helen Van Koevering

Tuesday 25 December (Christmas Day)

Luke 2:1-7

Incarnated wisdom

In those days a decree went out from Emperor Augustus that all the world should be registered . . . while Quirinius was governor of Syria . . . Joseph also went from the town of Nazareth in Galilee to Judea, to the city of David called Bethlehem . . . He went to be registered with Mary . . . And she gave birth to her first born.

(parts of verses 1, 2, 4, 5 and 7)

In just a few words, the very human events surrounding the birth of Jesus reveal the historic time and geographic place into which he arrived. Those usually remembered in history books – the famous rulers and leaders – are named, and the lowliness and ordinariness of the birth of Mary's firstborn son is quietly noted. The powerful political background of the Roman Empire, the humility of an engaged couple expecting a child, the exhaustion of a long, difficult trip, the poverty of the delivery for a new young mother, and the inhospitality of crowded Bethlehem – all are mentioned and the details left for our imaginations. For those who have known colonialism or dictatorship, the difficulties of unplanned pregnancy or travelling any long distance from home, feeling exhausted, unwelcome, uncomfortable in a strange place, the details don't need to be told. We know these situations ourselves: it's a shared wisdom. We recognise the shared human experience in Christ's birth, childhood and upbringing. Perhaps it is in the ordinariness around his birth that we recognise most clearly the humanity of Jesus and how like us he became. He shared our humanity – God's Son sent to share our lives, share God's love, joy and wisdom in this world.

† Lord, your Son shares our humanity in all its messiness, challenges, joys and sadnesses. I stand amazed today at your gift of love, joy and wisdom that came down through all time and space to this day and this place. Emmanuel, God with us. Amen

Wednesday 26 December (St Stephen's Day)

Acts 6:8-15

The face of wisdom

Stephen, full of grace and power, did great wonders and signs among the people . . . But they could not withstand the wisdom and the Spirit with which he spoke . . . his face was like that of an angel.

(verses 8 and 10, and part of verse 15)

The painter Van Gogh once wrote of the glimpse of eternity that is seen in the face of a sleeping child, and the eyes have been called the windows of our souls. Our faces tell a story through the laugh and anger lines etched there, in the brightness or lifelessness of the eyes or skin, with any scar or mark, blush or paleness. And others can read the story.

Angels are messengers, sent to announce God's message in the world. To describe Stephen's face as 'like that of an angel' is to add the presence of the divine mystery to all that could be read in his face. Artists' images of Stephen gazing serenely heavenward as he is stoned to death point not to the reality of the blood, sacrifice and pain, but to the inner mysterious understanding and knowledge of truth that held Stephen in life and death. Stephen's face is telling his story of love drawn from him through the call of his beloved Lord, peace discovered in obedience and companionship, fullness found in the grace offered within God's wisdom. Stephen's face reflects the angelic message for us even today, between the celebrations of yesterday and our ordinary lives tomorrow: wisdom accompanies us through all times, the celebrations and the sufferings and the ordinary days. And this wisdom is as real as the life we show to the world in our very faces, faces revealing the mystery of Love's wisdom.

† Lord, may the angelic message of the knowledge of your presence and the mystery of your wisdom be seen in our lives and remembered through every day, whatever that day may bring. And may others be drawn to you through our lives lived for you and with you. Amen

Jesus Christ, the wisdom of God   Helen Van Koevering

The light of wisdom

The true light, which enlightens everyone, was coming into the world.

(verse 9)

Jews saw God's word as alive and active from the creation when God had only to say 'Let there be...' for things to come into being; Greeks understood the word 'logos' as the logical rationality behind the universe; later Jewish belief included a feminine figure in Lady Wisdom, present with God at creation. John pulls all of these thoughts together with the amazing idea that the Word was pre-existent with God, divine and existing in the unity of the Godhead, yet distinct and also personal – simply, 'the Word was God'. And, more incredibly, John declares that the divine Word, the true light, has come into the world. This world, created 'good' by our loving God, rejects Jesus and becomes negative, the source of opposition to the light. But the light leads to the wisdom of God, and those who recognise and follow the light, like Nicodemus in John 3, will come out of the darkness to believe in Jesus, see the world anew, and become children of God, born again of the Spirit. That it is possible to re-see and re-know the world and our lives in it, be enlightened where our knowledge was darkened, is God's gift to us through the Son. To recognise Christ as the true light is like seeing the light at the end of a dark tunnel. It is to be 'born again'.

† Lord Jesus, the light of the world, draw us to that light which brings new life. Remind me throughout today that I am a child of yours, and let me be your light to those I meet. And may your light guide me and all those who know you, and bring light to the dark places of our world. Amen

Helen Van Koevering   Jesus Christ, the wisdom of God

Friday 28 December

Luke 2:8-20

A heavenly wisdom

The shepherds returned, glorifying and praising God for all they had heard and seen, as it had been told them.

(verse 20)

Luke is keen to emphasise that Jesus was born in poor circumstances, despite being in the line of David. His parents were migrants, unknown in Bethlehem, with nowhere but a hay-filled cattle trough to lay their baby that night. No extended family surrounded this newborn, as for John the Baptist. In Luke, Jesus' first visitors were shepherds (in Matthew, oriental sages), people regarded as unclean in later rabbinic tradition, and poor in anyone's eyes. But the wisdom of the angels is not of this world, with all its social divisions and expectations, mess and poverty. Their song is of the Messiah, born in the city of David, the fulfilment of all hopes and dreams, the Saviour and Lord. The angels recognise God with us now on earth. Sharing in heavenly wisdom, they proclaim who Jesus is, and waves of praise, song and joy move from this heavenly army to the shepherds and those who heard their news. As we hear, and as we desire to know Jesus our Messiah, so we also will praise and feel joy, because the Saviour of the world has come for us all. Emmanuel, God with us.

---

† Father God, words cannot express the joy of knowing that your love came down to us in Bethlehem. The mystery of your Word is revealed through your wisdom. Be with us today, we pray. For your honour and glory and power. Amen

Jesus Christ, the wisdom of God   Helen Van Koevering

Saturday 29 December
Luke 2:25-28

Revealed wisdom

It had been revealed to him by the Holy Spirit that he would not see death before he had seen the Lord's Messiah.

(verse 26)

When Jesus' parents take him to Jerusalem to fulfil the tradition of purification, they are greeted by Simeon and Anna, two prophets representing Israel: the patient faithful, a man and a woman. The life of both is centred on the Temple. Simeon is so full of the Holy Spirit that he is prompted to come forward at that exact moment to take Jesus in his arms, the fulfilment of God's promise to him personally as well as to Israel and all the world. Simeon's canticle reveals this child as salvation, light and glory; prepared, revealed and present to his own people and the world. The shadow of the cross hangs over the infant and his mother with Simeon's final words, but the welcome of God's Son has now been completed by the angels, the shepherds and the Temple prophets. Let us welcome him too.

† Jesus, my Saviour and Lord, brother and friend: my heart is full of the joy and love you have shown in your presence with me, in the desire I have to be changed by you and to follow you today and always.

For group discussion and personal thought

- Reflect on the readings this week in the light of any area of your life, personal, communal or national, and spend some time asking for God's wisdom for understanding, for peace and justice, for action, and for renewed prayer.
- How has this theme of wisdom altered your Christmas preparations and expectations?
- Did you receive any new insight from these readings? Share this insight with someone, and hold the thought with you for a few more days. Why do you think God revealed this to you at this time?

December

Helen Van Koevering   Jesus Christ, the wisdom of God

Sunday 30 December

1 Corinthians 1:18-24

Christ, God's wisdom

Christ the power of God and the wisdom of God.

(part of verse 24)

It doesn't make sense, does it? The baby born of a poor, friendless migrant couple more than 2000 years ago in a remote part of a powerful empire, who somehow influences life around the world, inspiring greater, more powerful people than himself – rulers of nations, captains of industry, leaders of armies, discoverers and explorers, and parents of successive generations. His teaching was distinctly uncomfortable – he taught about a Kingdom of God that threatened political leaders, and confronted religious leaders, upturned ideas about women, children and foreigners, spoke of forgiveness of enemies and love of your neighbour, of the poor being blessed and the fulfilment of the Law. He drew big crowds, but in the end they all betrayed him. It doesn't make sense to talk of his power and wisdom.

But that is what today's reading says. Some want to see signs of power, others want to debate wisdom, but Christ was both. He confounds the norm, turns the world around, shakes up conventional thought, reveals his power in the world's weakness. Our message today is of Christ crucified, God's Son who came to take our punishment under the Law in a brutal public death, but who conquered death by rising again. And through him, we now have new life, clean hands and pure hearts to transform our world and share with others who need to know this power and wisdom to simply and beautifully begin again – in truth, be born again. It doesn't make sense, but it's true.

† Living Christ, you died that we might have life, peace, love and joy, know God, and guided by the Holy Spirit do even greater things in your world than you did, limited as you chose to be in time and place. Go with us to share your love, forgiveness and salvation and make known your wisdom. Amen

Jesus Christ, the wisdom of God

Helen Van Koevering

Monday 31 December

1 Corinthians 1:25-31

Called to wisdom

Consider your own call, brothers and sisters . . . He is the source of your life in Christ Jesus, who became for us wisdom from God, and righteousness and sanctification and redemption.

(part of verse 26, and verse 30)

Our year has come to an end, and we look forward to the new one with mixed emotions and thoughts. It is good to be reminded, to look back before moving on. Look back now over this last year, note the times and places where you have felt grateful, joyful, fulfilled, and take a moment to thank God. Look back to other times which left disappointment, sadness, loneliness, and pause to praise God's abiding presence through it all. Look back and gently remember times of anger, non-forgiveness or impatience with others, and failure to love, and ask God's forgiveness.

To thank, praise and ask forgiveness of God is to recognise God as the source of our lives. To know that we are blessed, loved as dear children, forgiven, renewed, surrounded by loving protection, is to understand something of the wisdom from God, and the wisdom within the wonder of righteousness, sanctification and redemption. Discussions over the meaning of these words have filled two millennia, but the experience of each of them can be known in a second of thankful, praising or penitent prayer. And then go into the unknown life of next year, knowing God's word, life and love are with you always.

† Loving God, your Son Jesus came to live and show the way to a new life. Help me let go of the old and go with me into the new, just as I leave all that happened last year and move into the coming year. Your love holds me, now and always. Amen

Helen Van Koevering   Jesus Christ, the wisdom of God

All about IBRA

IBRA readings

The list of readings for the whole year is available to download from www.christianeducation. org.uk/ibra. You are welcome to make as many copies as you like.

IBRA books

Both extraordinary value at £8.75 each in the UK, with writers from around the world and many different Christian traditions.

IBRA samplers

From time to time IBRA publishes samplers using notes from *Light for our Path* and *Words for Today*, suitable for introducing new readers or for use with Bible study groups. Please contact us at the address below for availability.

IBRA Rep discount

If you live in the UK and purchase 6 or more copies of IBRA books, you can sign up as an IBRA Rep which entitles you to 10% discount off all your IBRA purchases. Just tick the IBRA Rep box on your order form and we'll do the rest.

IBRA International Fund

The IBRA International Fund enables the translation, printing and distribution of IBRA Bible notes and readings. For more details, see page 93. You can make a donation when ordering your books.

IBRA, 1020 Bristol Road, Selly Oak, Birmingham, B29 6LB.

International Bible Reading Association Partners

A worldwide service of Christian Education at work in five continents

HEADQUARTERS
1020 Bristol Road
Selly Oak
Birmingham
B29 6LB
United Kingdom
www.christianeducation.org.uk
ibra@christianeducation.org.uk

and the following agencies:

GHANA
IBRA Secretary
Box GP 919
Accra
asempa@iburstgh.com

INDIA
All India Sunday School Association
Plot No 8,
Threemurthy Colony
6th Cross, Mahendra Hills
PB no 2099
Secunderabad – 500 026
Andhra Pradesh
sundayschoolindia@yahoo.co.in

Fellowship of Professional Workers
Samanvay
Deepthi Chambers
Vijayapuri
Hyderabad – 500 017
Andhra Pradesh
fellowship2w@gmail.com

NEW ZEALAND AND AUSTRALIA
Epworth Bookshop
157B Karori Road
Marsden Village
Karori
Wellington 6012
Mailing address:
PO Box 17255
Karori
Wellington 6147
sales@epworthbooks.org.nz

NIGERIA
Hinderer House
The Cathedral Church of St David
Kudeti
PMB 5298 Dugbe
Ibadan
Oyo State

SOUTH AND CENTRAL AFRICA
IBRA South Africa
6 Roosmaryn Street
Durbanville 7550
biblereading@evmot.com

INTERNATIONAL BIBLE READING ASSOCIATION

1020 Bristol Road, Selly Oak, Birmingham B29 6LB, United Kingdom

You can order using this form or through your local IBRA rep, or online at http://shop.christianeducation.org.uk, or by email to sales@christianeducation.org.uk or by phone on 0121 472 4242

Please return this form to
IBRA, 1020 Bristol Road, Selly Oak, Birmingham B29 6LB

Order form for 2013 books

Name: _____

Address: _____

_____

_____

_____ Postcode: _____

Telephone no: _____ Email: _____

Postage in the UK is free. Payments in pounds sterling, please. If you are ordering from overseas and require more than one copy please contact us for a discounted price.

Code		Quantity	Price	Total
UK customers				
AA120201	Light for our Path 2013		£8.75	
AA120202	Words for Today 2013		£8.75	
	I am an IBRA Rep (see page 192)		10% off	
	I am ordering 6+ books and would like to become an IBRA Rep		10% off	
Western Europe				
AA120201	Light for our Path 2013		£13.00	
AA120202	Words for Today 2013		£13.00	
Rest of the world				
AA120201	Light for our Path 2013		£15.00	
AA120202	Words for Today 2013		£15.00	
			Subtotal	
	Donation to the IBRA International Fund			
			Total	

☐ **I enclose a cheque (made payable to IBRA)**

☐ **Please charge my MASTERCARD/VISA/SWITCH** (delete as appropriate)

Card Number: ☐☐☐☐☐☐☐☐☐☐☐☐☐☐☐☐ **Issue Number:** ☐☐

Expiry Date: ☐☐ ☐☐

Security number (last three digits on back): ☐☐☐

Signature: _____

IBRA themes for 2013

New Year Manifesto
John proclaims Jesus
Jesus proclaims himself

Living differently
But I say to you…
The new way
Hearing a different drummer
Living as children of light

Through Lent and Passiontide in poetry
Temptations
Enemies and opposition
Suffering and distress
Being overwhelmed
Separation from God
Protection and deliverance
The passion of Christ

Readings in Luke
Resurrection and Ascension
Going up to Jerusalem
The last days

Hosea
Covenant and faithlessness
God's continued forgiveness

Fire
Fire in the Old Testament (1)
Fire in the Old Testament (2)
Fire in the New Testament

Acts 6–12: From Jerusalem to Antioch
Disciples increasing in number
Light dawns for Paul and then Peter
The church spreads

Questions in Job
My servant Job
Job's friends venture a few words
Job calls God to answer
A happy ending?

Mountains and valleys
Mountains
And valleys

Paul for today
A re-formed life: in Christ, of one Spirit & always thankful
Sharing good news: healing in Paul's divided world
Grace talk: God-walk – with a difference
Living letters: negotiating challenges of life together

Contested sites
Promised or stolen land?
'neither on this mountain nor in Jerusalem'
God's vineyard

Navigating Numbers
Taking stock, counting heads
Journeying on
Beyond the plains

Mothers
God at the birth
Mothering continues

Facing death
Facing death in the Old Testament
Facing death in the New Testament
Facing death with God at our side
Facing death and beyond death

Readings in Luke
Jesus the teacher
The kingdom is among you

Isaiah 56–66
Soon my salvation will come
Your sins have hidden his face
Good news to the oppressed
You are our father
They shall not labour in vain